PRAISE FOR AMAZON

"Loraine Van Tuyl has drawn on an _____ary multicultural background and a career as a professional healer to produce a beguiling and insightful work of wisdom and compassion . . . Highly recommended!"
—MARK PLOTKIN, PhD, President, Amazon Conservation Team, Time's "Environmental Hero for the Planet" (2001) and bestselling author of *Tales of a Shaman's Apprentice* and *Medicine Quest*

"What a wonderful book and author! Loraine Van Tuyl is a clear voice to follow in the vastness of the mystical journey to discover the sacred and the divine."
—LISA TAHIR, LCSW, Host of "All Things Therapy" Radio Show, www.nolatherapy.com

"In a memoir that's braver than most, Loraine Van Tuyl shows how personal and ancestral stories and gifts breathe vitality into our life force. While taking us through a memory portal, she invites us to retrace our steps through our jungles of experiences, and dares us to recognize our own instinctual reactions at interesting crossroads in our lives. Her story of reclaiming and nurturing her awakening life force as a student, in the face of strong resistance, is valuable because it opens the door to how personal, cultural and spiritual truths and traditions can transform traditional Western psychology as well as individual lives."
—MARIA P. P. ROOT, PhD, Award-winning Psychologist, Reiki Master, Artist, and author of *The Multiracial Experience: Racial Borders as the New Frontier*

"A triumph of the heart! Amazon Wisdom Keeper reminds us of the essential need to connect to our authentic wholeness in order to provide service in the world. Loraine Van Tuyl has vulnerably and powerfully laid out her own journey along this path, inspiring growth, faith, and hope along the way."
—ANNE LOWE, MSW, Social Work Instructor, Salish Kootenai College

"Loraine's inspirational journey takes us from the jungles of Suriname to the United States and Europe as she grapples with a world that places more value on what can be seen and measured than the truth in her heart and in her past. Her process of shedding conventional thinking and expectations for the beauty, simplicity and truth of time-honored indigenous wisdom serves as a guide for a world that has lost touch with its inner truth."
—JENNIFER B. MONAHAN, Shaman and author of *This Trip Will Change Your Life: A Shaman's Story of Spirit Evolution*

"Loraine Van Tuyl has written a memoir that spans time and space, memory and precognition. She manages to escort the reader across the bridges she creates with skill and purpose so that the reader can begin to understand what is required to move from one realm to another and maintain equilibrium and balance. We can all learn from the courage and commitment to meaning and understanding Van Tuyl so poignantly demonstrates in *Amazon Wisdom Keeper*."
—ISA GUCCIARDI, PhD, Founding Director and Primary Teacher, Foundation of the Sacred Stream, and author of *Return to the Great Mother* and *Coming to Peace*

"Once Loraine Van Tuyl was separated from her beloved home, it feels as if she was always trying to get back to what she had lost. I loved the part of her trying to develop a multicultural dynamic to aid her thoroughly Western education in psychology and psychotherapy; her dedication, despite a growing sense of isolation, is impressive. I think the big lesson for me was a reminder, as a creative person, of the need to not only trust intuition and deeper feelings, but to continue to develop them until we can rely on them, until they're second nature, and trust that the intuitions and dreams aren't just a symptom or sign of a delusional psychosis."
—COFFEE AND INK SUNDAY BOOK REVIEW

"*Amazon Wisdom* Keeper richly mirrors the incongruence I experience as a sensitive psychotherapist working within a mental health paradigm that at times clashes with my own intuitions about healing,

and it instilled in me a sorely needed dose of validation, inspiration, and spiritual camaraderie. I suspect it will help catalyze and energize the visionary process of other sensitive, spiritually inclined healers, researchers, teachers, creators, innovators, and change-makers who also hear the call."
—KRISTA HARRISON, MFT, CHT, Intuitive and Shamanic Healer

"As we are poised at this critical time to evolve our conscious-ness, Loraine Van Tuyl has every reason to bring *Amazon Wisdom Keeper* forward to the public, and especially to therapists, to help us open ourselves up to the multidimensionality of our beings."
—DONNA MORRISH, MFT, Founder, Paths of Grace

"*Amazon Wisdom Keeper* is both a thoroughly engaging memoir and a timely, illuminating infusion of earth-centered wisdom. Loraine Van Tuyl has interwoven her rich and multilayered expe-riences and insights with stunning finesse, creating a ripple effect that continues to move deeply within me. I feel at once validated, strengthened, and inspired."
—JULIE SUZANNE BROKKEN, Artist, Poet, and Photographer

"All the tales are so validating and inspiring."
—DENISE COLBY, PhD, Founder, Integrative Wellness

AMAZON WISDOM KEEPER

AMAZON
WISDOM KEEPER

A Psychologist's Memoir of
Spiritual Awakening

Loraine Y. Van Tuyl, Ph.D.

SHE WRITES PRESS

Published 2017
Printed in the United States of America
Print ISBN: 978-1-63152-316-8
E-ISBN: 978-1-63152-317-5
Library of Congress Control Number: 2017944793

For information, address:
She Writes Press
1563 Solano Ave #546
Berkeley, CA 94707

Cover and interior design by Tabitha Lahr
Drawings by Yantze Li

She Writes Press is a division of SparkPoint Studio, LLC.

Names and identifying characteristics have been changed to protect the privacy of certain individuals.

Special thanks to: Brooke Medicine Eagle (www.medicineeagle.com) for permission to reprint excerpts from her book, Buffalo Woman Comes Singing: The Spirit Song of a Medicine Woman
Copyright © 1991 by Brooke Medicine Eagle

David J. Wallin for permission to reprint an excerpt from his book, Attachment in Psychotherapy.
Copyright © 2007 by David J. Wallin

To my dear husband, Robert Van Tuyl, and
my precious children, Terrance and Jade.

[Traditional] psychological theory too soon runs out for the creative, the gifted, the deep woman. Traditional psychology is often spare or entirely silent about deeper issues important to women: the archetypal, the intuitive, the sexual and cyclical, the ages of women, a woman's way, a woman's knowing, her creative fire . . .
—Clarissa Pinkola Estes

CONTENTS

▦ INTRODUCTION

FOR YEARS, THE AUTOMATIC THOUGHT that entered my mind after a near miss on my commute to my holistic psychotherapy practice in Berkeley, California, was: "No, I can't die yet! I'm not done with my book." Only then would the horror if I were to get in a bad accident set in, motivating me to drive extra carefully until I reached my destination.

Now that my book is done, I'm not sure if it will still be in my final thoughts when I leave this earth. It did form the basis of my first meaningful insight as a child, born and raised near the edge of the Amazon rainforest of Suriname, a former Dutch colony about

the size of Georgia located on the northern border of Brazil. Not many people have heard of Suriname or know that 95 percent of its landmass is covered by trees, officially making it the most forest-covered country on the planet according to the World Bank.

As a child, I loved to play and roam in the rainforest. Armed with a rusty machete and dressed in old clothes and oversized black boots, I pretended to be Mowgli, Tarzan, or a freedom fighter, like the famous rebel slaves Baron, Boni, and Joli Coeur we learned about in history class. Thanks to my three main girl role models and imaginary friends—Anne Frank, Helen Keller, and Joan of Arc—I began to grasp and channel "my book" around the age of eight, long before I knew what channeling meant and what my story would evolve into.

By then, I'd already gathered that some of my insights, interests, and reactions to people and life were not "normal." I seemed too sensitive, too particular, too precocious, too stubborn, too pensive, too wise, too opinionated, too perceptive, too intense, too passionate, too weird, too ambitious.

I began to separate and collect these parts of myself like out-of-place jigsaw pieces that belonged in a different box. Reading Anne Frank's diary unleashed a deep yearning to collect these rejected puzzle pieces for my own book—a "parenting" book that would show adults what really went on in some children's minds, modern-day Anne Frank-Joan of Arc-Helen Keller hybrids, like me, who were perhaps not abnormal at all but had gifts and important messages to share.

The more puzzle pieces I collected, the clearer it became that they were creating an image and story that had to do with far more than just parenting—these split-off pieces were influenced by the ancient mystical traditions and the soulful, but marginalized, worldviews of racial and cultural groups that were as diverse and commonplace as the air and wildlife surrounding me.

Because a diary was a luxury that kids my age didn't have, I tucked these insights and puzzle pieces away in a special file in my mind. And I'd regularly breathed in their wisdom, feeling it nourish my cells, blood, bones, and soul through connective karmic tissue that

Paternal grandparents. My father is standing on the top far left.

dipped into past-life memories, premonitions, and guiding dreams and through long, ancestral roots that spanned various continents—Asia, Africa, Europe, and South America.

My paternal grandparents were from a Hakka village in southern China. So was my maternal grandfather. My maternal great-grandmother was Creole (West African/indigenous Surinamese ancestry), and my maternal great-grandfather was a Dutch soldier with Portuguese-Jewish ancestry. My parents were born in Suriname but lived and studied in Holland for almost a decade before returning to their native country to start a family. The spiritual streams that run through my veins include Taoist, Buddhist, Catholic, Jewish, African spiritualism, and nature-based indigenous practices and wisdom.

In February of 1980, a military coup turned my life upside down and, three years later, at the age of thirteen, my family moved to Miami, Florida, in pursuit of a better future—free of violence, curfews, censorship, terrifying threats, and constant turmoil. Not until my potent, daily sanctuary was all of a sudden gone did I slowly begin to appreciate and water the seeds that had been sown in my fertile soul throughout my formative years.

Maternal Great-grandparents. My grandmother is standing second to the far right.

I didn't know yet how to dig up and unlock the secrets and hidden treasures that my soul had inherited from my ancestors and previous lives, but I sensed that they were sacred, mysterious, endangered, and important. A clear and passionate sense of purpose consumed and informed me that it was my job to safekeep them until I'd become "learned" and "the time was right to share them with the right person." I have a feeling that the time is now and that the right person is you.

PART ONE

Chapter 1

MY FIRST COMMUNION

The best remedy for those who are afraid,
lonely, or unhappy is to go outside,
somewhere where they can be quiet,
alone with the heavens, nature, and God.
Because only then does someone feel like
all is as it should be.
—Anne Frank

A HANDFUL OF MEN WITH white smudges of cracked earth on their bare, chocolate bodies made a smooth entry onto the playground of St. Bernadette Elementary School, the all-girl, Catholic school that my parents had entrusted with my primary school education. The men were wearing checkered, cotton loin skirts around their waists. The brown seeds around their ankles and wrists rattled while they unloaded and carried carved, wooden *apinti* drums and other belongings from their pickup truck to the playground.

Every now and then, delightful chatter, words of a familiar song, and occasional bickering and name calling in Dutch or the Surinamese Creole tongue, *Sranan Tongo*, rose above the cacophony that hovered over the playground. I was too busy numbering a row of square stone pavers to notice much of anything other than the relentless midday sun scorching my scalp through my shiny, dark hair. I patted the top of my head to circulate the hot air. Like most children born and bred in Suriname—a small Caribbean country and former Dutch colony almost entirely covered by muggy Amazonian rainforest—I'd gotten used to getting a bit sunbroiled in this tropical pressure cooker in the middle of the day.

"Come on, get up . . . let's play! Recess will be over soon!" Geeta pleaded while pulling me up by the elbow. Her hazel-green eyes sparkled next to her golden-honey skin.

Our grandparents were part of a band of contract laborers and grocers from India, Indonesia, and China who voluntarily moved to Suriname right after the abolition of slavery. While some, like my Chinese paternal grandparents, married within their ethnic group, others freely mixed with the existing melting pot that consisted of indigenous forest dwellers, freed slaves, and European, Creole (racially mixed), and (a few) Black plantation owners, government officials, and public servants. My Chinese maternal grandfather, a merchant and bachelor, found romance outside of his ethnic group. He married a Creole woman, my grandmother, who was of Jewish-European, African, and indigenous descent. Her ancestral roots spanned from our native Suriname all the way to Ghana, Portugal, and Holland.

Not even our bland, olive-green cotton blouses and gray, pleated skirts could neutralize my friends' diverse complexions, hair textures, eye colors, and facial features. We looked like the layered palette of a seasoned painter. Despite our differences, we all detested taking pages of notes in class until our fingers were about to fall off. If you happened to have nice handwriting, as I did, not only could you be copying an entire chapter from a tattered book onto the blackboard, you needed to copy it again into your own notebook after school.

There was one thing that I hated even more than sore hands and fingers. Watching "hopeless cases" get punished by some of the teachers. In just three years of grade school, I'd witnessed teachers fold these troublemakers over their desk, lift their skirts, and

I'm in the second row to the right.

swat them with a ruler on their bottoms in front of the whole class. Sometimes, they'd hurl a chalk eraser at their heads for talking too much, or dragged them by the ear to the principal's office.

It was never very clear to me why my friends had gotten in trouble. When I thought it was for talking back, someone else would get in trouble for not saying enough. I got in trouble for an entirely different reason: for shedding "crocodile tears" like a leaky faucet. I was often unable to stop the drip, which aggravated the grown-ups. And I was unable to explain what was wrong with me, which aggravated them more. My first-grade teacher took me to the principal's office when she couldn't take it anymore, and even Ma once raised her hand and threatened to give me a reason to cry if I couldn't provide one.

I didn't quite know how to say, "I feel sad, upset, and unsafe because adults like you, who should know better, are mean and are hurting us." No one around me did. When I got in trouble for crying, I tried to freeze up my tears and numb my bruised heart, copying some of my classmates. It only made me cry harder. When the recess bell rang, I was one of the first ones to bolt to the door, not able to stand another minute inside.

While waiting for me to finish drawing the hopscotch cross, Petra, one of the few Dutch girls at our school, rubbed her rock in her hands for good luck. Her freckled, apple cheeks had a red glow, and her blonde locks, sticky at the ends from sweat, gently framed her face.

The loud clamoring of the bell interrupted our play right before Geeta could claim victory. The head nun and principal of our school, *Soeur*, was vigorously swinging a short, thick rope underneath the heavy copper bell in the hallway in front of her office.

"Recess is over!" she bellowed. Dead silence settled upon the playground. There were a few pieces of broken chalk, not bigger than a fingernail, lying around. I swooped them up and dropped them in one of my front pockets like delicate gemstones. Hitting my thighs with open palms, I tried to get as much chalk dust off my hands and skirt as I could, turning my clean uniform into a rag in just one day, as Ma would say.

"Hey, where is everyone going?" I asked Geeta, confused that no one was lining up to go back to our classroom.

"Oh, didn't you hear? There's going to be a special cultural performance on the playground today," Geeta said.

"Really? What kind of performance?" I asked. "No one told me."

"I'm not sure." Geeta asked others if they knew what was happening.

"It's a *winti* thing," Sandra said in a spooky tone of voice with bulging eyeballs while signaling with her hand for us to come closer. *Winti*, wind or spirit, is the trance dance practiced by the descendants of African slaves, known as Maroons or Bush Creoles, *Bosland Creolen*, who escaped and resettled in the dense Amazon jungle in the eighteenth and nineteenth centuries.

The playground quickly morphed into an amphitheater, and those of us on the periphery stood on our tippy-toes to see what was happening.

"Girls, girls, please move back and open the circle," *Soeur* said, motioning her arms and palms back and sideways. She was short and stocky and no longer wore her gray nun cap. Because she had lived in Suriname for more than thirty years, the "hot potato" in her mouth, her Dutch accent, had considerably shrunk, but it still sounded smarter and much more sophisticated than the wide range of other accents that the rest of the teachers had.

"No need to push; everyone will be able to see," she said, and walked along the inside rim of the circle and opened it.

"Now, let's give a warm welcome to the dancers and performers and thank them for coming to our school," *Soeur* said, while clapping her hands and merging into the circle.

I wormed my way to the front as the circle expanded. The drummers began to beat the drums in between their legs, and my heart started to pound in unison, louder and louder with each beat. The springy feet of the dancers bounced on the beat and off the stone pavers as if their bodies were feather-light. It felt as if a bouncy ball had been released inside of my body, a funny sensation that made my perfectly still body feel anything but still.

I noticed that some of my schoolmates were intently pointing at the dancers. They had shocked looks on their faces. Eager to know what had caught their attention, I examined the dancers more closely.

Their hips were moving sensually from left to right and front to back, faster, faster, faster. This alone was enough to captivate my attention, but I got the feeling that the girls standing across from me were ogling something else.

Could they be looking at the white ceremonial clay, *pimba doti*, plastered on the dancers' skin, glistening with sweat? Wait a minute, that isn't glistening skin! Those are big, shiny safety pins! Your everyday, regular kind of safety pins, pierced all over their bodies through the skin of their arms, legs, and stomachs, without a drop of blood in sight.

I imagined how much it would hurt to pierce all those pins through my skin and shuddered. They didn't seem to be in any pain. Perhaps it was true that the sacred, mysterious powers of the white *pimba* clay could heal all flesh wounds. A sense of fearlessness and power started to swell inside of me, pumped up by the beat of the drums.

I let myself absorb the dancers' infectious joy until I was completely filled up. I felt more energized than I'd ever felt and much bigger and more grown-up than my usual self—clear, wise, loved, and invigorated, not at all on the brink of tears.

A similar surge of curious feelings grew inside of me once before when we learned in our history class about a daring slave who taunted, "Go ahead, kill me if you want. I am more free than you'll ever be," until he was tortured to death by his incensed tormenter. I somehow "got" the profound sense of freedom that the tortured slave was referring to. It stirred my blood and simultaneously gave me a sense of peaceful invincibility.

We also learned about Baron, Boni, and Joli Coeur, famous slaves who escaped (Boni's mother escaped while pregnant with him, so he was technically born free) and successfully revolted against plantation masters. After managing to escape a cursed life of mistreatment and misery, they instilled fear through their drumming and shouting at night. They burned down plantations and helped many slaves escape. I anointed them as my heroes until they were replaced by Anne Frank, Joan of Arc, and Helen Keller who were girls, closer in age to me, and easier to relate to.

The dancers in front of me were dancing just like my maternal ancestors had done for generations. Perhaps some of their descendants, my very distant relatives, still lived in villages deep in the jungle and were able to have their *winti* dance rituals whenever they pleased. The thought of this alone infused me with a sense of warmth, courage, and excitement.

Because some of these villages were strewn along the main roads on the southern fringes of Paramaribo, the capital, we got a glimpse of their homes and family life whenever we left the dank city to cool off in the creeks and rivers of our favorite jungle hideaways.

Their small wooden huts had beautiful, brightly painted, geometric hand-carvings on the doors. They were typically covered with dried palm leaves and scattered in between acai berry and coconut palm trees on a large stretch of communal land. Fine, glistening savannah sand surrounded their homes and marked the outside living space where children often played with each other or their dogs that were so skinny you could count their protruding ribs.

The women walking to and from their patches of land balanced big aluminum bowls of cassava roots, vegetables, and fruits on their heads. Like the dancers today, they wore nothing more than thin, knee-length cotton cloths wrapped around their waists and legs. With their voluptuous, bare breasts swaying freely from left to right, I imagined that these women were as welcome a sight to their children as Ma was to me when she returned from the Chinese grocer, *Omoe*, uncle, at the corner of our street.

I wondered if everyone around me was feeling what I was feeling. I looked at my teacher's face and the faces of the girls standing across from me. They seemed to be under the same spell that I was under. The performance lasted a little less than half an hour. As the dancers exited our circle, still dancing and drumming, *Soeur* enthusiastically applauded them with jiggly arms and loud claps high in the air, gesturing that we do the same.

After loud cheering and whistling, we lined up the way we usually did but were much rowdier than normal. There was more of the "Oh my God! Did you see that?" whispering going around, loud enough to annoy Mrs. Aardeveen, our third-grade teacher. She sharply shushed us with her finger on her lips, and threatened us with a "Quiet now, or else!"

"Because of today's performance, we will not be rehearsing your communion ceremony in church," Mrs. Aardeveen announced. Thank God. No jamming ourselves like sticky sardines onto the hard, wooden benches in the Sacred Family Church, a small Catholic church right next to our school. After we had settled behind our graffiti-covered desks, she explained that the Holy Spirit would somehow enter our bodies if we prepared our minds and hearts for this important moment. The experience sounded like what happened to me on the playground earlier today.

"You have come of the age to understand that by accepting the sacrament, the holy bread and wine, you are receiving the body and blood of Christ and giving yourselves to God. You will become one with God on your communion day. Your big day is just two Sundays away, so you need to be extra good, obey your parents, and pray every day," she said.

She said that we were all children of God, so it could happen for all of us, as long as we desired it and tried our hardest to follow God's example. Oh, how I desired it. I hoped that my first communion would feel as electric and uplifting as watching the dancers and listening to the drummers.

School got out a little after one in the afternoon. Ma was late, and I was one of the last kids left, sitting on the sidewalk, waiting, squirming. All the teachers had left. They were usually the first ones to leave after *Soeur* clanged the bell.

Where is she? Is she mad at me?

Ma was the principal of a junior high school just a mile up the street, and every so often got stuck in a meeting with her teachers. After she finally brought the meeting to a close, she picked up Mark, my younger brother, first. He attended the Thomas van Aquino all-boy elementary school, which was like the Siamese twin of my school, joined at the hip and only separated by a wire fence.

There she was. Her royal blue and white dodge swirled around the corner. It looked like a bedazzling vision compared to most other weathered cars on the road. I quickly wiped the tears off my face before she could tell me to.

"Were you worried? I told you not to worry when I'm a few minutes late. It's hard to get out of these meetings. Everyone keeps talking," she reassured me. I didn't respond, knowing that she wouldn't press me for an answer.

We stopped by a vegetable stand by the "big tree," a fairy tale–shaped tree with a giant umbrella-like canopy. It was next to one of the busiest paved streets outside of central Paramaribo. Ma bought long beans, *kouseband*, and large, heart-shaped leaves, *tayerblad*, that she blended and cooked into a watery, green mush. It looked gross, but it was actually quite tasty with some butter and salt. On Mondays, Wednesdays, and Fridays, she stopped by the milk man, *the melk boer*, to get fresh milk that often boiled over and dirtied the stove when no one was watching. On an occasional Friday, like today, Ma also bought a few bags of soggy cow manure. Lucky Mark and I got to load and unload them out of the trunk of her car.

"I know it stinks, but this is how you get tasty, juicy fruit and beautiful flowers," she said in response to our grumbling.

Why does she need manure? The dark soil around our house is so fertile that watermelon plants begin to grow after a seed-spitting contest!

I didn't say anything, because I didn't stand a chance. Ma knew her plants and trees inside and out, the easy as well as the finicky ones, the new branches that just sprouted, the sick roots and leaves, the blossoms on the verge of maturing, and the last dates our various fruit trees were harvested. Our pomelo, guava, avocado, cherry, mango, and papaya trees bore so much delicious, sun-ripened fruit that we bartered it for fish and shared it with our relatives down the street, the gardeners, and the housekeepers. We could go to the garden anytime and collect a full bouquet of orchid, hibiscus, bird of paradise, and anthurium flowers for a birthday celebration. Ma insisted that the soil was so fertile because of all the manure that had been folded in it.

We drove by half a dozen of Ma's siblings and their families, who all lived next to each other like nursing puppies. Growing up, my older aunties and uncles took care of their younger brothers and sisters, because their parents were far too busy to even say hello to them on a daily basis. Ma and Pa were middle children within litters of twelve. Actually, thirteen. In both of their families, bad luck struck the oldest sister in early adulthood; one died from a sudden infection, and the other from a broken heart.

Many parents sent their most ambitious and resilient children to Holland to get a university degree. Ma and Pa were among a handful of Surinamese students who quickly found each other and huddled together for warmth and support while studying in cold and desolate Haarlem, far away from home. Because of the dreary and long winters, they, like the rest of their friends, vowed to return to Suriname right after receiving their diplomas.

Pa got his degree in architecture. Ma received hers in education and taught bookkeeping and Spanish before she became the "boss lady" of the Pool school. Ma and Pa fell in love, got married in Holland, and moved back to Suriname the same year. They and half of Ma's siblings were the first in the neighborhood to buy a bunch of parcels from farmer Tammenga, who'd chopped up his land and sold sections of it as if it were a long string of licorice.

Pa designed and built our home on the far end of our muddy street when Ma was still pregnant with me. My neighborhood and I came into the world and grew up together. As I stretched out, took my first steps, became potty-trained, and grew bigger and taller, the streets also got longer and stronger, the trees fuller, electric posts and phone lines were put in place, street bricks were laid, and large sewage pipes were installed, which meant no more baby crocodiles making an appearance in the open sewers. Houses of all shapes, sizes, and colors—traditional wood-slated homes on stilts, a run-down, square shack, a large mansion with a super high fence, and a few other modest, one-story homes—popped up like mushrooms and proudly claimed their space on "our" street, the Dieter street, which some people teasingly called the Lieuw Kie Song Street after Ma's family.

Ma asked us to pile the bags of manure next to her orchid greenhouse and flower beds. After we had lunch—usually rice, some kind of meat stew, and vegetables—Mark retrieved his toys from a large, built-in cabinet in Pa's office where we kept our stuff. I climbed into my favorite spot: Pa's swivel chair behind his architectural desk that stood proudly in the center of his study. I twisted myself into a pretzel, turned the chair as far back as I could, then pushed myself off with all my might, spinning round and round and slapping Pa's desktop to pick up speed. There was nothing more fun than adjusting the heavy metal rulers up and down and left to right on a slanted desk top and trying to draw straight lines on a large piece of paper after I'd twirled myself silly.

A few stacks of savored architectural magazines—yellowish and worn from age, but still in impeccable condition—were within reach, resting on a built-in bookshelf on the back wall. The featured homes, mostly tropical and surrounded by serene settings and pools, were so beautiful that they looked surreal. With my belly on the cool floor, I strolled down their corridors and into their gardens and terraces without a care in the world.

I liked to look at buildings designed by Pa's idol, Frank Lloyd Wright, a famous architect. Pa wanted his buildings to similarly blend in with nature, just like Falling Water, Mr. Wright's famous house in the woods. It was Pa's favorite. Mine, too. Our snow-white, stone house had a similar, two-level flat roof and futuristic black and white linoleum tiles that you could play a giant game of checkers on.

Pa cared for and knew our home's skeleton and bones, its pipes and guts, its arteries and wiring as if it were a living thing. And, in some ways, it was, thanks to a built-in aquarium where fish were literally swimming in the dining room wall, and thanks to the back-patio pond, where Pa taught me how to call and gently pet our fish without damaging their oily layers.

"I need an assistant," Pa said when something needed fixing, which was almost daily. I enjoyed tagging along and helping him cement platforms and fix the brick fence, solidify the play structure, check the pool for leaks, make orchid beds, and tighten outside water faucets and pipes. After heavy rains, I was allowed to climb the extra tall ladder and play on our flat roof when Pa was drying puddles to prevent leakages.

Unlike most parents, Ma and Pa didn't seem to realize that I was a girl. Or perhaps they did, but let me to do a lot more than what I saw my girlfriends and girl cousins do. I never thought much about it. I just happened to be the one who outran and outclimbed the boys in our neighborhood when we played tag or hide and seek in the trees. I was always ready for the next adventure.

For birthday and holidays, Pa converted our four-car garage into party central by tying a few palm tree leaves to the hollow square bricks of the outside walls, and opened our round pool, the only one in the whole neighborhood, for swimming.

"Pappie, Pappie, can you turn the fountain on?" the neighborhood kids asked him one after another, whether blood-related or not, as if we were all part of one big happy family.

"Yay," we all shouted in unison after he turned on the "fountain," a single spray of water that entertained us for hours.

Ma was in charge of feeding my swarms of cousins and the neighborhood kids. The three big mango trees in our yard took turns bearing fruit, providing a year-long supply of half-ripe mangoes that Elfriede, our housekeeper, pickled for us. Pickled anything, but especially green mango, was my favorite treat.

Elfriede and I often hung out in her break room right next to the kitchen where she polished our shoes. Of all the housekeepers who'd been with us, Elfriede had been around the longest. There were times when we needed two housekeepers, one in charge of "large cleaning"—wiping off hundreds of glass window shutters, mopping the floor, cleaning bathrooms, and washing, hanging, and ironing laundry—and a second one in charge of the "small tasks," dusting, polishing shoes, copper and silverware, making beds, cooking and washing dishes. I sometimes needed to help gut, scrape, and brush shrimp, octopus, and fish, and could barely hold onto my own guts. Fortunately, the aroma coming from the stove whipped up my hunger pangs and wiped my memory clean when it was time to eat.

Even with all the help, Ma still managed to find plenty of leftover work to do or redo, and complained if our housekeepers didn't do a good enough job, broke stuff, or made stuff in the house disappear, like food, orchids, or a piece of jewelry. Or when the gardeners didn't show up or forgot to do what she asked.

"Go, go, go, we don't need your kind here. I'll take care of it myself," Ma huffed and puffed like the big bad wolf after a confrontation. She then took off like a steamroller, doing whatever still needed to be done, even if this was mowing the lawn, cleaning shutters, washing her car, raking, or dragging bags of manure around to fertilize her plants.

I was so glad that she treated Elfriede differently. Elfriede whistled all day and was allowed to finish her work in her own time. She lived on the outskirts of the city and often visited her family's Maroon village in the jungle. She liked to tell me stories about evil and dubious spirits, *bakroes* and *yorkas,* and about nature spirits, such as the Water Mother Deity, *Watramama.*

"Make sure you treat *Watramama* with proper respect or she'll drown you," Elfriede said. I usually hung onto her every word as if it were gospel truth, my feet dangling underneath the only table that I was allowed to sit on.

"How do you know when you are properly respecting *Watramama*?" I asked.

"Look out for *draaikolken,* whirlpools, spiral patterns in the water where *Watramama* could be swimming and pull you down if you don't honor her strength," she said. Elfriede made me promise to greet, observe, and listen closely to *Watramama* and the nature spirits whenever we went to *boitie,* our four-acre orchard in Saramacca at the northern edge of the Amazon rainforest, or took a weekend trip to soak in the creeks, rivers, and pristine natural world right outside of the city. I liked that she was worried about my safety and taught me special ways to protect myself from

Aunt Friede, Ma, me, and Mark

invisible and mysterious dangers. It felt like being entrusted with the secret behind an impressive magic trick that everyone else was dying to figure out.

My favorite thing to do at *boitie* was to wander to the far back of our parcel and hack through the tall growth with my machete while Ma and Pa spent the day planting, pruning, and picking tropical fruits and vegetables upfront. I loved playing peekaboo for hours on end with bold and shy, mesmerizing and hair-raising creatures—snakes, spider monkeys, parrots, Morpho butterflies, giant bugs, shrimp-sized coconut tree worms, bats, and the like. This sacred paradise of beautiful tropical plants and sheltering trees transported me into my own peaceful inner sanctuary of wonder where the jungle and I bled into one. It became my weekly salvation, offering me the spaciousness and safety I needed to reset my soul and explore, daydream, love, and feel loved without fear of being hurt or disappointed.

The dancers today exuded a quiet strength that I'd associated with Elfriede, who would never huff and puff, throw a chalk board eraser at someone's head, threaten to hit me, or ever grab a child by the ear if in trouble. I knew that for sure. Neither would she laugh if I'd told her about my fantasies of living in the woods and being raised by animals, like Mowgli.

Around Elfriede, it felt safe to be enraptured by nature documentaries about Maroon villages and indigenous tribes that lived in the farthest corners of the Amazon rainforest near the mountains where Suriname borders Brazil. And totally understandable why I'd run to my room, collapsed on my bed, and bawled inconsolably for an hour or longer after Pa told me that I couldn't join my older cousins on a trip to a popular waterfall deep in the jungle, because I was too young to get malaria shots and could get deathly ill.

"Superstitious nonsense," I overheard the adults say when stuff that Elfriede and I talked about came up at a party. I didn't understand why some people were so against something that made me feel so alive, strong, and wonderful. My aunties and Ma didn't mock the "fantastical" stories of the Maroons, but they didn't speak their secret language like Elfriede did. They usually came up with a few juicy stories of their own, like the one about a *bakroe* sighting, and another one about a kid who got possessed and died after venturing too far into the woods by himself. They also liked to talk about the healing ritual performed by a Hindu priest, a *pundit*, who cured Ma's fright after she fell out of a window and couldn't speak for weeks. She was just two years old when it happened.

Because Elfriede taught me how to talk to invisible spirits in nature, the invisible, mysterious things in my dreams and nightmares seemed less scary. For a very long time, I had a recurring dream of being a ninja warrior, dressed in black and masked, jumping from roof to roof and bouncing off walls. I was always running away from something bad that was out to get me. I couldn't see my own face, but I could tell that I wasn't mortified. Flickers of provocative boldness—reminding me of how I felt when listening to stories about Anansi, the trickster spider, ever since I was a teeny tiny tot—hinted that I was toying with this threat.

When I got too smug, the battles and attacks became fiercer and more frightening, determined to show me who was boss. A few nights in a row, I was locked up in Ma's car, and hands with sharp, bloodred nails were fiercely clawing at me, causing me to scurry inside the car like a squealing mouse. That's when I caved and reached out for comfort.

"I don't want to go to sleep. I'm having scary nightmares," I whimpered to Pa who usually tucked us in after pulling a story out of his big magic hat.

"Don't be scared. Dreams are not real. They can't hurt you. They come out of your own imagination. Aren't you right here and safe every time you wake up?" Pa said, then drew a cross on my forehead and gave it a kiss.

He was right. How could I get hurt in a dream?

When the hands reappeared in my dream, I carefully examined them. They weren't Ma's. She never painted her nails bloodred, and they weren't that long. But they somehow got stuck in her car and were after me. I managed to crack a window open, fight them off, and push them out.

As soon as I passed this challenge, another nightmarish nemesis appeared, and another, as if part of a never-ending Alice in Wonderland obstacle course. Fighting became my full-time job as soon as the lights went out, until I was, one night, stabbed and killed during a lightning-fast sparring match in a dark cave. I didn't see it coming. Not the knife nor the dying. I face-planted in the dirt and was certain that I was dead. The gods of the dream realm assured me that I was still alive. But someone told me that you couldn't die in your dreams, flashed through my mind. I heard that if you die in your dreams, you end up dying in real life too. I commanded myself to get back up, and to my surprise, my legs and arms responded.

Once you break the "you can't die in your dreams" rule and reawaken from your nightmare, everything changes. I couldn't remain stuffed in the cramped little box that I was in before. An ancient part of my soul got a taste of my immortality and reminded me of my superpowers.

Apparently, I'd lived, fought, died, and lived again many times before. I kept forgetting my previous gains, but this time was different. Some of my past learning had crossed over and gathered into a few pockets of my dream world like warm, golden nectar in the cells of a giant beehive. The nectar that had been saved up couldn't be accessed or depleted, no matter what happened to me. Once the fear of losing this golden essence dissipated, I relaxed and stood my ground like a mountain goat. Whatever was out to get me finally left me alone.

Until lianas, vines, began to choke me in a dream. They were connected to everyone in my life and weren't going to kill me, but they were also not planning on letting me go. I got my machete and cut through them with one determined whack. I was as aloof and brave as Ma once was when she chopped off a chicken's head to feed half a dozen hungry mouths, mine included.

Moments after I awakened from this intense dream, I felt horrible because of what I'd done. The next moment, I became aware that my callous rage didn't rise out of an evil heart, but out of a deep longing to be clear from suffocating pressures that kept entangling me. The people in my life and I were still connected at the roots but now we had more space to branch out into new directions above ground.

I didn't have the words to articulate the life-changing impact that these dreams and revelations had on me, but I knew that they were B-I-G. My imaginary comrades Anne Frank, Helen Keller, and Joan of Arc agreed. They nudged me to stuff my peculiar insights into a secret treasure chest deep in my psyche and far away from the adults until the time was right to bring them back out.

"Why don't you respond when I call you?" Ma asked, towering over me with her hands on her hips. Her irritated tone instantly jolted me back into Pa's study, still flipping through his architectural magazines on my belly.

"Auntie Chuny wants to know if you want to go over to play with Mayling," she said. I nodded and put Pa's magazines back.

Mayling, my paternal cousin, was a month younger than me and lived a few houses to the left on the street behind ours. If I biked fast, I could get there in a few minutes. While playing in the house or outside in the yard, Mayling and I sometimes mulled over adult topics of conversation, sounding more like eighty-year-olds than eight-year-olds. On this particular day, she wanted to share some really profound discoveries with me, sparked by our upcoming communions.

"My dad said that humans have tiny brains and are not as smart as God. Our minds are like a bucket of water while God's mind is like the ocean, so we will never be able to understand what God says with our little brains. All that knowledge just doesn't fit," she said.

I stayed silent, deep in thought. I tossed her insights around while continuing to dig through the dirt, not totally satisfied with her and my uncle's conclusions. I decided that my brain was more like a hole on the beach. Perhaps it wasn't as big as God's brain, but the same water and tides moved through us both.

What would happen to it during ebb or flow was still too far ahead to think about.

Chapter 2

 THE REVOLUTION

> *The true focus of revolutionary change is never merely the oppressive situations that we are trying to escape, but that piece of the oppressor that is planted deep within each of us.*
> —Audre Lorde

BOOOMMM! A deafening thud echoed in the distance.

Ma flew from the kitchen into Pa's study, a big frown burrowed in her forehead.

"What was that?" she asked Mark and me. We were doing our homework, Mark at a desk by the window, and me in my favorite position on the linoleum floor.

Another *booommm!* The earth underneath us shook in protest.

"That sounded like some sort of explosion," she said, peering through the trembling glass shutters. Mark climbed on top of the desk to look at the looming shadows above the rooftops and trees.

We waited for another blast, but the booms stopped as suddenly as they'd started.

Ma returned to the kitchen, her fingers making sharp half circles on the phone to find out what was going on. Mark and I went outside to play. I didn't quite know where to file "explosion" in my mind, let alone "bomb attack." The incident rolled like a stray marble in between the cracks of my mind, where all kinds of mysterious and strange occurrences, like bakroes, were clumped together.

Shredded ashes danced like silver snowflakes in the humid air. I tried to catch them. The smoke looked like it was coming from downtown, less than a ten-minute drive north toward the Suriname River. Was someone's home or store burning down? Maybe someone's tiny kitchen blew up, like Aunt Marie's, who didn't realize that there was a gas leak in her oven when she lit a match. Luckily, she survived, but I couldn't look very long at her face ever again.

"Let's go see what's going on," I said to Mark.

"Okay. I'm gonna bike. It's faster."

"Me too. Wait for me!"

We rode our bikes to the tallest and most mature tree in our neighborhood, our unofficial watchtower, that stood proud in Auntie Gerda's and Uncle Bram's beautifully landscaped front yard.

Knock. Knock. My aunt opened the door.

"*Dag tante.* Hi auntie. Can Janice and Robert come outside to play?"

"*Dag mijn schatje.* Hi precious. Yes, of course. I'll call them for you."

I monkey-climbed my way to the highest perch with the best bird's-eye view, but I couldn't see much, just a dark cloud turning the sky an ominous gray. Janice stayed on the ground.

I spotted Christa, my older cousin's best friend, flying around the corner as fast as she could. We swung down and jumped to the ground from a high branch.

"Christa! Christa! Over here!" I shouted.

Christa's long, dark curls, big brown eyes, striking eyelashes, and slender, but well-developed sixteen-year-old body made an impression on almost everyone she met, especially members of the opposite sex. Fierce and free-spirited, she looked like an Amazon goddess.

"You won't believe what I saw," Christa panted, leaning over the bike handles.

"It's completely burned down! I stood right there, in front of the police station, and watched it burn to the ground. No one did anything. No one tried to put the fire out. Everyone just stood there and watched!" she exclaimed in disbelief.

She seemed on the verge of passing out, breathless with excitement. I envied her for being able to witness all the action up close.

A television broadcasting later that evening confirmed her report. Desi Bouterse, a sergeant in the military, had given orders to bomb the police headquarters on the riverfront by firing missiles from military ships. The reasons for the "coup" were regularly broadcasted on TV, radio, or in the newspapers in between images of police officers in nothing but their underwear, either lined up or belly down on the lawn of a military base while armed soldiers calmly paced in between them.

The new military leaders wanted our five-year-young nation to wean off the financial aid provided by Holland, a ruthless slave driver and colonizer who'd graduated to post-colonial, meddling parent over a period of three hundred years. They claimed that the current government was pocketing most of this aid and crippling, rather than building up, the communities that needed it the most.

It was hard to believe that the coup was real and a big deal. It felt like watching a movie on TV, except the movies had much more action and violence. It was more like watching a school play, everyone still confused about their roles and not really getting into character.

Before the coup, my relatives and family friends often visited to tell stories, to *tak tori*, passing the latest gossip and news of the day around like a soccer ball. Flexing their comedic, *moppen-tappen*, joke-tapping, and juicy Anansi storytelling muscles was one of their favorite pastimes. Not much changed after the revolution, except that their jokes became darker.

"*Dan hoe dan*? So how does this work? You and I have been emancipated because of this coup? We are all grown-up now? *Ai boi*. Yeah man. Then why do we have a seven o'clock curfew? Did you have a curfew growing up? I didn't even know what a curfew was when I was a mischievous boy, an *ogri boi*, this size," Uncle Eric said, holding his hand up to the height of a six-year-old.

"That's because you were beyond help." The grown-ups on the front terrace snickered and laughed, shaking their heads.

"I've figured out what's wrong with you. You're too smart for your own good. Asking too many questions. Your head will burst if you don't watch out," Uncle Ronald said, offering some food to Uncle Eric.

"When you watch the Puppetshow, *Poppenkast*, on TV, do you see *Jantje*, Johnnie, asking the puppets, 'Why are you doing that?' No, he just sits back and enjoys the show. Right? Am I telling the truth or am I telling the truth?" he asked with his palms open and his head leaning a bit toward one of his shrugged shoulders.

Even though my ten-year-old brain only understood bits and pieces of the bantering, I enjoyed entering this rambunctious "adult arena" where the storytellers and comedians competed for the loudest belly laughs.

But when word spread that critics of the revolution were being singled out and uprooted like weeds, everyone in this untouchable domain of comic relief, sanity, safety, and sovereignty retreated like a snail touched with a stick. The grown-ups became much more careful about what they said in front of us and used code words like "divide and conquer" whenever the enemy introduced a new tactic, as if they were part of a top-secret, undercover mission.

"You can't repeat anything you heard here, alright? You never know who will tell the wrong person. Some people may be eavesdropping on our conversations, even through the telephones. People you may have known all your life may suddenly turn on us, so don't joke, or say anything, *anything*, about the coup or the military to *anyone*, you hear me? You don't want me or Pa to get picked up by soldiers, right?" Ma asked, looking each one of us sternly in the eyes.

"No," we said. Ma was telling the truth, but the gravity of her words didn't sink in. What did she mean anyone could turn on us? Anyone? Our immediate family, my loving aunties, uncles, and cousins wouldn't do such a thing, would they? Would my friends? I refused to believe that they would, but I suppose that they could accidentally repeat something they overheard me say and unintentionally make it sound far worse.

I could tell that Ma wasn't trying to scare us into behaving. She tried that once before with fabricated stories of masked robbers entering our house after I'd rescued Mark from his unfair imprisonment, ran away with him to Aunt Gerda, and forgot to close the doors. Earlier that day, Ma'd chased him like a madwoman for cursing at her and locked him into our bedroom. I don't think he even realized what he was saying. He was only six.

Ma's piercing eyes warned me that this was not the time to be *eigenwijs*. She was often on my case for being horribly strong-willed, *vreselijk eigenwijs*. *Eigenwijs* had a double connotation in Dutch. It could mean "my way or the highway" or "my wisdom." When Ma had a glimmer in her eye during moments when I didn't budge, it meant that I was being wise rather than stubborn, even when she was mad. Not today. The glimmers were as forceful and piercing as lightning bolts. From this day onward, I scrutinized every single word that crossed my lips. There was zero margin for error.

Shortly after Ma's warning, one of my good friends, Vanessa, came to school looking like her blood had been sucked out by a vampire.

"What's the matter, Vanessa? You alright?" I asked.

"Last night, two military guys with oozies banged on our door and took my dad with them. My mother cried almost all night until they brought him back. I hardly slept," she said, her eyes puffy and red.

"That's horrible. I'm so glad that they brought him back."

"Me too. I don't know what we're going to do. My mom said that she won't be able to sleep tonight."

I didn't know what to say or do either other than wanting to hold her, but I felt too self-conscious and young. Grown-ups did that sort of thing.

"Let's get a salted fish sandwich, a *batjauw puntje*," I suggested to get her mind off her miserable night. She loved *batjauw puntjes*.

After school, young soldiers handling their weapons like toy guns patrolled up and down our wobbly street in their rickety jeeps. Vanessa lived close to me. Were these the soldiers who'd picked her dad up? It seemed important and smart to fear them,

but my heart felt like a balloon. It popped right back to its original shape as soon as I got tired of squeezing, worrying, and despising. I wasn't used to being afraid for that long, especially not of a few soldiers who looked like harmless teenagers.

"Louise, Lucien, and the boys are moving to Miami. They got their green card," Pa said, using our thirty-minute drive to *boitie*, our weekend getaway outside of the city, to update Ma on the latest news of the week. Uncle Roy, Pa's youngest brother, had studied in Hong Kong, met and married my Aunt Ping, an American citizen, and settled in California. He'd applied for green cards for all of his siblings after getting his citizenship.

Oh no, not Auntie Louise! I'd nuzzled in her soft, matronly arms ever since I was a newborn. She was the sweetest godmother I could have ever wished for.

Ma and Pa didn't seem bothered by the news. They just continued to discuss politics, the food items on the scarcity list, and the current "situation" in big words that bounced around like bumper cars into all the feelings that were spinning inside of me.

After a fifteen-minute ferry ride, we hopped back in the car and passed a Javanese cemetery that looked like a miniature village. Small huts with benches hovered over and near the modest graves. A lively family was playing cards, eating and drinking, sitting on the benches, and leaning on the beams. I wished Pa would stop so I could get a closer look at this exotic dance between the mundane and mysterious that always whizzed by too quickly.

Pa turned onto a narrow, sandy street called Damalang Way, *Damalang Weg*. It had rained, and the sand was tightly packed. The puddles on the road were shallow, but he still maneuvered around them, making Ma's long dodge sway like a ship at sea. Long and narrow blades of grass and weeds that encroached onto the road were squashed by the tires of Ma's car.

"Make sure you rub this all over your thighs and around your groin," Ma instructed as she handed each of us half a clove of raw, sticky garlic over her shoulder. I discovered the hard way that grass lice, *patata loso's*, particularly like the warm crevices of your body. Their tiny little red bites itched like crazy. As much as I hated this ritual, I was at least not teased by my aunties for having to marinate my sausage with garlic.

Pa slowly pulled into our long, grassy driveway. I couldn't wait to get out of the car, antsy to zigzag and chase Mark between the rows of trees in our fruit orchard. Pa drove past the crude foundation of our house and parked next to a forsaken shack that housed a family of bats, a mini tractor lawnmower, some tools, supplies, soap, and our boots.

"You don't want them to fit too tight, or they'll be too small before you know it," Ma and Pa explained when making one-size-too-big clothes and shoe purchases for us. My boots were worn hand-me-downs whose origin I could not remember. I still thought that they were quite cool. Rimmed with dry mud, they looked rugged, felt solid on the bottom, and could withstand a lot more action than flimsy slippers with annoying straps between your toes that always popped out no matter how hard you squeezed them in place.

"Come on, let's go say hi to Grandma and Grandpa, *Mae* and *Pae*," Ma said. They were our elderly Javanese neighbors and endearingly called Grandma and Grandpa by the rest of our distant neighbors, most of them out of sight. We walked through a section of hip-high grasses to *Mae* and *Pae's* property. They were very wrinkled, miniature people, the tops of their heads not higher than Pa's chest.

"*Fai tang,* hello, how are you? *Mae, Pae,*" Pa said, while giving them each a warm handshake. Ma gave *Mae* a packet with some beef, and they gave each other a sideways embrace.

"Be polite and come say hello," Ma said while waving her hand to us to come closer.

I couldn't help but stare at *Pae's* bad eye, which had a foggy, grayish color and more pus in it than usual. *Mae* came over and stuffed a hand full of kernels in our hands to feed their roaming chickens that were always hungry. Her bare feet looked calloused, cracked, and as thickly padded as the muddy bottom of my boots.

In this safe haven, Pa continued to build up hope, even when important parts of our daily life, like school and work, were crumbling down. At *boitie,* we were shielded from the horrors and hearsay about kidnappings, arson, and "accidental" deaths, which held everyone's spirits in the city hostage.

After the foundation of our concrete jungle retreat had set, Mark and I were allowed to lay bricks that heightened our excitement and the exterior walls of our life-size play house. It took a good number of Sundays and steady dedication for the house—still unpainted and dull gray—to be in good enough shape for us to stay the night.

I was so excited that very first night, I couldn't sleep. The howling of monkeys and bickering of crickets, birds, and other wildlife was so loud in the early morning, it seemed as if we'd spent the night in hammocks in the middle of the jungle.

"Mark, Ma, Pa, wake up! Wake up! You have to see this!" I screamed. Hundreds of black beetles the size of golf balls had covered every square inch of the front patio.

"I'm scared. What are they doing?" Mark asked.

"They're harmless. They're just investigating, probably attracted to the terrace light that I left on," Pa said. "Stay inside. They'll go back to their dark hiding places when it gets brighter."

Pa was right. I could go outside in less than an hour to watch the last one of them return to their creepy, crawly holes, giving us a heads-up on what to do with the real vermin that got word of our weekend house.

That same afternoon, a military jeep dragged a puff of stale, polluted air all the way from the city into our pristine, safe zone. Two young soldiers pulled into our long driveway and swaggered toward Pa, who was suddenly both stiff and fidgety. Mark and I watched from our tree perches. Even the birds held their breath when Pa signaled for us to stay up there.

My mind side-tracked to the chilling news that I overheard Ma share with Auntie Gerda a few days ago.

"It was not an accident. Nonsense. He was shot for driving by the military base not even fifteen minutes after curfew hours. Deliberately shot for something this ridiculous. It only adds insult to injury when they come up with these ludicrous lies. Tragic. *Zielig.* Really tragic. *Echt zielig.*"

The military base was just a kilometer or so from our house in the city. I'd grown accustomed to hearing shots being fired in the evenings during routine practice. I couldn't believe that one of those horrible bullets had killed an innocent father, an acquaintance, swatting him dead like a dirty fly just for being in the wrong place at the wrong time.

The sight of soldiers at *boitie* suddenly made our secluded haven seem like the worst and most treacherous place to be. When one of the soldiers smirked at us, my clammy skin and insides recoiled like a poisonous snake. Blood and bile stirred in the pit of my stomach making my mouth taste like a piece of bitter gourd.

How dare they invade our sacred zone like nasty roaches?

"*Ey, brada, fai go? Na wan moi presi joe habi dja.* Hey, brother, how's it going? A nice place you have here," the first soldier said to Pa in Creole.

"*Goedemiddag, heren. Kan ik U helpen?* Good afternoon, gentlemen. Can I help you?" Pa said, using his most polite Dutch and the formal "you" when addressing them.

"*Goedemiddag, meneer.* Good afternoon, Sir. *Mogen we U een paar vragen stellen en even een kijkje nemen?* May we ask you a few questions and take a look?" the soldier replied in formal Dutch.

"Of course."

"We're looking for a traitor who may be hiding out in this area. Have you seen anyone around or noticed any suspicious activity in recent days?"

"No, we only visit Saramacca during the weekend. We live in the city. This is the first time that we've actually stayed overnight."

"So you wouldn't know if you're harboring a soldier on the run who can easily break in through those windows, would you?"

"No one has been here. Everything was exactly as we left it, and there were no signs of breaking in or foul play. Feel free to take a look inside."

The soldiers paraded around the house, inspected our belongings, looked in the dark shed, then the pickup truck, lifted the rusted well cover, and quickly closed the half-rotten, bug-infested door of the outhouse, *koemakoisie*, a deep hole in the ground covered by a wooden box seat. They didn't bother to inspect the densely overgrown back of the parcel where I would be hiding if I were on the run.

"*Bedankt, meneer, mevrouw.* Thank you, sir, ma'am. All clear. But remember to alert us of any unusual activity. Orders from the big boss."

I exhaled a sigh of relief while watching their jeep disappear behind the opaque cloud of exhaust and sandy dust that was closely trailing it. Ma and Pa went inside and started to pack up our stuff without saying a word.

We made a few more day trips to Saramacca several weeks later, but never again stayed overnight even though tensions continued to rise in the city.

As much as Bouterse tried to fuel his revolution by splitting black and white and tapping anti-Dutch, anti-elitist, and anti-colonial sentiments, the Surinamese population had become too gray, integrated, and layered to fall for his divisive tactics. Over the course of the next two years, the close-knit tapestry of communal connections and goodwill pulled in tighter the more he tried to rip it apart.

Almost two months after my thirteenth birthday in October, fifteen outspoken and popular journalists, university lecturers, lawyers, union leaders, community activists, and military servicemen were all picked up for questioning, all of them common household names: a popular radio host who talked nonstop, a relative of an in-law, a gregarious family friend, a schoolmate's concerned father. Three days later, every single one of these men had been tortured and killed in Fort Zeelandia, the deserted, spooky military post at the mouth of the Suriname River.

The *mofo koranti*, oral newspaper, was spitting out rumors faster than ever before. No one knew what really happened in the cursed entrails and morbid dungeons of this abandoned fort. I stretched my antennae as high as I could and picked up a few unnerving words. Counter-coup plans. Cigarette burns. Bruises. Lacerations. Torture. Gunshots.

"Where is Kiki? Has anyone seen Kiki?" I asked my classmates in a dizzying panic about a month after the murders. No one knew. In the past year, Kiki had become my dearest and most trusted friend. She'd been swallowed up by the night, like the thousands and thousands of other families who'd just disappeared from one day to the next. Entire planes full of families pretended to go on vacation without any intention of ever coming back.

"Kiki's uncle was one of the murdered victims? That's why their family fled?"

"Yes, they didn't want to tell anyone about their plans out of fear that these would leak out and put them in danger," Shanti, one of Kiki's close family friends, whispered while making sure that no one was around.

Kiki was the only person in the world who really knew me. Thanks to her, I realized that some mothers, like hers, stayed in *boitie* mode all the time, even in the city. They didn't switch back to stressed-out-school-principal mode, like Ma, as soon as the work-week started.

During lunch, it sank in that Kiki was really gone. All that I had left was a gaping hole in my heart, eyes full of tears, and an address in Holland to write to.

So write I did, desperate to know how she was doing, desperate to tell her how I was doing. Day in, day out, I faithfully checked the mailbox that Pa had built into our brick fence on the front lawn.

"A letter, a letter for me from Holland. I got a letter from Kiki!" I shouted, jumping up and down when I received Kiki's first letter, beautifully adorned with calligraphy and glittery Dutch stickers. Thank God, she was okay.

But I wasn't. My friends continued to evaporate into thin air, one after another. Within a few months, I wasn't only writing to Kiki, but to a dozen other friends who'd moved to Holland.

When I thought my crumbling world couldn't possibly cave in more, Ma dropped the bomb that we were moving too. Not to Holland, but to Miami.

"The situation here is not going to improve. Schools are on strike three out of five days, and the country is just a mess. America will offer you and your brother a much better education," she said in a matter-of-fact tone.

I held in a silent *noooo* because I knew it would be useless to protest. I still got an "I don't want to move . . ." out, half-numb from shock. I didn't bother to ask, Why Miami? All my friends are in Holland. Why can't we move to Holland? because I knew what Ma would say.

Holland is freezing cold and miserable eleven months out of the year. She would never in a million years live there again. I wasn't sure if I could tolerate the cold either. Miami was the logical choice. We already owned a house there that Pa had bought as an investment after the revolution and was renting out to Auntie Louise's oldest son, Victor, and his friends.

"We got our green cards. Mayling is also moving to America so you won't be there all by yourself. We need to move now, because you never know what this crazy government is capable of.

They could decide from one day to the next to close the borders and forbid people from leaving the country," she said.

I knew that Ma was doing the right thing and the hard thing. I'd heard about the stray bullets that shattered the windows of Pa's and neighboring offices. There was hardly any work coming in. Schools were a mess. Armed soldiers walked in whenever they pleased, ordered her to end all instruction for the day, and sent her students to the Independence Square, *Onafhankelijksheid Plein*, to rally on behalf of Bouterse's cause.

"Sir, I can't do that. I can send them home to ask their parents, but I can't just send them wherever," she bravely replied to the commanding soldier.

Ma was being strong for our sake. That was just the kind of person she was. When Mark was only five and fell, hitting his forehead on a sharp corner of her nightstand, Pa freaked out at the sight of his gushing blood. The more Pa panicked and lost himself in emotion, the more intently Ma focused on what needed to get done. She made sure that Mark got to the emergency room as quickly as possible.

"People have become apathetic. Like frogs in a pot of boiling water. That's why no one is doing anything, but the situation is getting worse every day. It's getting really unbearable."

We had about seven months to prepare for our departure before school started in September. We were the lucky ones: we could sell our belongings and carefully select and take our most prized belongings to Miami. It was a luxury that many others who left in secret did not have.

If we were so lucky, why would I rather be boiled in a pot of water on a fragrant Surinamese stove with the rest of my relatives who were staying? I had no idea what living in the US would be like other than what I'd seen in the movies or experienced during our short visits. It was one thing to leave everything that you love and know behind for something better. It was a whole other story to leave it behind for a complete unknown.

Getting rid of the few possessions and clothes that I had outgrown didn't bother me as much as selling things that had sentimental value: our ping-pong table, where cousins and friends cheered and played for hours on end; our dining table, the central hub of endless storytelling by the grown-ups; the party bar in the garage; our sofas; and our encased television that regularly transported me to the indigenous and Maroon villages nestled deep in the rainforest.

When Pa finally sold the house in Saramacca and the two uncultivated parcels in the city reserved for Mark and me, he had not only sold the precious memories of our past but also the dreams of our future. Their decision not to sell our house in the Dieterstraat was the only indication that they'd harbored some hope of returning, some hope that the situation could improve.

Ma and Pa filled a small cargo container with very delicate crystal and china, dozens of photo albums, Pa's favorite architecture books, a hand-hooked rug that took Ma months to make, and a plethora of worldly acquisitions and fond keepsakes from their travels abroad—a rosewood, carved Chinese oval table and tiny benches, a marble Mayan calendar, Peruvian cloth art, statues and wood carvings from Suriname and Asia, a souvenir teaspoon collection from a dozen different European countries, and other exotic little trinkets for the kitchen. Ma planned on carrying her expensive and fine jewelry in her handbag.

"This is your suitcase. Pack up your prized possessions and put whatever you don't want in that box. Leave clothes and shoes that are getting too small behind. No use bringing those," Ma said to each one of us.

"Should I pack now already? We aren't leaving until next month," I asked.

"Sure, it might help make up your mind what to leave and what to take," Ma said.

I didn't have many possessions that were worth keeping besides my first communion album, two little sticker books with poems, drawings, well wishes from elementary school friends, and some clothes and shoes that either fit or were a bit too big. The things that I wanted to keep I couldn't pack: our street, our neighborhood, my relatives and friends, our house, *boitie*, the jungle, and the animals.

Two weeks before our departure, I biked to visit Elsbeth, my oldest cousin. She lived close to the river, in between two warehouses of the largest department store in the city where her husband worked. She had a small, in-home salon and had cut my hair two or three times before when it desperately needed trimming.

"I want it just like that," I said, showing her a magazine picture of an American blonde with a spunky crew cut.

"You sure?"

"Yes," I said decisively.

Locks of waist-length hair dropped onto the floor.

In just ten minutes, one-inch, spiky hair covered my head like a splotchy round duster and looked nothing like the blonde, gelled coif in the magazine. Months of stuffed-down tears welled to the surface and blurred the awful new me in the mirror.

"The good news is that it's hair. It will grow back if you don't like it," Elsbeth said.

I hated it. But I also liked that I hated it. My horrid hair reminded me of a battle scar or amputated limb stubs. It spoke for me how I felt about my wild locks no longer able to blow free in the wind, like the untrimmed tree branches in the jungle. It felt as if I'd just lost my only lifeline.

Our flight was scheduled for early Sunday morning, but it was not early enough to stop a bus full of relatives from accompanying us to Zanderij, the international airport. We'd been saying goodbye for weeks, Ma reminding herself and everyone how bad things had gotten and Pa joking himself and everyone out of any sad feelings. As for me, I no longer gave a damn that I looked like a plucked chicken or that we were leaving.

Zanderij was about an hour away from Paramaribo, right where savanna and rainforest merged into one. The road was narrow and lined with a few mom-and-pop grocery stores, a mosque here and there, and wooden houses where the bottom floor served as carport. I watched the sun slowly rise above the dark silhouettes of dense rainforest canopy and revive the colorful Maroon huts and tiny villages from their gray slumber when we neared the airport. The loud laughter and chatty talk of my relatives and school friends during our many bus trips down this very same road to "Cola Creek"—a popular retreat for birthdays, field trips, and family gatherings—rang in my ears. I didn't have the faintest idea just how much I'd miss these outings.

After we arrived at the airport, Ma and Pa focused on practical matters. My heart felt as hard and heavy as a rock. An announcer said it was time to leave. We haphazardly hugged and kissed our relatives one last time and joined the shuffle of moving bodies behind a clangy, metal gate that was rolled in between the passengers and those staying behind. I looked around and saw longing eyes and faces and hands everywhere, reaching through the holes of the gate. I wasn't sure who had the shorter end of the stick, they or we, and whose fate to feel worse about.

I followed Ma and Pa to the airplane in a silent daze. A long row of trees with outstretched branches lined the entire runway, as if offering one last embrace. I looked down and kept walking.

Chapter 3

 SHELL-SHOCKED

Death is not the greatest loss in life.
The greatest loss is what dies in us while we live.
—Norman Cousins

"I LOVE THIS SYSTEM. See that, the avenues run this way, and the streets run that way. These numbers tell you exactly where you are and how many more streets to go. You can't get lost here," Ma said, admiring Miami's concrete and efficient infrastructure on the drive from the airport to our new home.

"It is such a treat to drive on nicely paved streets," she sighed, as if to reassure herself that we'd done the right thing by leaving our hellhole of troubles and chaos behind.

We might as well have landed on Mars instead of Miami if you'd asked me. It looked like a colorless movie set with fake storefronts, building facades, phony landmarks, and make-believe caricatures—a black and white wasteland of two-dimensional, empty skeletons. Nothing could change my tragic outlook. Not the glitzy, shimmery coat on everything around me, not Ma's upbeat talk. I had no idea how to resuscitate my shell-shocked body and soul back to life.

"Uncle Eugene and Auntie Chuny are cleaning up and waiting for us," my cousin Victor said. He turned onto a cul-de-sac and then the driveway of a plain, one-story home painted an avocado-green that reminded me of the hideous school uniform I wore throughout elementary school.

Ma's enthusiasm dropped a notch when she got out of the car and noticed the barren sea of lawn that hugged the house.

"Hallo, *gudus*, sweeties, come in. Welcome to your new home," Auntie Chuny said, opening the front door. An obnoxious, orange-brown, worn carpet covered every square inch of our new house, and bleak white walls stared back at us from every direction. It was surreal. This could not possibly be my new life. Disgust, sadness, resistance, survival guilt, and a twinge of curiosity competed with one another for space within my heart.

"Come see your room. It's right up front. You can see all the action from here," Mayling said. She was going by Karen, her American name, and seemed to be handling all the recent cultural conversions in her life just fine. She and her family lived "close" to us, in Ft. Lauderdale, an hour drive from Miami, and I would be able to see her "often"—once every few weeks or so.

Ma made sure that we got to Miami just before the start of the new school year. I'd be entering the eight grade; Mark the seventh. On our first day, I searched high and low for our junior high school, perplexed that it was the huge, concrete, jail-like warehouse right in front of me.

Ice-cold air escaped through the solid metal doors. Not only was this our school, the inside was a giant freezer chest that would keep us cold all day long, as if we were pieces of meat that would otherwise rot in the humid Miami heat.

"They even have carpet inside. Everywhere," Mark said, feasting his eyes not just on the clean carpet, but also on the brand-new furniture, shiny books, and enticing stuff visible through the long rectangular glass windows in the middle of the doors. Kid-friendly posters decorated the walls, and bright projects hung from the ceilings. Some of the classrooms were full of typewriters; others had pianos and musical instruments. There was a large gym with basketball courts and sports equipment and an art room with paints, crayons, pencils, and papers in all the colors of the rainbow.

These classrooms were nothing like what we'd been used to. A fully stocked middle school classroom in Suriname had beaten-up, wooden desks covered by profanity, obscene drawings, and pen holes, a blackboard, a few pieces of chalk, glass-shutter windows with gaps here and there, and dreadfully old textbooks.

I wanted to try these alluring offerings, but resisted the urge. I was too afraid of forgetting the past. The truth was already fading and slipping like sand through my fingers, and I was hellbent on holding onto every single last grain that I could. I refused to gloss over the fact that, from now on, we were going to spend our days in a refrigerated jail, in a barren, spiritual desert without any of my friends and relatives, far away from Suriname, the mystical, rainforest womb that had birthed and nourished me all my life. All because of a stupid revolution that robbed us and thousands of other families from our beloved homeland.

I felt like an alien from another planet, and, next to the stiffly lacquered bangs, blue and purple streaked hair, stylish, brand-name clothes, perfectly traced eyes and lips, and fine jewelry of my classmates, I'm sure that many of them also thought that I looked like one. Even I could tell that my duster hairdo painfully clashed with the ruffled, turtleneck, polka-dot mini dress that Marie, our seamstress in Suriname, had sewn using a picture that I'd ripped out of an American fashion magazine—not sure what year.

"Hey, goody two-shoes. If the bus driver asks you if you're stoned, say yes, okay?" Danny, one of neighborhood boys, snickered while waiting at the bus stop the next morning. His friends were puffing on cigarettes behind some tall bushes and cracking up.

It didn't take a rocket scientist to figure out what "goody two-shoes" and "stoned" meant. But why was he picking on me? Just because I didn't speak English very well? What have I ever done to him?

The two girls who lived next door, Jackie and Melanie, were cousins, mixed and Asian-looking like me, except that they were from Jamaica. They were the only non-white kids in our neighborhood, two of the five—now seven, if you included Mark and me—kids responsible for the recent "Asian Invasion" at my school.

"Sniff it," Jackie insisted, holding up a Ziploc bag with white powder under my nose. I did, so glad that they were trying to befriend me.

"It smells like baby powder," I said, confused.

"It is! Don't tell anyone," Jackie squealed, pleased that I was in on their little secret.

Is she serious? She reminded me of a helium balloon on a flimsy string, bobbing all over the place in the wind. I had trouble holding onto my center of gravity around her, around everyone for that matter.

My teachers were kind, but my last name, Tjenalooi, and my background stumped every single one. I was from a country no one had heard of. I spoke a language, Dutch, that no one else in any of my classes spoke. There was not a single TV show or thirteen-year-old cultural reference I could relate to. There were very basic things that I didn't understand and that bewildered me, like placing a paper plate with food in a plastic oven—a microwave oven that is.

The only familiar place that I could retreat into was my inner world, filled with memories of the past. Rather than paying attention in class or doing homework, I wrote my name in 3-D shaded block letters on the edge of a notebook, wondering what time it was in Suriname and in Holland, and what my friends and cousins were doing.

"I have no idea what's wrong with these kids," I wrote to Kiki. "It's just like what you see in the movies. They are so immature and do the stupidest things to get attention and appear cool. They smoke cigarettes and carry baby powder around, pretending it's cocaine. I'm not kidding. Everyone is put in some kind of racial box, and they're so mean. Especially to foreigners, like us."

After pouring my heart out to my friends, I had no desire to engage in frivolous talk. I was in a private Cold War with everyone around me for almost a year, including my family. They left me alone, too busy trying to make ends meet, and attributed my

moody stone-walling and silent treatment to hormones and adolescence. That probably had a lot to do with it, but there was so
much more going on that no one seemed to get or care about. I
hated that I had to start all over again, from scratch, not in my first
or even second language. In my third, the broken one, the one that
evoked teasing and chuckling when I mispronounced a word in
class or made other embarrassing mistakes.

While Pa searched for job leads in the newspaper, Ma tried to
grow roots, flowers, and fruit trees in the rocky dirt in the backyard. We helped Pa stuff and mail more than a hundred cover letters, but, for some strange reason, not one architecture agency in
the whole big city of Miami and surroundings was hiring.

The arrival of the container with our belongings was the biggest highlight in months until Ma realized that her beloved oval
rug, that she'd hooked, strand by strand, was gone. Stolen. A trickle
of tears streamed down her face all day long. This was the first time
I'd seen Ma crack and cry. I didn't know what to say or do.

To make matters worse, the black-market inflation back in
Suriname had shriveled up Pa and Ma's life savings and shrank
the income of my relatives back home almost two-hundred-fold,
which put them in an even worse predicament than we were in.
Consumed with survivor guilt, I converted every dollar that I
had into Surinamese currency, to calculate what kinds of grocer-
ies they could buy with my pocket change, and was hardly able to
spend any of it on myself. Ma and Pa were just as worried about my
relatives. Every so often, we went to the airport on weekends, and
asked random Surinamese travelers or an acquaintance if they'd
be willing to take a care package along.

I eventually got used to my new normal and became interested in typical adolescent activities like the rest of my peers. I was
thrilled when Ma let me get some make-up. When I attempted
to apply my latest acquisition—cheap, chalky, flea market eye
shadow—in the hallway one morning, a girl with perfectly feathered hair and make-up walked by and sneered, "Don't bother,"
while rudely smacking her gum. I looked up. She clearly meant me.
What's her problem? She wasn't trying to impress anyone

with her insults. There was no one else around. Maybe she's not even trying to insult me. Maybe I look so hideous that she felt compelled to keep me from making a fool of myself.

Something inside me spoke. *You know better. You know that this has nothing to do with you. This is all her stuff.*

What stuff? I don't get it. And why would she be mean to me because of her stuff? That makes no sense at all.

At home, my family was subjected to a similar streak of random attacks. The tree in front of our house was TP'd, and the back window of our car was busted with a brick.

"Someone is specifically targeting you. Do you know why?" the police asked Pa. "The rest of the trees and cars in our neighborhood have been spared." We had no clue.

The next day, for no reason at all, Danny, the kid who'd picked on me at the bus stop, called Mark a "motherfucker" and told Ma to suck his dick when the three of us were in the front yard, minding our own business. Mark froze and didn't say a word.

I'd never even heard grown-ups curse at each other with such contempt, let alone a child at an adult. Not just any adult. Ma. I wanted to beat the shit out of him. Ma probably would have gone after him like a wild animal if we still lived in Suriname, but, here in Miami, she submitted, as if she were prey. The United Stated was not the Wild, Wild West like Suriname. There were a lot of strict, unfamiliar rules about child abuse that Ma was learning about and respected. She didn't understand them well enough to know if her ideas about physical discipline were out of line and would rather be safe and shut down than sorry.

I marched behind Jackie, Melanie, and Danny into his house. I didn't care about getting in trouble. I needed answers. Could he and his friends have broken our car window and TP'd our tree? It was late afternoon, and no one seemed to be home. Danny flung a bedroom door open, and all of us paraded in.

"Who said that you could come in? Get the hell out of here! And close the damn door behind you!" a body slumped in a wheelchair bellowed, oozing hatred as tar-black and sinister as the walls and window shades of his dark prison.

Danny shut the door and went back outside with a steel face. "Who is that? What's wrong with him?" I asked Jackie.

"It's his older brother. He was in a car accident about two years ago and can't walk anymore. He hates everyone and shouts a lot. Don't take it personal," she said nonchalantly.

"Where are his parents? How can they leave him like that and let him paint his room black? I'm sure he didn't do that," I said, unable to erase what I'd just witnessed from my mind. I'd never seen anyone in such despair and misery before. Jackie just shrugged her shoulders. I felt silly and like a goody two-shoes for being so bothered by everyone and everything.

For months, I tried to ignore Michelle, the loudest and most obnoxious girl on the bus, but she was crawling and festering under my skin like a painful, swollen zit that had finally come to a head and needed to be popped.

"Who do you think you are? The Queen of the bus?" I snapped at her one morning when the humidity was already as thick as a wall.

She was, as usual, taking up a whole seat and cackling the ears off the girl behind her, too self-absorbed to care that the rest of the seats were all taken.

When I made it a point to sit next to her every morning, she said that her Cuban, bodybuilder friend would beat me up. Sheryl, my six-foot-tall Black classmate from Barbados, heard what happened, went up to her, and said, "So, where's your Cuban friend? I'd like to meet her." That was the end of that. Michelle never mentioned her Cuban friend again.

It wasn't hard to find a new target for my wrath: Ricky, a scrawny boy who sat behind me in English and kept sliding down in his chair to touch my butt with his knees until I couldn't stand it anymore.

When the bell rang, I turned around, grabbed him by the balls, and said, "If you don't stop touching me, I'm going to rip these off."

He squirmed, blood draining from his face, his eyes as big as marbles. I didn't care that I'd scared the living daylights out of him. I had bigger things to worry about than his puny testicles.

Pa was moving to California to look for work, while the rest of the family—Ma, Mark, and I—needed to stay behind. We couldn't afford to move again so soon, especially since we didn't know for sure if Pa would find any work there. I shouldn't say any work. I'd been doing any work, any odd job that I was offered—babysitting, selling kabobs, *sates,* at a street fair, serving stuffy guests at an extravagant wedding, filing paperwork at my school's office, washing cars.

Not Pa. He was set on staying in architecture and was devastated when he failed the costly state license exam by a few points after months of studying. Uncle Roy suggested that he try his luck in California. I didn't get why. Uncle Eugene had given up his job at IBM in Suriname and was filling vending machines for a living. It didn't kill him, and he seemed to be making enough money to support his family.

But no. Pa was moving farther away from us than our relatives in Suriname, acting like that kind of work was below him. We'd managed on very little—even furnished part of our living room with a vinyl outdoor patio furniture set—but he'd made up his mind. Yeah, whatever. I forced myself to keep my mouth shut. I knew that this was extremely hard on him. He used to love his job and was really good at it. Everyone in Suriname knew that. And what did I know about finances and surviving in a brand-new country at fifteen?

With Pa gone, I realized that Ma was even more self-conscious about her English than I was about mine. So, I ended up answering the phone, talking to the doctor, the dentist, teachers, church ladies, and Jehovah's Witnesses, who knocked at our door and ate up our entire afternoon.

Once my English improved, school started to get a lot easier. I'd bumped up from ESOL classes to honors level classes in English, world history, biology, and math. Because I dreaded getting clumped in with the nerds, I tried to shoot for grades that were good, but not too good. B pluses or A minuses were fine. I could get away with looking sorta smart, but not weird smart.

"Ms. Loraine, is it necessary to lather your homework in suntan oil when the two of you hang out at the pool? Could you bring in homework that looks a bit more decent than this?" Mr. Andres, my math teacher, asked while waving a rumpled sheet of paper pinched between two fingers, oil stains clearly visible.

I smiled and slyly slipped the nail clippers that I was using to cut off my split ends into the palm of my hand, darned pleased with myself. My *eigenwijze* daring self was making a comeback, and my goody two-shoes reputation was becoming a thing of the past. I was determined to keep it that way, even if that meant that I needed to distance myself from any and all goody two-shoes who roamed the world, including Mark.

When my high school's glamorous Golden Girls drill team strutted their tails at my first pep rally to songs like "Thriller," "Super Freak," and "Don't You Want Me," I bit. They had the irresistible appeal that every high school girl and guy desired, and I

was gonna get me some, no matter what. I practiced for days on end, auditioned, and was, within weeks, bobbing and undulating to "Egypt, Egypt," decked out with a bronze choker, chiffon genie pants, and golden skin.

"Work it, ladies, work it," our team captain shouted during practice and warm-ups for our halftime show on football game nights. Not that any one of us needed the reminder. We knew how to rile up the entire student body in our white, knee-high boots and super-short, black velvet mini-dresses rimmed with sparkly, gold sequins. White cowboy hats topped with fluffy yellow plumes completed our head-turning look.

After the game, we worked our charm some more, got chummy with the football team, and danced in the parking lot, tipsy on beer that the guys would sneak into their gym bags.

"*Tsssss*, you girls are too hot to handle," Eric, one of the football players said, while whipping his head around in a pivot turn.

"Look who's talking, Mr. Hotness himself," I said.

"Mr. Hotness?" Eva said, choking on her beer, which caused

spurts of laughter and giggles. "Since when do you like him? How much did you have to drink?"

I didn't respond. They were too out of it to notice or care that I could get goofy and high on just water or soda. Redemption was sweet.

"That's a beautiful ring. Did you get that from your boyfriend?" I asked Eva on the bus ride back. I'd felt most comfortable around her, perhaps because of her tendency to suddenly retreat into sober reflection.

"No, I got it from my dad," she said, her delicate face and voice solemn.

"He must love you a lot. I don't know anyone with a ring like that," I said.

"I actually don't think he does. I hardly ever see him. He just buys me expensive gifts," Eva said, sounding more defeated and tired than most grown-ups I knew.

"I'm very sorry. I hardly see my dad either. He visits every two or three months from California," I said, saddened by her predicament.

Even though Ma and Pa had never been to a halftime show, football game, drill-team performance, or award ceremony, and couldn't afford any of the expensive jewelry, clothes, or cars that the parents of many of my friends lavished on them, I at least knew in my heart that they loved me a lot. Pa wrote often, and had just sent pictures of his new "bedroom" and "bed," cardboard boxes under his desk at work so not to overstay his welcome and burden our relatives in California.

He kept his belongings in the car and showered at the gym. His boss apparently agreed to this arrangement after he'd shown himself to be a good worker, and he sounded happy and grateful to have a well-paying, steady job that was in his field. I drew him a picture of a Chinese guy, hanging upside down, his shoe and foot caught on a corner swirl of a pagoda. I titled it "Hang in There, Pa," in my best chopstick letters, my way of making peace with his decision.

At home, Mark and I moved around each other like oil and water. Mark was home most of the time and only went to wrestling practice, math meets, and school events; I was home as little as possible and came and went as late as I pleased, even during week-days. Ma was black pepper; her presence lightly sprinkled in both of our lives. I figured that all that she really cared about were my grades, because she never asked me about anything else. It never occurred to me that she may not have a clue what to ask, just like I had no idea what to ask her or Mark. And the heart-to-heart talks that I used to have with nature spirits and my soul every weekend were a thing of the past. I'd concluded that as long as we were fed, clothed, and thriving in school, Ma and Pa's sacrifices had been worth it.

My friends and their friends' friends drove me wherever the action was on any given night—street parties, birthday parties, dance clubs, the beach, *Calle Ocho*, Coconut Grove, you name it. If we didn't have a ride back, we figured that we'd meet at least one cool guy with a car who was out to meet a few cute girls and would be willing to give us a ride home. Luis, a friend of a friend, often came to the rescue when we were left stranded.

"*Chinita*, come here. Talk to me. Why won't you talk to me? Don't you see how much I love you? I don't even want to talk to any other girl. See that beautiful girl? Not interested. I just want to be with you," Luis pleaded while holding me by the arm and pulling me closer. He was a junior, but three years older than me: dark, handsome, very buff, and the black sheep in his family. I wasn't sure if his family treated him like the black sheep because his skin was darker than theirs or because he had a dark side.

"There is no one else in the world who will love you as much as I love you. Don't you see how crazy I am about you? You can ask my friends. I always talk about you. They call us *Negro y China*, Black and Chinese. Doesn't that sound good together?" he insisted.

Even when my friends were in his car, he showered me with a special kind of attention that I'd never experienced before and that seeped into the parched cracks of my famished soul. He shamelessly got me whatever he thought would win me over—his sister's driver's license to get me into night clubs, food and drinks whenever I just looked hungry and thirsty, stuffed animals at the fair to cuddle with at night, audio tapes with love songs that expressed how he felt.

Our entire interaction consisted of him orbiting me, and, when I could no longer disavow his effort and perseverance, I figured that he must be right. He had months' worth of proof that no one loved me as much as he did.

There was never a set moment in time when I officially became his girlfriend. He never asked, and I never said yes, because it never occurred to me that I could have feelings of my own that could be different than his. I assumed that if someone loved you this much, you were obligated to love him back. Or perhaps that's what I began to believe after hearing him say it so often. I was pretty sure I loved him. I'd listen to "Faithfully," "Open Arms," and other Journey songs that he'd dedicated to me until I had become intoxicated by the passionate feelings that came straight from his heart. If this wasn't love, I didn't know what was.

Drunk on love, I had no time or interest in going out with my own friends, let alone write letters to childhood friends who'd become ghosts. Sporting jaguar eyes, bronze jewelry, a golden tan, skintight jeans, and boots, I preferred to prowl with Negro and his posse through the sultry streets and throbbing nightclubs of Miami until the wee hours of the morning.

Some nights, we gyrated with a mass of sweaty bodies to salsa and techno beats; other nights, we hung out at South Beach, daring each other to jump off a thirty-foot wooden dock into the dark water below. On the weekends, we went jet-skiing with his brother and girlfriend, or fooled around by the lake near my house.

"*Chinita,* baby, I love you so much. I can't imagine my life without you," Luis said while we were making out in his big pickup truck in the parking lot before school, our bodies swooning to a new set of sensual love songs that he'd compiled for me. There were times that the sparks got so intense that we needed to finish what we started in the janitor's walk-in closet, skipping a period of class here and there.

"You are going to give your father a heart attack," Ma said when I sat down for breakfast at about one in the afternoon on an ordinary Saturday. I had no idea what she meant. Because I stayed out late? Why was this all of a sudden an issue? It irked me that she was acting all dramatic and putting Pa's life in my hands in an attempt to get me to "behave." I missed the old Ma. I wished that she'd just yell at me, that being a single immigrant mom—with Pa gone so much—hadn't sucked the life out of her, and that she weren't so afraid of giving it to me straight up.

She must have complained to Pa about my behavior, because he wrote me a long letter about all kinds of abstract stuff, like the care that is required in handling a sharp knife. The knife isn't good or bad, but a child may not have the finesse, the maturity, that is needed to use it properly and may accidentally cut herself. What the hell was he talking about? Sex? Apparently so, because he talked a lot about temptation, like craving ice cream or cake. Kids without any self-control gorged themselves full on it. Was he implying that I was acting like a little kid? Well, he didn't need to worry about any of that, because I knew how to handle a knife just fine. As a matter of fact, I knew how to handle a ton of adult matters just fine, and I wasn't gorging myself full on ice cream.

I was able to appreciate Pa's letter a bit more the next day, just bumming in my bed and staring at the ceiling. My mind spun around like the rows in a big slot machine. It kept going until all the symbols had lined up, until I had a better sense of what was up and what was down.

Pa didn't say to put down the knife, which was kind of cool. "My Dutch liberalism," he would have said if he were here. I still wished that he was more direct and clear about his sentiments, like James, the student director of our school's performing band.

"What do you see in that asshole?" James asked me when a bunch of us were hanging out after band and drill team practice.

"You mean Luis?" I asked.

"Yes, that asshole," he said. He was clearly annoyed, but I could tell that he wasn't criticizing me for being with an asshole. I wasn't sure what he was getting at, but his boldness piqued my interest.

"Why do you say that?" I asked.

"Something about him, the way he carries himself, tells me that he's an asshole. I can just see it," he said.

"Well, you're wrong. You don't even know him," I retorted.

Luis wasn't an asshole. Sure, there were rumors going around that his family smuggled drugs, but that's what kids at school said about all Colombians and Cubans with nice houses and cars. That would include at least a thousand kids at my school. I couldn't stand it when people stereotyped me, so I purposely didn't ask him what his dad did for a living. Nor did I care why his brother once had a handgun in his glove compartment. It was none of my business.

James just didn't know the real Luis, the Luis who shed tender tears when he told me that he loved me, the Luis who was crazy about me and showed it in a million ways. I was the center of his world.

Why did James go off on Luis? Did he like me? His comment kept popping up in my mind. He had flown underneath my "cute guy radar," because of his super short hair and flipper ears. What had suddenly changed? Why did I suddenly care what he thought?

He wasn't part of the popular crowd, but he was respected by his band, his teachers, and the smart kids. Even if he liked me, it was clear that he wasn't saying things to impress me or win me over. When I was little, Ma used to say, "If you care about someone, you tell her or him the truth." He was the kind of guy who couldn't help but tell people the truth just because he cared and wanted the best for them.

I wanted to be more like James, an honorable rebel who dared to look truth straight in the eye, just because it was the right thing to do. I'm not sure what drove that truth home other than James helping me to lift a veil of deception and revealing painful aspects about my life that I couldn't confront on my own. It was like being injected with a reality shot that broke the addictive spell that Luis had put me under.

I could no longer shake the diehard truth that was staring me straight in the face and sizing me up from all angles. Sure, Luis loved that I could rile up a crowd, but he hated that it couldn't be a private show just for his pleasure. The sad truth was that I felt flattered by his jealousy. I also enjoyed it when guys undressed me with their eyes from the bleachers or sidelines of the dance floor or "accidentally" rubbed up against me with their hard-ons, even though I twisted their groping hands and wrists and dramatically shoved and punched their shoulders. I didn't want to admit that the Corvette-driving physician or the bridge-playing math teacher who hit on me were just as perverted and horny as these scumbags, attracted to the same filthy Band-Aids stuck on my neglected wounds. I believed that their attention—measured by their status or by number—was truly elevating my self-worth. Until James helped me to see that I had stooped lower than ever before. I could no longer deny the devastating truth—I was addicted to sleazy, sexual vibes to soothe my lost and aching soul.

The following weekend, Luis' cousin, Enrique, drove us to a nightclub. He and Luis were gabbing away in Spanish. I didn't realize that they were wasted until Enrique almost rammed straight into a steel railing at a T-crossing. Luis grabbed the steering wheel and pulled the bottom toward him. The car screeched loudly, swerved, and skidded around the corner, then wobbled over the ribbed edge of the street, missing the railing by less than a foot.

When Luis laughed off this near miss, everything came to a boiling head. What an idiot! My wise voice asked, "*What happened to all the lessons about your superpowers and immortality? This is not what I meant.*"

"I want out. Right this instant," I yelled. I wanted out of the car, out of the relationship, out of the illusion that Luis was my caretaker, my protector, my everything.

Why did you think that he'd be using his head? The only head he cares about is the one attached to his penis.

True. He insisted that the "pulling out" method was a reliable form of birth control and only backed down after having it his way much more often than I liked to admit.

"Hey, *hombre*, man, turn around. China wants to get out. Drop us off over there."

Enrique dropped us off at a busy shopping center where cruisers floated by for hours on the weekend. Luis grabbed me by the wrist and dragged me to an alley behind a movie theater. I went along to avoid a scene.

"Let go of me, you asshole. Get your fucking hands off me," I snarled when we were alone. He had never seen this side of me in the two years we'd been together.

"You are breaking up with me, aren't you? What happened? *Do you like someone else?* Tell me the truth," he shouted.

"No, I don't," I said. I chose not to answer the first two questions.

"Then why are you acting this way?" He sensed that I was done. Done. *Done.* Like a leathery, overcooked piece of meat. *"Why are you doing this to me?"* he cried through angry, despairing tears, while slapping and hitting the rough cement wall, his palms and knuckles scraped and bleeding. He looked like a volcano that was fuming and fighting with itself, wanting more than anything for me to be the wall. Instead, he grabbed me by my upper arms, shoved me around, let me go, and started the cycle all over again, sounding like a dying animal stuck in the swamps of the Everglades, pleading and begging not to be abandoned.

My stomach swirled and somersaulted while tolerating an hour, and another, of Luis' unraveling while the substances in his system wore off. I huddled into a ball to shield myself from his hurricane of rage and destruction, pondering what to do within the few tiny, clear spaces left in my mind.

"You *have* to believe me that I can't live without you. What am I going to do? You are *killing* me inside. *It will be your fault if I kill myself,*" he said, trying out different moves to corner me. I thought about his brother's gun for a moment. My mind went frantic, but my body didn't respond to his bluff. He quieted down every so often, then, as if armed with a freshly cocked gun, he attempted a new strategy to convince me to stay with him. I held out as long as I could, determined not to budge an inch, until he threatened to show Ma and Pa a steamy letter that I'd written him. Checkmate. He knew that this was my Achilles' heel. I couldn't bear the thought of worrying and hurting Pa and Ma after all that they'd already been through.

What he didn't know was that Pa had saved up enough to

buy a house in Sacramento. A few days ago, I wouldn't even look at Ma when she delivered the devastating news that we were moving to California at the end of the school year. I hated her for forcing me to move again and forcing me to leave Luis. Who would have guessed that in less than a week, I couldn't wait to start over and be free from Luis? What was six months? During our final years in Suriname, I'd held my tongue for much longer because of another deranged lunatic.

"Let's go and see where everyone is," Luis said, sensing that I'd surrendered. He gently pulled my exhausted, slumped body up by the wrist and off the ground, and wrapped his arm around my waist. I fought the urge to pull back, wiped a lone tear off my face, and accompanied him to lights . . . sounds . . . people . . . action.

Chapter 4

 PILGRIMAGE

Life is a long pilgrimage from fear to love.
—Paul Coelho

"ARE THESE BRUISES?" Gianna asked while lifting up my sleeve and scrutinizing my face.

"Kind of. They don't hurt. Don't worry about it," I said. She was Luis' friend, but we'd gotten closer over the past few months, hanging out every now and then on Sunday afternoons.

"Did Negro do this? What an asshole. Where's your phone?" she asked while throwing my comforter and pillows around, looking for my phone under piles of books, notebooks, and stuffed animals.

"Gianna, calm down. Please don't call him. He didn't hit me. He just squeezed me and didn't even realize that he was bruising me."

"What the hell got into him?"

"I don't know. He went berserk, because he sensed that I wanted to break up with him. I don't know what he's capable of. At one point, he said that he'd kill himself, then he blackmailed me with a letter, threatening to give it to my parents if I left him."

"Kill himself? *Pff.* That's a bunch of bullshit."

"I think he was drunk and maybe took something else. He's

never acted like that before. We're moving to California in six months. I'm pretty sure it won't happen again if I just lay low and don't provoke him," I said while pulling on the cord of the phone in her hand.

"Do you know how long six months is? You shouldn't have to put up with this for one minute!" She elbowed me out of the way and gave me a look that said, *Back off, or else.*

"*Negro,* jerk, *cabrón. ¿Qué te pasa,* eh? What's the matter with you? *¿Estás loco?* Are you crazy? Did you see the fucking bruises on China's arm?" she yelled. I could hear him yell back in Spanish, and they went at it for a while until Gianna slammed down the phone.

"He said that he's coming over right now. Let him. I'll spit in his face," Gianna said.

"Gianna! Ugh. My parents are home. I don't want them to know about any of this. They have enough to deal with. Let's go outside." I took her by the elbow and pulled her outside.

Ten minutes later, Luis' car screeched around the corner and stopped in the middle of the circle. He jumped out with a piece of paper in his hand, leaving the car door wide open and the engine running.

Gianni pushed up from the parked car that we were leaning on, and charged at him full force. Luis shoved my steamy letter in her face, and said, "*Mira, mira lo que escribió, mira, es una puta.* Look what she wrote. She's a slut."

Gianna read a bit of my masterpiece, carefully crafted during a boring math class, and said, "So what? I don't fucking care." She snatched the letter out of his hand and crumbled it up. Luis began to shove Gianna around, and something in me snapped. My protective fierceness shifted away from my parents and laser-beamed onto Gianna. My insides growled like a black jaguar, wanting to pounce on Luis and get him out of her way. Instead, I ran inside and got help.

"Ma, Pa, hurry, Luis is outside, and he's acting crazy. Look what he did to me," I said, holding up my sleeve and showing each of my parents my bruised arms. "You have to stop him. He's going to hurt Gianna too."

They rushed outside and found Luis and Gianna standing by the door like two children in trouble for fighting.

"Luis, I'm not going to call your parents, but, if you don't stay away from my daughter, I will. And I'll also call the police. Do you understand?" Pa said. He sounded calm and concerned, treating Luis as if he were his own son.

"Yes, sir," Luis said, looking down. Ma stood next to Pa in the doorway, thick silence enveloped her like the muggy evening air. That was it. *That was it?* I wished Pa would yell at him and punch him in the face, but he didn't. That's not who Pa was. And Ma's sharp tongue was twisted in a knot, too afraid of stumbling over unfamiliar English words and falling on its own razor edge.

After Luis and Gianna left, we each went about our business as if nothing had happened. No questions. Not even a "What happened?" "What did he do?" "Are you alright?"

"It's not your fault," Mark said, poking his head around my bedroom door. "I saw on a TV documentary that girls who are hit by their boyfriends blame themselves for it. I just want you to know that it wasn't your fault."

"Thanks, I appreciate it," I said, swallowing the lump in my throat. I didn't realize that he'd been following my drama from behind the scenes.

"It never really crossed my mind that it was my fault. He went nuts imagining me with someone else, but, thank God, he didn't hit me. I figured that if I could hold off with breaking up, I'd spare Ma and Pa unnecessary headache and worries in having to deal with this."

Even though I didn't feel like I deserved to be mistreated, I believed that I needed to protect others from my poor choices. My reasoning made as much sense to Mark as it did to me. Ma and Pa were big into self-sacrifice and led by example. They'd become more "hands-off" in their parenting, especially after our family was pried apart in four different directions after moving to Miami. It was up to us to detect the glistening nuggets of their guidance, either accidentally dropped along the way or intentionally sprinkled along our paths. They never directly conveyed what they thought or wanted.

"He just needs to stew a bit in his own juices and learn from his mistakes," I overheard Ma say to Pa not too long ago, referring to someone who'd messed up. Pa didn't respond but seemed to agree. Ma has said more than once to Mark and me that she would not bail us out of jail if we ever got ourselves in trouble.

Their thinking explained why they had no qualms whatsoever about letting me steep in my own mess now. I picked at my cold serving à la mode, not able to find its warm, soothing center. I had to trust that it was there despite a lack of evidence.

Yes, of course they love you. They know that you lost your way and that you can do better. Much better. I just wished they'd given me a concrete map and some instructions on how to find my footing, but they seemed to be as clueless as I was, or perhaps even a tad more, on how to help me.

What am I supposed to do if Luis doesn't leave me alone at school tomorrow? I fretted in bed while staring at the ceiling. *He's chicken shit. He won't bother you. If he does, just call the police and get a restraining order.* Reassured, I dozed off into a deep sleep, not giving him a second thought.

Luis fortunately did leave me alone the next day, and all the subsequent days that followed. He replaced me with another *Chinita* in fewer than two weeks and, whenever he saw me, would pull her close and nestle his leg in between hers like he used to do to me, hoping to get me jealous. All I felt was huge relief that he and all of his friends, except for Gianna, were out of my life for good so I had time to think and regroup.

Luis had been the asshole, but I'd been his accomplice. I'd fed on and fed his needy possessiveness, confusing it with love. I even gorged on it at times to soothe the persistent aching for my old life—my friends, my relatives, Pa, my old home, and the innocent, inquisitive, and happy me—until his sick attention had completely hijacked my body, heart, and mind.

Pa and Ma's love was very different. Sober and steadfast. I'd never even seen them hold hands or kiss.

"I don't get these celebrities. They fork over all this money for their extravagant weddings. And what do they do the following year? Get a divorce. It's all show business and drama without any substance and can blind you if you don't pay attention," Pa said while watching some Hollywood entertainment show on TV.

I knew what he meant now and added this gem of truth to my collection of other introspective treasures. Many of the kids at my high school looked and acted like mini-celebrities. Whatever immunity I used to have for this kind of peer pressure had gradually worn off. Not the case with Ma and Pa. They had remained as devoted as ever to us and each other, trying to reunite us on higher ground. It was time for me to get on board with their program.

That Sunday morning, we sat and kneeled and sat and kneeled on the hard, wooden benches of our neighborhood parish that Ma, Mark, and I attended every weekend. I was glad that Pa could join us before heading back to California in a few days, but, once we all sat down, I felt so ashamed about the Luis catastrophe, I wanted to hide under a rock.

I'd felt this worked up once before. My fourth-grade teacher used to tell us that we were disobeying God's will and that we were gonna go to hell whenever she needed us to quiet down and behave. I asked Pa if it was true.

"Don't get too hung up on words and literal commands. Humans have throughout history tried to capture what God is all about, but we can never do God justice. God would not make any boastful or harsh claims or judgments or order us what to believe or not to believe. That's not God-like. Just use the Bible as a guide and listen to your heart to determine what's right or wrong, because even the Bible is translated and compiled by humans and therefore is an imperfect representation of God's ways and words. Every culture and religion gets things partially right. If any of them claim that they have it more right than others or that they are 100 percent right, run in the other direction," Pa responded. He could make all of my worries disappear with just one whirl of his magic cape and wand.

Our circumstances had changed a lot over the years, but Pa's comforting presence was the same. So was the soothing, melodic murmur of choir hymns. They enclosed me in a cocoon of deep peace in the vast stillness of my being.

Out of nowhere, a vision of a little girl, sweet and spontaneous, appeared in my mind's eye. I leaned forward and hid my face in my hands, softly clasped in prayer.

The little girl who'd appeared was my precious and precocious younger self, the forgotten and rejected wild me who loved to roam through our jungle sanctuary every weekend. She peeked her head out and darted back and forth in the dark, subconscious woods of my mind like one of the elusive, iridescent Morpho butterflies I used to chase. My heart rejoiced and longed for more time with her, just like we used to have. Tears welled up in my eyes and rolled down my cheeks.

She stopped, cautiously examined my face, then flew into my arms. I imagined kissing and embracing her, inspecting her for scars and bruises. I used my long hair—that had grown back—to hide the stream of tears that resulted from our dramatic reunion. She clung onto me, relieved that we were both more or less unscathed. Pangs of remorse and sadness coursed through my body. I promised her that I'd never abandon her again, a heartfelt promise that I'd make over and over again every subsequent Sunday during mass until we moved.

"What are you doing this weekend? Do you want to hang out with us tomorrow?" Cheryl, one of my drill-team friends, asked me, not long after Luis and I had broken up. She must have noticed that I was no longer entangled in his grubby tentacles and was in need of new friends. I knew her boyfriend and recognized a bunch of her other friends. They were in our school's band, in my honors classes, and on the football team: all of them preppy kids who were dialed into a more wholesome radio station than the one I'd been listening to.

"Sure. That sounds fun," I said.

They picked me up at five in the afternoon, the earliest I'd ever gone out on a Saturday evening, and introduced me to venues in Miami where teens gathered and enjoyed simple pleasures—

bowling, watching a movie at one of their homes or at the theater, hanging out at the community pool, a nearby shopping center, the fair, and getting late-night dessert at IHOP or Baskin Robbins.

These friends were my new cool to emulate, but I wondered if it was too late to save my soul. Romping silhouettes in the dark corners of my old hangout spots still flashed in and out of my mind like the flickering images from an old movie projector.

Of course it's not too late. Even if one of your new guy friends turns you on and sets you off like a box of fireworks, no big deal. Don't panic. Don't act on it. This is where you go wrong. Just stay put, feel, and enjoy. Then, let it go.

The very next time we all hung out, playing foosball and sunbathing by the pool, I practiced my "staying put" skills on Charlie, who liked to lean in and get a bit too close when he talked to girls. Perhaps to show off his perfectly chiseled face and tanned body, but more likely because he was so adorably clueless what impact he had on us and especially me. I inhaled his scent, his model looks, and his charm, and slowly exhaled the sensation of blood draining from my brain into my lower torso, hips, and thighs, slowly winding around like thick, hot lava in an awakening volcano.

See? It's just like entering a bakery full of delicious, buttery pastries. You can enjoy and appreciate them without splurging on every single one.

After a few hard weeks, the worst was over. The grip that sexual arousal had over me loosened so much that I stopped trying to appear normal and blend in. I just did.

About a month after Pa'd returned to California, Uncle Henk, his best friend, crashed his lanky, runner's body on our L-shaped sofa. It was his bed away from home every three months or so while visiting for business.

He was an oddball. On the one hand, naive, idealistic, and mellow. On the other, well-read, widely traveled, and worldly with an impressive handle on foreign languages, especially English and Spanish.

"Je zal het niet geloven, maar zo praat ik met Robert over zijn liefde's problemen aan de andere kant van de aardbol. Jullie zouden het zo goed met elkaar vinden. You won't believe it, but this is how Robert and I chat about his love life and girlfriend problems on the other side of the globe. You guys would get along so well," Uncle Henk said after I told him that I'd dumped Luis because he was a creep.

"What are you doing tomorrow? I'm going to run a half-marathon in the morning and squeeze in a shopping marathon in the afternoon, he he," he said, pausing with a raised eyebrow after his punch line and signature chuckle. "I need a good buyer's eye."

He often solicited my input when buying sneakers, T-shirts, and athletic clothes for Robert and his younger brother, Dean, the sons of his other best friend, Uncle Jan, and his wife, Aunt Anita, who lived in Holland. He usually moved from our sofa straight to theirs, his customary pit stop before continuing on with his travels in Europe.

Even though I'd only met Dean and his parents once before in Suriname, it often felt as if I'd known them much longer, because Uncle Henk had, especially in the last few years, intertwined our lives into a tight braid. One, because of his comings and goings from Miami to Holland. And two, because he lived in their house in Suriname, which he had furnished with our old furniture from the Dieterstraat.

When he visited, he brought us homemade delicacies and goodies, stocked up on the latest gadgets and supplies for his telecommunications business and home, and left with packages and mail for friends and family, keeping our close bonds alive and kicking despite the distance. It was this safety net of love and enduring family bonds that prevented us from hitting rock bottom more than once during our lowest points.

"This is the plan. Uncle Henk, Uncle Jan, Aunt Anita, and the boys agreed to help us move to California. Uncle Henk will drive the U-Haul truck. His daughter Monique is driving down from Atlanta in her station wagon, which we will pack up too. I'll drive ours," Ma said.

"Uncle Jan, Aunt Anita, Mark, and Pa are flying to California after Pa wraps up the sale of our house. Robert and Dean will be driving with us, so every driver will have a passenger. We'll start early in the morning, and break around two or three to do a bit of sightseeing and relax by the pool in the afternoons."

I liked the sound of this.

"How long will it take for us to get there?"

"About two weeks."

I hadn't seen Ma this excited and energized in longer than a decade. When I was only six years old, I trotted the globe with her for a good eight months to use up the vacation time that she'd accrued as an academic. She allowed me to skip most of the first grade, deciding that homeschooling me during our travels would teach me a lot more. We mostly stayed with relatives who had immigrated to the United States, Canada, and several countries in the Caribbean, Asia, and Europe: *Hakka* Chinese relatives who were like us, nomads at heart as well as by heritage.

In Hong Kong, Ma dragged me by the wrist through polluted, muggy slums and sketchy nightclubs in search of some distant relatives. And, on the balcony of *Apoh's*, grandma's, condo, I discovered that one of my uncles, Pa's distant cousin, had swum from China to Hong Kong through ice-cold waters, unsure if he would ever make it to the shores of freedom. This is when Ma first noticed my *eigenwijze* feistiness. She smiled proudly when I fired question after question at my uncle.

Now, I was the one smiling quietly. Her love for adventurous travel and the quickly approaching Californian horizon, already sprouting with fresh potential and second chances, was doing her good.

Driving all the way to Sacramento was going to be a pilgrimage for me too. I was not only moving to a brand-new state, but also to a brand-new state of mind and being, a fresh new beginning where no one knew my past, and I'd for sure not find any freaky fingerprints on my bedroom window. I swore that nothing could ever make me stray again, not even being called the nerdiest goody two-shoes that ever walked the earth. California was going to be the place of my true redemption.

"Thanks for the ride, guys. I don't think I'll be able to hang out tomorrow. We have visitors from Holland, and I need to finish packing up my room. I'll call you," I said to Cheryl and my friends, who were jammed in car one. I scooted to car two and car three for a last flurry of lingering arm caressing and loud, smacking hand kisses.

"Don't get arrested in California! And you better write me!" one of them shouted, referring to the surprise goodbye party they had thrown for me the previous Saturday. I smiled and shook my head, remembering the moment a male stripper, dressed as cop, walked through the front door and asked for me. I grunted and cried tears of embarrassed rapture during my squirmy roast that fortunately didn't venture beyond the stripper's red spandex G-string. There was no greater tribute to the taming of my tempestuous libido than this moment. I waved my friends off with deep fondness until they were out of sight, my heart constricted by pangs of sadness and, at the same time, wide open to greet the next chapter of my life.

A sputtering lawn mower and the fresh smell of cut grass welcomed me home. I walked to the back and looked around the corner of the house. A broad, shirtless V-back was pushing it, creating neat rows in the green carpet.

Oof. That must be Robert.

The lawnmower swiveled around. The eighteen-year-old, upgraded version of the cute thirteen-year-old boy I'd once seen in Uncle Henk's wallet smiled at me, his competitive swimmer's chest and stomach muscles bulging and relaxing with each stride.

He lifted a few fingers to greet me then casually went back to work. I slipped into the house. Pa, Mark, Uncle Henk, and our new guests, Robert's family, were zipping in between stacks of boxes, busy sorting, lifting, joking, and deliberating how to best pack up the small U-Haul truck and two station wagons with all of our stuff. Uncle Henk, Robert's dad, and Dean, his younger brother, were also shirtless, Surinamese style, and shiny with sweat.

"Are you trying to fit all of this in the smallest moving truck possible to show how smart you are or how cheap?" Uncle Jan asked

Pa, shaking his head with a grin on his face. Teasing laughter and familiar waves of comfort and safety warmed my heart.

"*Hallo lieve schat,* hi dear, *hoe gaat het?* How are you? *Al ingepakt?* All packed up?" Aunt Anita asked. She was helping Ma in the kitchen.

"*Bijna.* Almost," I smiled, while kissing and hugging our guests. The sliding door opened.

"Hallo," the heartthrob said while nodding at me, the only one who he hadn't formally met yet.

"Robert," he said and shook my hand. I blushed, my heart beating frantically.

"It's really hot here. Can I take a quick shower? I got grass all over me," he asked Ma.

"*Natuurlijk.* Of course. Loraine, get him a towel and show him where the bathroom is," Ma instructed.

I signaled to Robert to follow me. My body railed in confusion. The familiar ways of his family and his platonic, brotherly vibes were not able to pacify my hollering inner mare. She had no interest in just breathing in this fine-smelling scent, especially not after Robert came out of the shower with just a towel around his waist.

He has a girlfriend for God's sake. Just treat him like one of your handsome cousins.

It's not working!

What happened to your convictions?

They're not holding up. He's making it impossible for me to stay on track.

No, he isn't. He's just a good-looking guy. It's not like you haven't been around other good-looking guys.

But he's different . . .

It doesn't matter. He's here to test your self-control. Just breathe and pull yourself together.

Okay, okay. Give me a break, will you?

I went to my room to pack while the rest of them continued to work in the living room, hoping distraction and physical barriers would prevent me from spiraling into a dangerous and slippery hole. It worked.

Within the next few days, Pa, my uncles, and the guys had packed up the whole house, and stuffed boxes, furniture, and loose items into every nook and cranny of the U-Haul truck like a 3-D puzzle. When the long-awaited day finally arrived, we began our journey without much ado. Uncle Henk and Dean led the way in the U-Haul. Robert, Monique, Ma, and I followed close behind in two fully packed station wagons.

"So, what do you think of Robert? I convinced his parents that driving across the US would be educational and really good for them," Uncle Henk asked me with a sly smile when it was my turn to accompany him for a while in the bumpy U-Haul truck.

"What do you mean? You're not trying to match us up, are you? You said that he had a girlfriend."

"Nah, that won't last. And there is no harm in meeting each other, right? Who knows what the future has in store for you," he said while pulling out of the gas station. I looked out of the window, not sure what to do with the information, and remained quiet. He dug his foot onto the gas pedal and the loaded truck shook and sputtered until it picked up speed on a sudden downhill stretch.

Perhaps it was being able to speak Dutch for days on end, perhaps it was seeing Ma giddy and witty, relieved to be saying farewell to our trying Miami years. By the time we got to Texas, my spunky, carefree, and relaxed younger self had become a permanent part of me. Even when I watched Robert's muscular arms and speedo bum glide up and down the pool, I remained the master of my domain.

"Hey, can I drive a bit with you during the next stretch?" I asked Robert, trying to get out of the awkwardness of sitting next to Ma or Uncle Henk for hours on end.

"Of course," he said.

It didn't take long before I chattered Robert's ears off while secretly admiring his strong, long fingers and hands around the steering wheel, his creamy, tanned skin, and his perfectly shaped mouth occasionally cracking a sweet smile.

"How come you haven't called your girlfriend yet?" I added onto my list of random questions.

"I don't really miss her, and I doubt that she misses me. She wants to be in an open relationship and is seeing some other guy right now who's much older than her and has a Porsche. She doesn't have to get on a train to see him. He picks her up and takes her places," he said.

"Why are you still with her?"

He gave me a sideways glance of intrigue mixed with appreciation.

"Probably shock and confusion. I thought I loved her, and, since she's not sure about him or me, I'd hoped that she'd pick me and dump him."

"Ah, I know that feeling of confusion even though my situation was a bit different. I was with a jerk for a few years before I realized that I never loved him at all. I decided that I'm never trying that hard again to make a relationship work. I think there's a lid for every pot and, if a relationship doesn't feel natural and easy from the start, it's probably not a right fit. It'll only get worse when the going gets rough, and, trust me, the real tests will come. They do as soon as the sparkle of newness wears off."

"I always struggled just to get noticed. I was teased as the white boy in Suriname, and, in Holland, I'm the brown boy. And short. Most of the girls there are at least six feet tall. No one would ever go out with me unless I made an effort to get their attention."

"That totally surprises me," I said, sizing him up. He was several inches taller than me. "You're not short here and would be in great demand. I'm sorry about being teased. I was made fun of too after I moved here. It sucked."

"You? I thought you were Ms. Popular. I saw your friends dropping you off in a caravan of cars."

"Yeah, now perhaps. It was hard in the beginning. Very hard. I felt like an alien."

Robert's openness and vulnerability were like a refreshing breeze, filling me with a warm tenderness that I rarely felt when talking to a guy. It upped the gauge on his attractiveness meter with each passing mile.

Without any warning, Robert took my hand and started to

play with it. He stirred his finger in the palm of my hand which ignited little tingles up and down my spine and radiated from my navel into every direction. I panicked for a moment but decided to keep quiet and work on my tolerance skills.

Surrounded by miles and miles of sizzling desert and blessed with all the time in the world, he carefully ventured farther out to the side of my thigh, twirling around in torturous spirals and spinning me in a trance of heat as dizzying as the squiggles above the asphalt.

I didn't say a word, trying to keep my cool and indulging for as long as I could in the sensations, as if they were an ice cream cone that had just dropped out of the sky.

"I need to get gas, and there's a station coming up soon," he said. "The others are too far ahead to signal. You have the address for the hotel, right?"

I nodded.

He took the next exit, pulled behind a forsaken gas station and turned toward me. My face and eyes must have looked like a blinking green light framed by clumsily suppressed heaving.

"Come here," he said, and pulled my body, now throbbing with anticipation, toward him.

The instant our lips touched, they longingly opened and bursts of sweet pleasure pulsed through me. His luscious lips and tongue carefully explored mine, causing gushes of desire to well up from the bottom of my being.

An unbridled magnetism accumulated in the gap between our bodies and amplified every conceivable yearning that much more. Within this gap, my soul was holding the reins around my body and letting me experience for the first time what it was like to feel completely unleashed and uninhibited, yet contained and in full control.

There was no pressure to do anything that I wasn't ready for. I could tell that Robert was leaving it up to me to decide how far we'd go, a decision that I wasn't used to making and that paradoxically made me want him even more. The only way I'd know where exactly to draw the line was to slowly inch my way toward him. But, instead of leaning in closer, I reluctantly peeled my lips off his.

"We should get gas and catch up with the others," I mumbled.

"Okay," he complied with an irresistible sideways glance that said, "to be continued," while starting the car.

We did continue, but in a much lower gear. We finger frolicked on the middle console of the car until we caught up with the others at the hotel about an hour later. That night, Robert and I snuggled next to each other on one of the beds, bellies down, to watch a movie. The rest of the crew was scattered around, except for Ma who'd already retreated to the other room.

I didn't follow what was happening in the movie, too taken in by Robert's hand slowly exploring my bare back under my oversized sleep shirt. It felt as if his curious fingers were caressing the front of my begging body, mercilessly melting every part into an indistinguishable, throbbing blob.

Just inhale, exhale, inhale, exhale, and you'll get through. I breathed through an hour and a half of maddening arousal as indifferently as I could and somehow slept off my sexual frustrations.

From that day onward, we stuck to each other like two magnets. We held hands in silence or talked non-stop during long stretches of boring road, then wrestled and splashed each other in hotel pools. When we got to California, we excitedly ran up the stairs of my family's brand-new home in search of my bedroom, went on neighborhood strolls, and explored my new surroundings.

We came close to, but never crossed, my abstinence barrier. I was still waiting for some sort of sign, something more convincing than our parents' approving glances.

During one of our sight-seeing afternoons on the grassy lawn of Union Square in San Francisco, we rolled on our backs and watched fluffy clouds scroll by. Out of the blue, Robert sang to me in his best bass voice, "I left my heart in San Francisco." I burst out in giddy laughter. He turned to me, leaned on his elbow, and stared at me for a long time.

"What?" I asked.

"I love looking into your big brown eyes. They're so beautiful." Nervous flutters tickled every cell in my body. I knew what he was about to say but wasn't ready to hear it.

"You're perfect for me. We're meant to be together," he cooed.

"How can you say that? We just met. Your head is way up in the clouds. Way up there," I said dismissively while pointing up.

"What do you mean? What happened?"

"This is just a summer romance. The best I've ever had, but just a summer fling without a future. Let's just leave it as that."

A light shower of sobering reality began to drizzle down on us.

"I wish I could, but everything about us fits perfectly together. You're too good to be true, too good to just let go."

"This seems too good to be true, because it is. It's just an air castle, a fantasy of perfect love, and wonderful while it lasted. I don't even know who I am and what I want out of life. I still need to date a bunch of guys, go to college, explore my career options, travel, and do lots more before settling down. And, besides, you live all the way in Europe. It would make no sense for us to get into a long-distance relationship that has no end in sight. That's just crazy!"

"I'm just telling you what I feel right now."

I looked at his vulnerable, sincere eyes, sighed, and gave into a sweet kiss, but neither one of us brought this topic up again until our final goodbyes a few days later.

He held me for a long time, then said, "We'll meet again, you'll see. We were meant to be together. Mark my words."

I smiled appreciatively, and decided not to kill the moment by telling him what was really going through my mind. Yeah, right. Like how? What's up with you guys? You're such dreamers and sweet talkers. I'm not falling for this again.

While the rest of our families said goodbye to each other with boisterous hugs and kisses, Robert leaned over the back seat of the car and gave me a penetrating look that insisted, "You'll see."

Fine. If we were meant to be together, it'll happen. Someday. But I'm continuing on with my life as planned, and so should you, my eyes replied during our stare off until he faded into the distance. When the car turned the corner, I turned on my heels and went into the house.

I strangely felt more full than empty, not in the least sad. It was all so new. I didn't quite know what to make of it except for sparkle. Whatever he'd done, it definitely raised the bar for all future romantic suitors.

Chapter 5

 # THE RIGHT LID

> *You don't find love, it finds you.*
> *It's got a little bit to do with destiny,*
> *fate, and what's written in the stars.*
> —Anaïs Nin

"COLLEGE WILL BE THE BEST TIME of your life! Make sure you live in the dorms to get the full experience," my English teacher, Ms. Weiley, advised us while passing around a sheet with tips that could help us with the essay part on our college applications. She was the first person who'd ever talked to me about college.

"I have heard so often from my students who commuted that they missed out on all that was happening outside of class. By the time you graduate, you'll realize that all those extracurricular activities and dorm parties are just as educational as the classes you'll take over the years," she said.

I clutched onto her every word. There was no doubt about it. One of those cool dorms had my name on it. The quiet lull of vast and mellow Sacramento was exactly what I needed to get off the popularity train that I was on in Miami and board the high-speed brain train at my new high school. For the first time in years, my books saw the inside of a backpack and were regularly opened. I paid attention in class and took copious notes. I turned down invitations to go out and instead wrestled with impossible physics and calculus homework assignments until late at night just for the thrill of occasional victory. There was truly no senior student I knew of who was more immune to the senioritis bug than me.

My calculus teacher, Mrs. Bakelas, better known as "the drill sergeant," also shared her thoughts in regard to higher education.

"You're all smart boys and girls," she said in a thick Greek accent, the ugly black frame of her glasses on the tip of her nose. "But you need to keep your focus! There are a lot of distractions that you'll encounter in college that have nothing to do with a good, solid education, like the one you're receiving here in my calculus class. There are plenty of Mickey Mouse majors, like psychology, that you can pass with a bit of common sense. Don't take the easy way out just because you can. Work hard and you'll get far."

Hmm. Psychology. Is that like analyzing characters and themes in English class? I love breaking out in groups and talking about the moral of the story and searching for all the clever tricks like foreshadowing and good dialogue that make a book interesting. For sure, it's way more fun than cut and dry math problems. There's actually a college major to study this?

In spite of the contradictory advice from teachers, I was certain that college was a wonderful playground for the curious and carefree. My dream of going to college was getting so near, I could almost taste it.

Right when my future plans started to stick in place, Pa came home, looking like he'd been electrocuted.

"I got laid off," he said, barely audible. "I left my previous job a few months ago because Harvey insisted that he had a lot of work. He knew that I was buying a new house and bringing my family over. How could he do such a thing?" Pa said to Ma, shaking his head in disbelief. He slumped into a chair in front of the television and stared straight ahead with zombie eyes. This lingered on for days, weeks, and months.

Ma said that Pa needed to recharge and that it was her turn to step up and step in. She didn't disappoint. She applied for a job at a Montessori Preschool and supported us on her minimum wage salary while Pa cooked, did some light cleaning, and "just needed some time to grieve."

"I'm learning so much about disciplining children the right way. No one ever teaches you stuff like this in Suriname," Ma beamed over dinner. She was clearly one of the favorite caregivers at her new job, endearingly referred to as "grandma" by children, parents, and co-workers alike.

College applications were due in a few weeks, heightening Pa's stress about money. When we filled out the financial aid portion of my applications, I learned that Ma's modest salary scraped together with dwindled dividend income still fell into the lowest-income bracket.

"There is a community college just two exits from our house. We cannot afford to send you to a university. And why would you want to live there when you have a roof over your head right here?" Pa asked. It hit him hard that I'd grown up—a lot—while he was scrambling to reunite us as a family.

"Isn't getting a good education the whole point of moving to the United States?" I said, playing the same hand that I was played for so long. "My English teacher said that the life experience you gain while living on campus is an important part of your education. Maybe I can get financial aid to cover the costs."

I watched my college dreams morph into a big question mark. Why was Pa acting like it would be the end of the world if I moved out? Isn't he used to being separated by now?

I'd struck a very old, raw nerve. Pa, already quite resilient and social at twelve, was sent to a boarding school with Uncle Erwin, his younger brother, so that their three cousins from out of town could move in with my grandparents and enroll in city schools. After a few years of limited weekend time with his family, Pa was shipped to Holland to get an education at age sixteen. When he lost his father a few years later, he decided to miss the funeral in Hong Kong rather than miss his final exams. This saved his mother the cost of another expensive school year overseas.

Without needing to spell it out, Pa was clearly fed up with being the bigger person and continuously robbed of what he valued the most—uninterrupted time with his family. After all that he'd gone through, it was my turn to make a sacrifice.

≈

About two months after I'd sent off my college applications, I opened an admissions letter from UC Davis.

"I got it! I got into UC Davis!" I shouted. The best part: I'd received enough financial aid and scholarships to stay at the dorms during the week and visit Ma and Pa, who were just twenty minutes away, on the weekends. It was a dream come true that even Pa felt proud about and could live with.

"Many adolescents don't know how peer pressure operates, and I don't think grown-ups understand what kids and teens are confused about," I explained to a panel of interviewers for a freshman scholarship. "When I told one of my friends that he was using drugs because of peer pressure, he told me that I was wrong, because his friends would be happier if he didn't touch their drugs so that there would be more left for them."

After noticing a few pleased looks and slight nods, I made a bold claim that I didn't even realize had been marinating in my subconscious.

"I would like to study psychology, because some of the worst decisions that I've made in my life were due to peer pressure. I'd like to steer teens and kids away from making the same mistakes that I made."

I heard by the end of that week that I was awarded the scholarship. While it greatly boosted my interest in pursuing a psychology major, Ms. Bakelas' depiction of this career field as frivolous haunted me and created mountains of self-doubt. Only after I received the highest grade in my freshman Calculus class, along with a B in Psychology, did I believe that psychology was not a Mickey Mouse major . . . and that I did not have a Mickey Mouse brain. It was important to me to study something that made my heart rather than my head swell. Was there anything wrong with that?

To be safe, I'd chosen to live on the quiet floor of Malcolm Hall, and met some really nice friends who were studious but fun. They reminded me of my friends in Miami. We enjoyed each other's company and always ended up having a good time no matter what we did. Watching cheap movies on campus, getting ice cream downtown, dancing at the cheesy shopping center night club across the street, driving all the way to Sacramento for midnight chow mein and fried rice. We always had a blast.

On an adventurous Saturday night, Sherri, a few other floor mates, and I decided to party hop down Russell Boulevard. It was the busiest street in all of Davis and teeming with frat houses. I'd watched the boozing and schmoozing scene for about an hour when a dissatisfied gnawing got louder and louder.

The words, *been there, done that, let's go,* kept grinding on my nerves until I mustered up the courage to pick up and leave.

"I'm gonna go home," I whispered in Sherri's ear. She looked puzzled.

"You okay?"

"Yeah. I'm fine. Just tired."

"You sure? Want me to go with you?"

"No, no, stay. Really. I'll be fine. It's plenty busy and lit along the sidewalk. It will take me five minutes to cross the street and get to my room."

"Okay. Be safe," she replied.

That same feeling of boredom snuck up on me again during my jazz dance class. While my body replicated the sassy, sensual moves of our gorgeous student instructor, Kelly, my mind kept wandering off, distracted by the modern dance team, stretching in front of the wall length mirror and waiting for us to finish.

I stayed behind and watched them practice their routines, captivated by their eccentric poetry in motion, their primal music, and their fearlessness in being wild, intense, weird, even grotesque, if that's what their artistry called for. This was unlike anything I'd ever seen and what my soul had been craving.

A flyer in the hall indicated that the team was having auditions that same week.

"Welcome to Nexus, ladies, and thanks for trying out," Bonnie, one of the team members said to us during tryouts. "Nexus means coming together. Coming together to dance. Coming together to our center to share ourselves with our audiences. The first part of your tryouts will involve learning a new routine, where you'll have a chance to show off your dance technique. The second, and more important, part will be improv. You will be asked to portray a tree."

A tree? I can do pretty moves, have good body awareness and control, and can imitate other dancers, but I'd never choreographed a dance on my own. How in the heck do you portray a tree?

The first part of the auditions went smoothly, but when asked to depict a tree, I went out on a limb. I dug deep within, and decided to begin as a seed, hunched into a tight, compact ball, feet firmly planted. Next, roots and toes carefully wiggled out and poked into the ground. I cracked and burst open, naturally and easefully, my body remembering the many times I'd communed with nature spirits and plant devas at *boitie*. I knew, after all, what to do.

A tiny, vulnerable little leaf the shape of my hand shot out, waving above my head, looking for the sun. My torso trunk slowly elongated, thickened, and firmed. In minutes the length of months and years, I stood tall, sturdy, my branches gently swaying in the breeze. A broad canopy of leaves the width of my outstretched arms prayed to the sun while rustling and rubbing against each other. Energy ran and shivered up and down my body from the bottom of my feet to the top of my head and back. I felt elated, more rooted, authentic, beautiful, alive, and fulfilled than all my years of dancing, performances, wins, and awards combined.

The team loved my piece. By the following week, my body and those of a dozen other dancers were contorting and shape-shifting into the private pain of bulimia, the horror of an impending atomic bomb, the silliness of colorful, body-sized, stretchy pillow cases, and the desperation of an abused woman longing to be loved, safe, and free. This mosaic of dances for our annual winter production and the popular Whole Earth Festival shared one common theme—exposing and expressing what was forbidden, unsaid, hidden in the margins.

For the first time, despite my years of dance training and experience, I felt like an artist instead of a photocopy machine, mimicking someone else's creation. I was able to tap into an eternal, timeless space where I flourished and soared and danced on music that streamed through the universe, nature, life, the dancers, the audience, and all things. In our synchronized dances, we moved like a flock of birds without leaders or followers. We were all one.

"Really? You've never heard of flower children? The hippie movement?" Margie, our potluck host and the oldest member of Nexus, giggled. She was dressed in a white cotton gown with eyelet lace on the sleeves and liked to jam on her guitar during get-togethers.

"I moved to the US in 1983, and didn't watch much television in Suriname. I know about it from hearsay and movies, not from up close, like you guys," I replied.

"Yeah, some of our parents were hippies and instrumental in growing the Whole Earth Festival on campus to the size it is now. This little town is full of history. I even got arrested once during peace protests right here in Davis," Margie said. She was a mother of three, and returning to school to get her degree in Women's Studies.

Wow. Flower children, now returning students and rebellious moms, who've been arrested for protesting? I was beyond intrigued.

Brent was a regular at their potlucks and showed up in faded jean shorts, a ripped shirt, and bare feet.

"You must be one of the newest members," he said.

"I am. And you?"

"An old friend of Bonnie's."

Brent turned out to be everything that my dorm friends, frat boys, and other cookie cutter college guys were not. He was five years older than me, a pre-med major, very laid-back, and full of life experience. A worldly military vet and a bit of an outcast, he brimmed with overseas stories of courage, loneliness, hardship, and friendships that developed between him, his comrades, and the Korean prostitutes who slow danced with them during the holidays.

This was the brighter story.

The darker one revealed the reason why he joined the military. He desperately needed to get away from his "dysfunctional family" and divorced parents—his "alcoholic father," a wealthy lawyer, and his "enabling mother."

"They lost their way and still haven't found it. Confused by the ways of the world. Money. Business. Success. Failure. Especially in relationships."

"Do you talk to them?"

"Hardly. It feels shallow. We don't have much to talk about, so I'd rather not. I like to live in the present moment, in the here and now. I strive to be free from the past, from societal rules, from their cultural legacy that doesn't reflect my ideals. They don't get that. It always causes contention and conflict between us. So, I've decided to live and let live. I can't change them, but I can work on myself and find my own way," Brent said in a soothing tone.

"I don't think I'd ever be able to do what you do," I said, in awe. Finally, a guy with some substance, a deep thinker who wouldn't judge my unruly Miami years.

"Do you like to read?" Brent asked.

"Yeah. Don't have a lot of time these days because of my hectic dance schedule, but there's nothing more eye-opening and thought-provoking to me than reading."

"I have a great book for you. It's my favorite book. Have you heard of *Jonathan Livingston Seagull* by Richard Bach?"

"No. What's it about?"

"The journey of a seagull finding freedom from the flock and learning to soar on his own. I think you'll find it helpful. You're welcome to borrow it. I usually hang out on the lawn by the quad on Tuesdays and Wednesdays after my OChem class. Come find me. I'll have it with me," Brent said.

The following Tuesday, I encountered Brent as well as Darla, his loyal golden retriever, on the quad. We met regularly and discussed Richard Bach's book, Buddhist philosophy, and the fascinating teachings from my religious studies class. Brent and I eventually became an item even though he acted more like my spiritual teacher than my boyfriend. Ma and Pa didn't seem too excited about his stiff presence. When I brought him over for dinner and

asked if we could spend the night, in my room, of course, Pa looked
at me in shock and shook his head no.

"That's fine. If we can't stay here, we'll just drive back to Davis
after dinner. We're more comfortable at his place anyway," I said.
Pa quietly got up, and started to clear the table. I felt a dash of guilt
for stabbing him in the heart, but I was convinced that it was a
necessary evil for asserting my freedom and independence.

One afternoon in Davis, Brent's older brother and girlfriend unex-
pectedly swung by for a visit while we were in the bedroom.

"Stay here. Let me see what they want."

"So, still rocking the cradle?" I overheard his older brother,
who I hadn't met yet, say in an amplified voice.

"She's not a baby. She's nineteen."

"Oh my, she's nineteen. Technically an adult."

"What do you want?

"Just dropping by to say hi. Are we not welcome?"

"If there is nothing else that I can help you with, please go."

"Let's go, Gloria. I think we stepped on someone's toes. You'll
thank me later, Brent. Take care, buddy."

"What's their problem? What was all that about?" I fumed.

"He was probably drinking. Don't let him get to you. He's just
jealous. He blames me for being the favorite and he loves to pick
on me."

"Well, he was picking on me too. He's a jerk, and I wished you
stood up for me. You could have said she's more of an adult than
you'll ever be."

"I don't want to stoop to his level. And neither should you."

"Standing up for me and yourself is not stooping to his level.
I don't think I could stoop to his level, even if I tried to," I said,
getting more upset because of his rationalizing.

"This is exactly what he hopes to accomplish: to get us to
fight. Let's watch a movie and get him off your mind."

"I'm sorry. You're right," I said reluctantly. "I'm just baffled
that someone's direct family can be as mean, cold, and calculated
as this."

"I don't let him get to me," Brent said.

"How?" I asked.

"Just ignore him," he said nonchalantly.

By the time summer rolled around, our relationship had gotten rockier. Sharp gravel and pointy rubble covered almost every arena. I had trouble accepting his brother's animosity, and it didn't help that Brent insisted that I just ignore him. His clumsiness in dealing with feelings in general became a major issue—like saying that I had no reason to feel jealous or insecure when he openly admired other women who were a whole three or four years older than me.

I was on the verge of breaking up with him but decided to visit my friends in Miami first. Maybe the distance would give me some clarity. We'd been together for eight months. I was still confused if I needed to become less emotional, if he needed to become more emotional, or if we both had it all wrong.

"Why don't we meet up and go to Disney World for a few days? It will be fun and will do us good. This quarter has been busy and stressful for both of us," he said when he heard about my plans.

"Okay. You may be right," I said.

But not even the magic of Disney World and Epcot Center combined could salvage our relationship. I continued to feel insecure. Brent continued to dismiss my feelings as unfounded, which infuriated me to no end.

I returned to Miami on my own but still coupled, too paralyzed and unsure to make a move. I was stuck in this hazy confusion when the shrill ring of the phone brought me back to my senses.

"*Hallo, met* Robert. Hello, this is Robert. I called your mother in California. She told me that you were in Miami and gave me this number."

"*Hallo* . . . What a surprise. How are you? Where are you?" I asked. Gulp.

"Here. In Miami with Uncle Henk in transit to Suriname. He's stocking up on some inventory. I've been driving crisscross through Miami to help him with his marathon shopping."

I heard Uncle Henk laughing in the background.

"Want to join us? What are you doing tomorrow?" Robert asked.

I'd received a handful of postcards during the past two years, but hadn't given him much thought. I'd completely closed that chapter of my life off so I could focus on my future.

Yes. Go. Given the current state of your romantic affairs, sure, why not?

"No plans for tomorrow," I replied. "I've seen my old friends already, and Brent, my boyfriend, just left."

"Hm, boyfriend, huh?"

"Yeah. I think. I'll tell you more tomorrow."

Robert and Uncle Henk picked me up the next day in a van packed with office supplies, old tires, and telecommunications hardware.

"Tires?" I asked.

"Don't ask," Robert replied.

We gave each other a friendly peck. Robert looked and smelled as great as I remembered. On our way to Uncle Henk's old business partner and friend in southern Miami, we caught up on family affairs and life in Suriname, Holland, and California. Once alone, Robert and I continued right where we left off, only this time around, I was the one complaining about my questionable relationship and problematic boyfriend, Brent.

"I sometimes wonder if he has a pulse. I'm not kidding. He's so detached about everything that it's hard to believe that he really cares about me. He takes all kinds of BS from his family and some of the insults include me. Anything to get to him. I think he's lonely and in love with the idea of having a girlfriend, and I happen to be that girlfriend, but I don't think he really cares about me as an individual. Or perhaps they're making him doubt our relationship so much he can't go further. Whatever is going on, I feel dispensable, replaceable, and miserable."

"I'm sorry to hear that. Maybe you've been working too hard to make this work. Remember what you said to me? There is a lid for every pot?"

He raised his eyebrows up and down, as if to say, "like right under your nose."

Did he just repeat to me what I said to him two years ago? No one even listens to me, let alone repeats what I said two years ago!

Rows of dominoes toppled over and converged in the center of my heart. The fog lifted in an instant.

"You know what? You're right. This lid is not right for me. I needed to break this off months ago. I see it now."

"Are you sure? That was fast."

"Remember what you said about your ex? Maybe I never loved Brent either because all I feel right now is huge relief. I was too afraid to make a clean cut and didn't trust myself. I've dated and gotten to know a bunch of different guys, but I never again experienced what we shared and what I feel right now, after just an hour talking."

I paused, reluctant to completely bare my soul. Fortunately, I was too cognizant of the little time that we had left to hold back. I dared to feel my true feelings. Darn. He'd been right all this time.

"It's so easy to be myself and to feel connected to you. I feel important and central, in a healthy, non-obsessive way. This simple thing that we have is what truly makes me happy and what I've been seeking," I said.

Robert smiled with tears in his eyes and gave me a quick kiss.

"Hey kids, hungry? Ready to go?" Uncle Henk chirped. He seemed pleased with his business transactions and with our rekindled romance.

"Can you give me a hand unloading this stuff?"

"Where should we have dinner?" he asked while we piled tires and boxes into his partner's garage to be sent to Suriname.

"Hmm, wherever you guys feel like. I'll be happy with anything right now," Robert said, winking at me.

We reminisced about our road trip adventures over dinner. It felt great to be among old friends again.

"Noon tomorrow? Bring your tennis shoes and bathing suit. We can have a nice lunch at the hotel and hang out by the pool," Robert said.

"Sounds good. I'll be ready," I said, and gave each of them a hug.

That night, Brent gracefully accepted my break-up call.

"Before you hang up, I want to thank you for helping me get in touch with my feelings. I know it may not seem that way to you, but my heart was frozen, and I'm able to feel so much more now than in the past because of you," he said. I could tell that he was feeling a bit sad, but it was so fleeting, it hardly had any impact on me.

"I appreciate your kindness and for letting me know, and I'm sorry for all the times I was impatient, bratty, and demanding," I said, feeling calmer and more composed with him than I'd been in a long time.

"You speak from your heart, and that's admirable and brave. Take good care. I'll see you around when you're back," Brent said before hanging up. It was the easiest and fastest break up ever, completely the opposite of what I'd experienced with Luis.

"I did it! I broke up with Brent," I announced to Robert and Uncle Henk the next day. I felt as free as a bird and couldn't stop yakking. After lunch, I dashed from left to right on the tennis court, more often laughing deliriously at fly balls than hitting any.

"This is futile," Robert said, shaking his head. "Let's go to the pool."

Uncle Henk struck up a conversation with a hotel guest and stayed behind to play a game of singles. Robert swam a few laps before joining me in the jacuzzi. Everything about us was exactly the same as two years ago, except for my mind and my appreciation for him, which had exponentially matured during our time apart and our short time back together.

"If you don't know me by now, you will never ever know me," Robert sang along with the poolside radio. Both of his arms were leaning on the side of the jacuzzi, and he wore a seductive come-hither look on his face.

That moment, I decided to go for it. He was leaving the next morning, and I didn't have all the time in the world to sort everything out. What did I have to lose? Nothing. If it didn't work out, no big deal. It was now or never.

I slowly swam toward Robert, my lips going straight for his. This time, there was no holding back. I got closer and closer until our bodies were plastered together, skin-to-skin, except for the few places where our thin, stretchy patches of bathing suit fabric created the flimsiest of barriers. Strong massaging hands and a whirlpool of sensations—hot, wet, hard, slippery, strong, weak—quickly heated my body to a boiling point. I plucked my lips off his to catch my breath, and whispered, "Let's go to your room. Uncle Henk will be busy for a while and won't bother us."

We surrendered to each other's bodies as if we'd had two years of foreplay. All I needed to do was press "play" to continue right where we'd left off in the car the first time we kissed, on the hotel bed watching a movie, on our backs watching the clouds at Union Square. All my dating and relationship experiences that happened in between only served one purpose. To help me catch up to Robert's clarity and knowing that we were a perfect fit, a fit that his athletic body and graceful butterfly thrusts confirmed the second he entered me, and we melted into passionate waves of long-awaited ecstasy.

Chapter 6

 COMMITMENT BOOTCAMP

No love can be bound by oath or covenant to
secure it against a higher love.
—Ralph Waldo Emerson

WHILE WAITING FOR ROBERT the next day, the loud ticking coming from Cheryl's kitchen clock grated on my nerves like a time bomb. A heavy, looming pressure had amassed around our impending separation and threatened to shatter my heart into a thousand pieces. Fortunately, Robert and his loyal accomplice had "accidentally" missed their flight that morning, granting us two stolen days. It didn't seem like much, but I had a feeling that even two days could make all the difference in adjusting to the big changes in my life, absorbing the magnitude of Robert's love, and coming up with some plan for how to cope while apart.

"I gotta go. Have fun and tell me all the juicy details tonight," Cheryl said on her way out.

Shortly after, Robert rang the doorbell. I threw my arms around his neck and gave him a grateful and adoring kiss. He walked me to the van, wiped his forehead, and asked me if I wanted to go to the mall.

"Sure, good idea. It's way too hot and humid to be outside now," I said. It would be easy to kill a few hours or so in the mall, talking, window shopping, people watching. I didn't really care where we went or what we did. Just feeling Robert's arm around my waist or having his face close to mine was enough to shoot me out of the stratosphere in a rocket fueled with bliss.

"I want you to know how serious and committed I am about our relationship. I'm not letting you go again," he said, grabbing me by the hand and maneuvering me into the jewelry section of a busy department store. He scanned over a case with rings and wedding bands and said, "Let's get promise rings. Which one do you like?"

My heart fluttered with joy for a few beats before Ms. Vigilante barged in and listed her cautionary conditions.

"This is the craziest idea, but as long as we don't hold each other back . . . why not? Promise me that you won't deny yourself anyone, anything, or any opportunities in life because of me. And the same goes for me. I've made that mistake before in the name of love, and I don't think that's what love is. We just have to be really honest with ourselves, and each other, and clear any issues right away. If we can promise each other that, I'm good."

"I can do that. I didn't deprive myself of anything the last two years, even though I didn't date anyone. I knew what I was looking for and wasn't finding it. Just the thought of you inspired me to become a better person. I know that I'll be much better off with you as my girlfriend than I was before."

"You're too sweet," I said, melting on the inside.

"I'll write you as much as I can, and I'll visit you during Christmas. My semester exams are in January. I'll just bring all my books with me and study at your place. Even if I have to retake them all, it'll be worth it," he said, holding my face in his palms.

"See what I mean? Not good. I don't want you to fail because of me."

"I'm not going to fail because of you. I'll thrive because of you. *Alles gaat op zijn voetjes terecht komen.* Everything will fall in place. You'll see."

I believed him. I wasn't sure how he'd done it, but the part of me that felt desperate and insecure with Brent just a week ago had been replaced by a fierce Amazonian goddess. Is this what happens when you're in love . . . for real?

We strolled through the mall, my eyes continuously drawn to the elegant, simple, double band of rubies on my finger and the bold wedding band that accentuated his.

I can't believe that we're doing this. Rings? This is insane.

Chill already. Dutch people do this all the time when they decide to go steady.

While my wary mind disapproved of this impulsive move, my heart knew and celebrated that we'd just gotten married in some parallel universe.

After a good hour of breaking in our relationship status as if it were a new pair of shoes, we strolled into a Hallmark store.

"To keep you company at night," Robert said, handing me a white, fluffy teddy bear.

"Aww. Only if you let me buy you this one," I said, giggling, and handed him a brown one in a pink dress.

"Okay," he said and accepted it without a sign of self-consciousness.

In the next aisle, I got ahold of a cool diary with a lock, the kind that I would have entrusted with my secrets and big dreams, like Anne Frank, if I'd owned one as a child. The cover had an image of an adolescent girl staring at the stars from the windowsill of her room and four lines that I read to Robert:

"Sometimes I need to be alone,
thinking, dreaming on my own.
Trying to see what makes me Me
finding my own special path."

"Isn't it beautiful? I have to get it," I said, overcome with old yearnings.

"It is. It's so you," Robert said, enamored with the free-spirited dreamer in me.

Wedded to my new bear and diary, I could conquer the world. Not even an entire ocean and continent could get in between us.

"Thank you for giving us a chance. I know that we just got together, but I'll do everything in my power to make it work. You're my soulmate. I've never felt so sure about anything. I love you," he said, full of conviction. I felt the same way.

"I love you too," I said. We kissed, savoring and magnifying every sensation and tingle as if it were our last.

"Let's go to the beach and have dinner somewhere over there," Robert said.

We made out some more on the beach, bewitched by an infinite love with mysterious origins—a familiar yet strange love that spilled over the edges of reason and freely colored outside the lines of my usual mind. During dinner on an outside patio, a bright, full moon illuminated and blessed our special bond and this magical day with her enchanting presence.

I showed Cheryl my ring and caught her up on the exciting details and developments of the day as quickly as I could. My unleashed heart had drifted somewhere else, far away. I excused myself, dove onto her guest bed with my brand-new diary, and landed on a deserted island of my subconscious mind where I'd buried a treasure chest full of childhood insights and dreams; it was time to dig it up and unlock it.

On the thin, purple lines on the first page, I wrote:

I have been wanting to do this for years, and, finally today, I saw you, and I knew right away, this is the diary I want (even though you were twelve dollars!) . . . I'll tell you a secret. I had always been so interested in having a diary because I wanted to remember what it was like to be a kid while I was a kid. I already wanted to be a very understanding mother (back then) and do even more now that I'm almost twenty . . . One of my dreams is to write a book to help parents with raising children. I don't know enough right now, but all this information can help me when I'm a "learned" person. Maybe the right person will get to read this someday.

The tucked-away memories and dreams didn't fly out all at once or gush over me like a tidal wave. Instead, they slowly bubbled up, one secret treasure at a time. Before my childhood wings were clipped, they knew no limits nor fear. While playing in the forest, they lifted me up and carried me to a realm beyond time, language, age, education, life experience, and familiar roles where I could just be with myself, my dreams, and my calling to tell adults that children were much wiser and knew a lot more about the secret to happiness than they let on. When I entertained these ideas, I felt a lot like how I feel now: high on love.

I concluded that only a few rare birds—like Anne Frank, Joan of Arc, and Helen Keller—were able to convince grown-ups what they knew as children because their circumstances, stories, and gifts were so extraordinary. That's why they were forever memorialized in books. I, on the other hand, needed to become "learned" and grow much older and powerful before I could realize my dreams and share my gifts with the world. These gifts could be distilled into my insights about nature, God, and getting along. They were similar to Anne's, about fighting for freedom and social justice; similar to Joan's, about trusting extrasensory perception and divine guidance; and, similar to Helen's, about pushing myself beyond preconceived limitations. These girls were my closest friends and my inspirations, and I didn't care that we never met in the flesh or couldn't play hopscotch together. They understood my secrets better than anyone and significantly lightened the load in my heart and soul.

Many years had gone by since repressing these insights, my soul patiently waiting for the right time. My clipped feathers had grown back and were strong. I no longer needed to censor myself to protect my family from harm. Plus, cutting off my voice didn't exactly protect anyone from harm, considering my trying and reckless years in Miami.

The courage to speak up in the midst of turmoil was the thing that inspired me the most about my heroines. This was precisely what helped them to tell and write their stories and end up in books: by not remaining silent. I needed to revisit the lessons about life and death from my dreams: fear was a tool used to keep us small and prevent us from realizing our true nature, immortality, and spiritual freedom. It was the reason my spirit stopped flying, especially after the revolution and after moving to Miami. The time had come to cut myself loose from constricting lianas.

The last hours prior to Robert's departure to Suriname moved in slow motion. I'd stuffed every last moment that we shared in a time capsule for later, just like I'd done after Kiki left, after many of my other friends and relatives left, after we left, after Pa left. I strung the time-capsules together like a roped buoy when it was time for Robert to leave. It was the only thing that stopped the unbearable sinking feeling and kept me afloat.

A little package from Robert arrived at my dorm room mailbox in Davis about two weeks later.

"Testing, testing, one two, one two, left ear, right ear . . . It's me, baby, how are you?" his voice echoed in my ears. I fumbled with the volume of my new Walkman, almost falling off my bike.

His first letter was long and delightful, but listening to his sweet voice on a tape cassette was so much more comforting and intimate. He seemed so close, as if standing right behind me and telling me about his day, about the ticket he already bought for his upcoming visit in a few short months during Christmas break, and about counting the days until we'd meet again. I kept him up-to-date in the same way by capturing little snippets of hot-off-the-press news throughout my day in writing or on a cassette.

"I have really great news, too. I found out that I can participate in a year-long study abroad program that starts next summer. Holland is unfortunately not one of the participating countries, but Spain is. I can double major in Spanish and Psychology. My parents want to go to Hong Kong for my grandmother's eightieth birthday and visit a village in China where our *Hakka* ancestors are from. Since my language intensive program in Spain doesn't start until late July, I can fly from Hong Kong to Holland and spend a few weeks with you before I go to Spain. Isn't that great?"

The more serious and passionate our future plans, the more adamant Ms. Vigilante became in protecting me, making sure that I spoke my truth, bared my soft underbelly, and did whatever was necessary to avoid any recurrence of self-compromise. Ironically, my loyalty to myself and my needs ended up strengthening rather than sabotaging my commitment and relationship to Robert.

To prevent major Robert withdrawal, I funneled all my superfluous love and energy into my studies, reaching new heights of excellence that I didn't realize were possible. Robert did the same, passing all the exams that he'd failed right after our Christmas reunion and three-week long rendezvous, the longest we'd ever been together as a couple.

He sent me a cassette with Richard Marx's song, "Right Here Waiting," that helped him through the roughest patches of being apart. I listened to it whenever I missed him. Being able to trust

Robert and anchor my heart into his love—no matter how far away—paradoxically inspired my soul to take flight. Every time I told him about my dreams, he was all ears. His sweet talk wasn't a bluff. He encouraged me to feed my wanderlust, life-long curiosities, and bold soul-searching as much as I could before settling down, and I urged him to do the same.

That upcoming summer, all eleven of Pa's siblings and their families and more than a hundred other guests attended *Apoh's* eightieth birthday banquet in Hong Kong, gifting her a beautiful life-size golden peach that symbolized long life.

Apoh was my paternal grandmother and oldest living ancestor. She moved from Suriname to Hong Kong after *Apak*, my grandfather, died. I could not imagine a more fitting way to jumpstart my year-long journey of adventure and self-discovery than by interviewing her about her life with my late grandfather, a beloved leader of his birth village in southern China.

"*Hakka* people are curious explorers from the north. Their ancestors were nomads, like the Mongolians, and their women were tall and strong, like *Apoh. Apak* took a boat to Canada, then a train across, and another boat down to Suriname. The journey took months. He was a soybean farmer and saw opportunity all the way over there. What would possess him to do that? It's in our blood. That's why you'll find *Hakka* immigrants all over the world," Pa said, choking up whenever he talked about *Apak*.

Apak's valiant journey paved a trail of opportunity for many. Within a few years, he made a fortune in Suriname as a grocer, returned to China, and convinced his new bride, *Apoh*, his friends, and his distant relatives to follow him to an unknown faraway land, on more than one occasion. Robert's maternal grandpa, also a grocer, tried his luck in Suriname for similar reasons. Our grandfathers became friends and were part of the same Chinese organization in Suriname.

"*Apoh*, what was *Apak* like?" I asked.

Apoh answered me in broken Creole, the only language we

shared, or in *Hakka*, her Chinese dialect, which Pa, Uncle Erwin, or one of their other siblings translated to English.

"He liked to make people laugh. When everyone was bored on the boat, he pretended to mow the lawn and do chores," *Apoh* laughed with a reminiscing fondness that made me feel proud of and loved by a man who I'd never met.

In the forsaken village in Southern China, where their home and antique belongings had been cemented in a caked-on layer of dust, a mysterious someone, perhaps a distant cousin, had updated the family tree on the wall of a desolate shrine. It looked like a Christmas tree, topped by one female ancestor—perhaps a young maiden accompanying her family and tribe—who many generations ago migrated from the far north from the land of tall people down to this auspicious lap of land and nearby lake.

I paused to take it all in. Adaptability, courage, robust and strong matriarchs, a craving for adventure, and a sixth sense for better opportunities crackled and popped through my veins like the feisty red firecrackers that had invigorated my bloodline for many generations. The time had come for me to heed my childhood dreams and honor the calls from my ancestors.

At the Hong Kong airport, Pa was both beaming that I was following my heart and broken that I'd be gone for longer than a year. My mid-year visit to renew my green card clearly didn't count. I gave him a firm hug and said that I'd be back home in no time. Tears were streaming from his eyes.

"Don't you worry about a thing. We'll be fine. Have the time of your life. I'm so happy for you," Ma said while hugging and kissing me. Her unwavering support reminded me of our unforgettable journey around the world and of all the times she'd come through for me and supported my mission. She was our rock.

"Thank you. I'll miss you so much, and I'll call as soon as I arrive," I said. I turned to my brother, and said, "Have fun at UCLA. I know that you'll do great, as always."

"You have a great time too and be safe. We'll see you soon," he said. After I hugged him, I slipped through the gate and waved them a goodbye drenched in spikes of exhilaration, a twinge of

fear, and a low hum of sadness, realizing that we'd soon be farther and longer apart than we'd ever been as a family.

I couldn't wait to see Robert again. We'd been separated for months. He and his family welcomed me at Shiphol, the Dutch international airport, with arms full of roses. Robert and I refueled our romantic gas tank in no time, which left me plenty of time to revive special relationships from Suriname that were plucked from my life like mangoes stolen from our trees. To my delight, I caught up with Kiki, a few other childhood friends, and relatives with such ease that you'd think the detours along each of our journeys had never happened.

Not only did they spoil me with their warm hospitality and masterful cooking, there was a *warung* or a *toko*, a Surinamese eatery, at almost every corner and market in well-known Surinamese neighborhoods and markets in the Hague, Rotterdam, and Amsterdam. I shamelessly stuffed my face with *roti, pom, saoto, moksi alesi, heri heri, bara, teloh*, and many other delectable homecooked dishes and delicacies not for sale in any restaurants or stores in the US. If it weren't for the climate, the subtle hints of Dutch cynicism in the wry, city air, the brick roads, and the bland buildings, you could have fooled me that I was back in Suriname.

We topped my two-week stay with a camping trip to Southern France and Switzerland. About twenty of Robert's closest family friends and relatives, all of them of Surinamese descent, came along, making up for all the years I missed being surrounded by close-knit community. When it was time to leave for Spain, I was full to the rim.

En route to Madrid, Robert and I stopped a few days in Paris, leisurely strolled through Montemartre, admired the gorgeous city of lights from the top of the Eiffel Tower and were embarrassed by a bus full of clapping tourists when we passionately kissed by the edge of the Seine River.

Our train entered Madrid early in the morning. A soft glow of sunlight embellished the many statues and monuments smack in the middle of street intersections, sidewalks, and parks, like the pieces of exquisite art in the Louvre and some of the other impressive museums we visited in Paris. Rich history and culture saturated every living corner we peeked into, from the flea market to underground flamenco and *tapas* bars, restaurants, and even at the university where I'd be studying, *Universidad Complutense*, one of the oldest and largest universities in the world.

A stern matron dressed in a black dress opened the door of our modest hostel. She seemed displeased, perhaps because of the short shorts and tank top I was wearing that day, or perhaps because she'd grown into a bitter spinster. Not even her judgmental frown could bring me down when we arrived at her place night after night exhausted from exploring my new home on foot.

Robert took a plane back to Holland. Being on the same continent and separated by a short flight felt more comforting than I'd anticipated. The next day, I joined about a hundred University of California students from various campuses to attend a six-week Spanish language intensive in Santander on the northern coast of Spain.

"Hey, I'm David. I'm from Irvine. What campus are you from?" one of the students across the bus aisle asked while stroking his long locks back with a sideways swipe. Like many of the Spanish men, he was wearing dress shoes, instead of sneakers and socks like the rest of us.

"Davis. Is it your first time here?"

"Nah. I have some Spanish ancestry and a few relatives here. I'm studying Spanish to get back to my roots. Do you know anyone here?"

"No, just got here a few days ago."

"Meet Kim," he said, while tugging her on the sleeve, "and this is Megan."

"Hi, nice to meet you," I said. They reminded me of two sorority sisters who shared the same bedroom. After flashing their pearly whites, they resumed their animated conversation about the hot Spanish guys they'd met at a bar in Madrid.

Fortunately, David seemed fine with just marveling at the ancient aqueducts and charming cobblestone towns at every pit-stop on the way to our destination. After being assigned our dorm rooms in Santander, he and a bunch of others decided to go to the beach, where every young person in Santander apparently hung out during the summer.

"*Vamos a la playa.* Let's go to the beach," he said.

"*Sí,* yes," I said, curious and grateful not to be left by myself.

The beach was swarming with bodies. Seeing the many topless sunbathers aroused a burning desire in me for similar release, freedom, and uninhibited communion with the sun, the sand, and the sea. I didn't dare do what seemed like the most natural thing to these women, who must have been tourists from France and northern European countries. The disparity between our hostel keeper and a young, half-nude Spanish sunbather was too wide to reconcile in my mind.

"I'm gonna go for a walk," I said after sweating it out for a while and getting increasingly more restless.

"Do you want me to join you?" David asked.

"If you want to, but you don't need to."

He tagged along, powering through soft, dry sand, his eyes perusing the beach scene. Every so often, I glanced at his runner's body while looking for shells and rocks along the high tide lines and wave swash. When we reached the edge of the beach, he turned around, ready to jog back.

"What's the matter?" he asked when I wasn't following. The jagged, sharp-as-knives, rocky cliffs of the *Costa Quebrada*, the Broken Coast, were begging me to climb them.

"You go ahead. I'm going to explore these a bit farther on my own if you don't mind."

"Okay, but I'll come check on you if you stay out too long."

"I won't. Don't worry about me. I'll be fine."

I carefully climbed the ridges on hands and sandals with nothing more than a small fanny pack, a bottle of water, and a light beach wrap around my bikini and shorts. Once on top, I peered far into the distance ahead. Not a single soul in sight.

Without hesitation, I ventured toward Spain's northernmost edge, lured by the distant sounds of mighty waves crashing on the cliffs. The farther from the beach, the more comfortable I felt shedding the items of clothing that had created a barrier between me and my own true North—my body's intuitive sense of direction, purpose, and inner wholeness. The sun warmly embraced my face, bare breasts, and glowing skin as I carefully approached the steep edge of the cliff. There were a few fleeting moments when I felt like a foolish captain of a boat, mesmerized by the dangerously seductive voices of sirens, but it was too late to turn back.

My inner compass still worked and didn't let me down. I settled into an incredible, scenic spot just a foot or so from an edge that sharply dropped at least thirty feet. Endless vast blue stretched from my far left all the way to my far right making the broken coast appear like a small rock in its immensity. I lay my bare back on a smooth, sun-soaked boulder, my head, legs, and arms spread in the four directions, then closed my eyes, absorbed the rays of the sun, and let the sound of the roaring waves below embrace me until I no longer had a sense of myself.

In this magnificent solitude, I heard what my body was trying to say. I'd overcome huge obstacles and setbacks, and had reached the apex of some sort of personal Mount Everest. The awe and love that I'd experienced as a child in the rainforest had stretched

through time and across continents, spanning from Suriname all the way to Spain. I was much older and wiser as a result, but my primal soul was still wild, free, and fearless. My union with nature felt more unbreakable and sacred than ever.

I relied on my freshly recovered inner compass while navigating through Spain and getting around Madrid and surrounding cities, such as Sevilla and Granada, but also when doing everyday things, like shopping for food, exploring new friendships, and deciphering dense, university-level course material taught in rapid-fire *castellano*, Castilian Spanish. None of the inappropriate sexual ordeals and impulses that I struggled with as an adolescent ever came up in Spain, even though I was often still out and about in restaurants, bars, and dance clubs until the break of dawn.

I used my tiny apartment just to study or sleep, mimicking the lifestyle of most Madrilenians, even those with babies and small children. I studied hard and played hard, either with Robert on my mind or by my side. When the year was over, my trust in my intuition had sky-rocketed. I felt healed, confident, and reborn, ready and eager to give back to society.

Chapter 7

▦ THE FINISH LINE

We can do anything we want if we stick to it long enough.
—Helen Keller

UPON MY RETURN TO THE US, I reexperienced a wave of culture shock that caught me off guard. Mellow college life and student preoccupations in a small town like Davis dramatically differed from daily life in Madrid, a lively, cosmopolitan Mecca full of cultural and spiritual intersections and stimulation. It felt as if a vacuum could suck out my soul through my porous, thin skin unless I sought out activities that could serve as some sort of buffer. Much to my surprise, the soulful aliveness and sacred spaces that I was looking for existed in obscure pockets of society where people regularly stared death in the face.

One of these places was Yolo Hospice where I provided office support—administrative tasks, filing, and program coordination. The other was at a senior home, where I offered night-watch care to a ninety-year-old woman, Mrs. Weiss, three days a week. She enjoyed our hearty, meaningful talks, just like Barb, the office manager at Yolo Hospice who was about the same age as Ma, did.

Barb had a gentle presence and deep connection to nature. It was very easy to let my guard down around her.

"You're such an old soul. You have a maturity that's well beyond your young years," she used to say. She encouraged me to look into counseling and gather information about my career options by talking to one of the counselors at the psychology department. I trusted Barb's guidance and approached one of the graduate student advisors during her office hours.

"So, let's see. You won't find a job with just a bachelor's in psych. The only things out there are internships and peer or crisis counseling positions that pay peanuts if you're lucky. In the state of California, you have to go to grad school and get a PhD to become a psychologist. This applies to researchers as well as clinicians," she said.

"These here are the best grad programs. They offer both research and clinical training, unlike our department, which has a heavy research focus. University-based programs are super competitive, though. They'll accept maybe two to five candidates out of a few hundred applications. Seriously. Then you have the professional scientist-practitioner schools that are half-research, half-practice oriented. They are super expensive, but their incoming class is pretty big, so you have a good chance of getting in. Given your stellar grades, all you need is some research and clinical experience and above-average GRE (Graduate Record Examination) scores, and you'll be set. And take the abnormal and clinical psychology pre-reqs now if you can."

"Okay. What about these programs, the California Institute of Integral Studies and the Institute of Transpersonal Studies? Are they any good?"

"Those are the touchy-feely programs that don't require you to do a dissertation to graduate. Just a thesis paper. They are totally focused on practice and are a lot less rigorous than the university programs and the professional schools," she said.

As soon as she called these programs less rigorous and touchy-feely, I scratched them off my list. I gathered that they were second-rate and somewhat dull, appealing to students with a syrupy, bleeding heart. My instant turn-off may have been the combined result of my academic department's emphasis on research, public stigma around mental illness, and "abnormal" behavior, Ma's concerns for my safety around "crazy people," and my unfamiliarity with any careers in psychology. Whatever the reason, just shifting my focus and interests from developmental to clinical psychology was already causing me heart palpitations.

I stuck to my inner sense of true North despite feeling uncertain and afraid, and decided to conduct mental health–related research to strengthen my undergraduate transcript. Noting some of the differences between American and Spanish women in regard to their bodies, I designed an honors senior thesis that examined body image, eating, and acculturation patterns in female, college-aged students. I gained enthusiastic support from my Abnormal Psychology professor, David Walter, who agreed to supervise my study. John, a computer lab tech assistant, helped me to get through the complicated factor analyses as well as the longest six months of my life. There were a few intense moments when I wanted to jump him just because he was male and alive. Most of the time, however, I was clear who I wanted to be with. It was still Robert and only Robert, and he fortunately felt the same way about me.

"Angie? *What is he doing here?* Don't tell me you don't know!" I screamed at my roommate when I entered our apartment and recognized the hands and shoes of the stranger who was on our sofa, hiding behind a newspaper. I wasn't expecting Robert for another week.

"It's really sweet of you to skip your graduation and surprise me, but I can't spend any time with you right now. I really have to buckle down," I said, my arms around his neck, not sure how to break this to him.

"What do you mean? You'll do just fine even if you take your tests with your eyes closed," he said.

"You don't understand. I could blow off these exams and still graduate, yes, but I need to ace them all to get this honors recognition. I worked too hard to throw it all away now. I'm this close to getting it," I said, showing him the millimeter between my pinched fingers.

"Just ignore me. I won't bother you," he said, kissing my hand and arm.

"I can't when you're doing that. Please, I'm serious. This is not Holland. I can't just retake my exams if I fail them. My two graduate school options are either super competitive or super expensive, and my parents are still struggling financially. They're leaving soon to check out the situation in Suriname and won't be here to bail us out. Our future hinges on these three days. If I do well, my grades can get me into grad school, lead to scholarships, get me a job, you name it. I know that it sounds a bit dramatic, but it's true. I need you to help me do this," I lamented, peeling his arms off me, and wondering if I was going overboard.

"Okay. Don't worry about me. I'll go to the pool and the gym and stay out of your way. Just pretend that I came and left. You can do this. Do it for me," he said, finally getting it.

"I love you so much and will make it up to you, I promise," I said, and gave him a big fat smooch, then grabbed my backpack and books and biked to my favorite café.

This was the moment of truth. Robert played Houdini during the day as promised. I still needed to scrape the bottom of my soul and gather up all the strength and determination that I had in me not to hop over to the gym. I'd missed him so badly these past months, I'd fantasized about hijacking a plane to see him and hated that he put me in this torturous tug-of-war.

It was almost impossible for me to concentrate. My heart was too elated, and I kept thinking and daydreaming about him. This sweet gesture to shave off a few days from our agonizing time apart was what I loved the most about him: he understood that a little romance and few stolen days—that he gifted me today and three years ago when he missed his plane in Miami—meant everything to me. How I wished I were done and off to play instead of peering into my books and notebooks.

I dug deeper than ever and eventually managed to zone him out and zoom in on my studies. I aced my finals, was recognized by Dr. Walter as a "rising star" in the field, received a prestigious research award from the American Psychological Association, and graduated with the highest honors. Not even a month later, I pocketed my return-on-investment. I interviewed for and was offered one of three Air Force Family Support Center management trainee positions nationwide. It not only paid well but would allow me to climb the ranks at an accelerated speed that was unheard of with just a bachelor's degree in psychology. Best of all, I got my first choice location, Travis Air Force Base, only half an hour from Davis.

Just in case Barb was right about the military being one of the most dysfunctional bureaucracies to work for, I agreed to help a clinical psychology graduate student with her dissertation to strengthen my research skills. Three times a week, I drove to UC Berkeley after work, napped in my car, watched videotapes of arguing couples in the bowels of their dingy psychology department, and coded cultural expressions of emotion until late at night.

One of Pa's good friends in civil engineering arranged an internship position at the county office in Sacramento for Robert. It wasn't quite in his field—industrial engineering—but it met his last internship requirements and allowed us to be together.

"I know that you've been here for only two months, but do you realize that your visa will expire in four months? I don't know about you, but I can't do this long-distance thing again. We need to put our heads together and decide now what we're going to do," I said to him while lounging on his lap in a reclining chair on the back patio of my old Sacramento home.

"You know that I want to marry you, right . . . ?" he said, his eyebrow raised. "I just don't want to rush into anything."

"Rush? Are you kidding me?"

"I mean in planning a wedding. I just got here. People will wonder if you're pregnant or if I'm trying to get a green card. I can't even ask your dad for your hand. He's all the way in Suriname, and the phone lines are overloaded these days. You can't get through."

"I really don't care what anyone will think, and you don't need to ask my dad for my hand. You're not marrying him. How's waiting a month or even two going to make a difference?" I said and got up, annoyed that Robert was letting small-town gossip and thinking get to him.

"Sweetie, come back, I'm just thinking out loud. I don't even have a job or a salary. Just give me a moment to think this through," he said, holding onto my hand and gently pulling me back in his lap.

"Why does that matter? I have a job. We've been pushed to our limits. Let me speak for myself. I've been pushed to my limit these past three years, and I can't do it again," I said, my lips quivering and my eyes piercing into his. "Are you having second thoughts about me or about moving to the US now that you're actually here and we're living together?"

"No, no, come here," he said, wrapping his arms around me and rubbing my back. "I love it here, and I'm more sure about us than ever. You believe me, don't you?"

"I do . . . but this is a big step and precisely because I don't want to rush things, we need to get going now. Four months is a really short time to plan a wedding, even a simple one. We need to pick a date, look at a few places, shop for a dress, have you fitted in a suit, and tons more."

"You're right. I'm sure everyone overseas will also appreciate it if we give them an early heads up," he said.

"Exactly."

A few days later, we were back in our favorite hangout spot on the back patio.

"What's that?" Robert asked.

"What's what?"

"There, in the pond. Looks like there's something on the waterlily pad."

I squinted my eyes at him suspecting he was up to no good.

We walked over to the pond, and he held my hand while I dangled over a waterlily pad to retrieve a small, velour jewelry box that was on top of it.

"It's just a formality, but, you know me, I'm a hopeless romantic," he said while I played along with my hand on my heart, my face donning a look of surprise. I nestled back in his lap and, despite trying to keep it light and silly, I was choking up.

"You didn't need to . . . I still love the one you bought for me at the mall," I said, twirling the band with rubies around my finger like I had countless times right before seeing him or after we'd said goodbye.

"I know. That's why I love you," Robert said. He carefully wiggled the engagement ring out of the box, held it up to me, and asked, "Will you marry me?" with his signature, endearing smile.

I uttered a hoarse yes, pressed my lips on his, and dissolved into his loving arms.

"I can't believe we pulled all this off in four short months," I said to my cousin, Yvonne, while examining my carefully made-up face in the mirror. Her swift and graceful hands were turning my long, straight hair into waves of beautiful curls. I chuckled. Was it really a decade ago when I sat in front of a mirror with my other cousin, Elsbeth, and asked her to chop off almost all of my hip-length hair? That was one of my boldest moves, to me as radical as shaving my head and tattooing middle fingers on it.

I never thought I'd be getting married at twenty-three. Twenty-three sounded so young, like a day-old, freshly hatched chick. Oh well, what's new? As far back as I can remember, age was a confusing marker. I often felt ageless or ancient or both. I'm not quite sure how I distinguished between these two feelings.

When I felt ageless, it seemed as if I was floating: a talking voice without a body, like a radio station, broadcasting timeless wisdom. When I felt ancient, my body felt like the pyramids, Mayan temples, Stonehenge, Greek ruins. Heavy and solid, made of stone and earth, salty sweat, and forgotten blood, mortared together in messy human history, heartache, and mysterious breakthroughs. Definitely not floaty.

Ageless or ancient, Robert and I had been together for so long, it felt like an eternity, especially during the times when we weren't physically together. Boy, was I glad that this chapter in our relationship was now over.

"What a gorgeous gown," Aunt Anita, my soon-to-be mother-in-law, said. She admired the beading on the long sleeves, high collar, and long train of my dress while Ma helped me to wiggle into layers

and layers of material. Ma looked stunning in her mother-of-the-bride dress and so proud.

"Yvonne, can you take a picture of the three of us?" Aunt Anita asked. Even though the initial news of our whirlwind wedding came as a shocker to both sets of parents—who all happened to be in Suriname at the same time—they had a toast and a few drinks on us, calling us back a few days later in the best of spirits. I locked elbows with my future Ma on the right, with my old Ma on the left, and felt doubly blessed and held.

"Are you ready? Pa is right outside. We need to get going, but we'll see you in there, okay? You look beautiful," Ma said and gave me a kiss.

I could feel everyone's eyes burning into me. I clutched Pa's arm for support as we walked in between familiar faces of family and friends, their mouths in slight smiles, their heads in puppy-dog tilts. Behind them was a curtain of loosely curled strings hanging from pearl and lavender balloons. Themed teddy bears in black hats and wedding gowns topped our wedding cake and were

scattered here and there next to purple orchids and green ferns, reminding me of Suriname's rainforest.

I stared into Robert's eyes, red and doting. They pulled at unbridled feelings and my desire to evade the limelight. When it was time to repeat our vows, I sounded reticent, feeling overexposed and uncomfortable. I finally came undone and let tears wash over me when Kandra, my maid-of-honor, sang the lyrics of our song, "Right Here Waiting," that had comforted me so many times before: on bus and train trips to quaint little villages in Spain, during quiet evenings in my apartment, while walking home and goofing off late at night, or whenever my heart ached for Robert.

It was suddenly real. We were husband and wife! We didn't go insane and we'd more than survived this romance. Ma, Pa, Robert's parents, Uncle Henk, family and friends sympathized— everyone who'd offered us a boost, a laugh, and a lift throughout our epic, long-distance relationship was either dabbing away a tear, clapping, or smiling broadly.

After the formalities, Uncle Roy, our MC, turned the cake-cutting ceremony, garter belt and bouquet tosses, and his speech into an entertaining class act, and made sure that everyone had a good time.

We slipped out before the festivities were over and checked into our honeymoon suite in downtown Sacramento. I dropped on the bed with my arms spread out so that my aching feet, back, and shoulders were no longer perishing under the weight of my leaden dress. I'd never run a marathon before, but, at that moment, my taxed body was convinced that it just had.

"That was one crazy stunt, these last four months, these last three years . . . the last five years," Robert said.

"We did it. Our letter writing and sex tape days are over!" I giggled. I thought of the round popcorn tin that I once received for Christmas, now full of letters and a few hot and steamy numbers.

"Oh God, where are they? I hope that no one accidentally finds them," Robert said. He took off his tie and jacket and walked toward me, looking dashing and quite irresistible, but not enough to revitalize my wilted body.

"In the garage, sealed. No one will find them. Come over here and lie down next to me," I mumbled, patting my hand on the bed, my arm as heavy as dead weight.

"Would you accept a raincheck for tomorrow morning?"

"Sure," he said, cupping and massaging my feet, "but I won't be offended if you change your mind."

PART TWO

Chapter 8

BORDER LIGHT

*The intuitive mind is a sacred gift and
the rational mind is a faithful servant.
We have created a society that honors
the servant and has forgotten the gift.*
—Albert Einstein

OUR AIRPLANE BUMPED, jolted, dropped, and shook during patches
of rough turbulence over a thick green blanket of rainforest that
covered almost all of Suriname. Robert squeezed my hand, leaned
in, and gave me a kiss, while I tried to offset the painful pressure
that was building on my eardrums with quick nostril puffs. He
was just as thrilled as I was about paying our home country a long
overdue visit.

I'd landed at least half a dozen times before at Zanderij—the
only international airport in the entire country—when I still lived
here, but this was my first time back as an adult. When we left
Suriname in 1983, I was a month short of turning fourteen, which
meant that, at twenty-eight, I'd lived the first half of my life in
Suriname and the second half in the United States.

I reflected on the unique challenges that each time period
posed and what I'd say to my old friends and relatives if they were

to ask me how I've been. How have I been? I'd been through so much it was hard to say. Living in a military state as a preteen and being forced to leave everything and everyone I loved during such a delicate period of my life was hard beyond comprehension. All the footholds that I'd ever relied on were gone. The trying Miami years that followed were marked by steep learning and trial and error, mostly error, exacerbated by intense hormonal changes and unruly feelings of loss, loneliness, and displacement, especially after Pa moved to California and Ma, Mark, and I stayed behind. Our eventual move to California, my adventurous college years, and my long-distance romance with Robert resurrected my old self back to life. I was able to catch my breath and reset, just in time for the next phase of tests and tribulations. The last five years following our wedding had once again been turbulent, jarring, bumpy, and painful—due to sudden drops and unavoidable external pressures—just like this descent.

"Are you okay? You're so quiet," Robert said, able to read me like an open book.

"Yeah, I'm fine. I've got a lot on my mind and am wondering if any of it relates to my dissertation. Maybe I should jot my thoughts and feelings down," I said, and pulled my research notebook out of my backpack. Reassured, Robert went back to reading the business magazine he'd brought along.

Our relationship was still solid, often the one thing that centered me in the midst of scattered thoughts, puzzling experiences, and feelings of uncertainty regarding my graduate studies in clinical psychology. It seemed to offer Robert the same secure home base when he grew disillusioned with corporate America and his new job. Over the years, he learned to accept my need for quiet mulling and problem solving, most likely a leftover pattern from playing in the rainforest for hours on end while simultaneously sorting through childhood troubles.

I was now in my fourth year of my graduate program, my dissertation year. This was the year when everyone was doing their most important research—aka their deepest me-search—myself included. My research had a dual purpose. I was, on the one hand, overjoyed about gathering novel data about the multiracial experience in Suriname, and, on the other hand, feeling unmoored, hoping to find answers to questions that hadn't fully formed in my mind. I was wrestling with strong impulses to break out of the usual mold of doing psychotherapy and longing to examine psychological struggles and healing from an intuitive and spiritual perspective. The only caveat: my ideas clashed with almost everything that I was learning.

Because I was so sure that this program was right for me when I first enrolled, I was blindsided by this realization. I'd left my previous job at the Family Support Center precisely because I was being groomed to become a central director in charge of public administration. This didn't interest me at all. My favorite part of the job had been offering direct services—individual and group counseling—to military personnel and their spouses.

The innovative cross-cultural dissertation research that I was doing with the psychology graduate student at UC Berkeley was also tugging on my heartstrings and begging me to pay attention. I got the impression that there was at least one more cross-cultural research study stirring inside of me.

This clinical psychology program, offered by the Pacific Graduate School of Psychology, sounded like an ideal fit. It was a scientist-practitioner model that valued my two primary passions. The best part: the school was offering a full-tuition scholarship to one incoming ethnic minority student, even though affirmative action scholarships had already gone out of fashion almost everywhere else. When I got accepted and was granted the very last scholarship as well as a California Psychological Association Foundation Award given to promising new students who could increase the cultural diversity in the field, I took it as a serendipitous sign. This was where I belonged.

It took only a few months for the excitement of being a graduate student to wear off. Even though I loved most of my teachers, my classmates, and the fascinating new information I was learning in my classes, it bothered me that my intuitive insights into the root causes of psychological suffering weren't mentioned.

For instance, we learned that attachment theory, a key concept in modern psychotherapy, suggests that our development is largely shaped by our relationship with primary caregivers in early childhood. As children, we unwittingly adopt our parents' and caregivers' relationship patterns and repeat these in adulthood. This made sense to me; I also considered myself a product of my cultural environment and recognized parts of my parents in me.

Nevertheless, a part in me objected. This part wanted to honor nature and the rainforest for serving as my ideal parent; they'd offered me peace of mind, insight, and validation on countless occasions when I felt let down by the adults around me. This soulful part had also been in charge of sifting through and rejecting what didn't sit well with me. I didn't just blindly adopt what the adults did or wanted me to do, even as a child, which was the reason why Ma called me *eigenwijs* and accused me of driving her crazy. I was making all kinds of decisions and choices—when to listen to Ma or Pa, when to ignore them, and when to pay closer to attention to Elfriede, an auntie or uncle, or a friend—even when I lacked the words to explain what I was doing. And I sometimes got the impression that I was reshaping their views of the world and themselves as well.

Just when I decided that it would sound too bizarre to say in class that I regarded nature as my mother, my Sikh friend and neighbor dropped by out of the blue to lend me the book, *Living with the Himalayan Masters* by Swami Rama. I had a nagging sense that there was a message for me in it. Sure enough, in the chapter, "My Mother Teacher," Swami Rama's interaction with Mataji, a ninety-six-year-old yogi, spoke directly to my heart.

He was very sad when it was time to say goodbye to her after being immersed for two and a half months in intense study directed by her loving guidance. She said to him, "Don't be attached to the mother figure in my physical body and personality. I am the mother of the universe, who is everywhere. Learn to raise your consciousness above and beyond my mortal self."

I felt humbled and wanted to bow when something like this happened. What were the odds for this obscure yogi from the

Himalayas to be sharing my worldviews? And how in the world did her message reach me all the way in California when I needed it the most? The universe was orchestrating this and bending the laws of physics, no doubt. These serendipitous miracles were rare, one-time events, but they had a greater impact on my mental health and sense of integrity than messages I may have heard my whole life but that didn't resonate with my soul. This miraculous, guided healing is what interested me. It was much greater and more powerful than the sum of our parts and psychopathologies.

Within my rigorous academic program, however, revering phenomena like this felt wrong and frankly, disconcerting. I didn't dare test it out. When I was at school, I had my thinking cap on. My intuitive mind felt misaligned, illogical, wishful, and superstitious compared to the crisp and logical treatment plans that my peers and teachers were formulating. Who was I to advocate for my weird views about mental health?

My intuitive perspectives remained dormant, just like my Dutch or Spanish language abilities. It would be strange to speak in one of these languages rather than English when everyone else was speaking English. I was an expert at adapting and blending in, but that didn't keep the unspoken rules and biases embedded within my program from gnawing on every little edge of my confined soul. My mind started to daydream about the mystical rituals and experiences that I was exposed to as a child whenever I longed for a deeper perspective in class and drifted off into my own wildly imaginative world.

Some of my fellow classmates of color did speak up and expressed their dissatisfaction with our course curriculum, which wasn't all that different than the majority of clinical psychology curricula across the nation. They complained that Western-based theories about mental health and the experiences of white, mainstream, college-aged Americans were overrepresented in research studies, class discussions, and readings. I volunteered to support, colead, and organize this group of students but discovered soon enough that our priorities were also different despite our shared concerns.

I became increasingly more interested in my Taoist *Hakka*

roots and in cultivating a non-dualistic (no polarities), paradoxical mindset that fostered a sense of wholeness and psychological resilience, while they wanted to create a safe space within the program by prohibiting white students from attending our meetings. Amidst this support group, I began to perceive myself like one of Picasso's cubist images, mutated and distorted into racialized split parts.

The bulging canopies and sparse city lights in the far distance captivated me and whizzed me back into my window seat in the plane. My primal connection to the untamed natural world below welled up and moved through me like a wave of fierce passion. This feeling reminded me of the drum beats, sounding like distant background noise, that accompanied my daydreams during boring lectures. They every so often still echoed in my inner ear.

I knew that the visions and drumming were creative variations of my wise voice but they sounded awfully similar to hallucinations when examined through a clinical psychology lens. Because some of my memories—starting with the healing dance ritual of the *Winti* dancers at my elementary school—were laced with a sense of urgency and the threat of extinction, I assumed that they were sparked by rumors about an Indonesian logging company wanting to buy a good chunk of Suriname's rainforest.

I wondered if I was hearing the cries of nature spirits because the forest was in trouble. Fortunately, the negotiations fell through but the drumming and dreadful sense of endangerment continued. Perhaps my primal self and intuition were, like the rainforest, in danger, threatened by the rational ways of being and thinking in my academic program. I couldn't be sure. My insights were streaming together like the water from creeks, streams, lakes, and an ocean at the mouth of a grand river. From the perspective of my logical, concrete, and overbearing conceptual mind, each stream was too indistinguishable from the other to draw any definite conclusions.

But when I paid attention to my feelings, I could tell that the drum beats energized buried reserves of courage in my heart and belly, reminding me of my childhood heroes, Baron, Boni, and Joli

Coeur, who'd escaped and hidden in these same dense jungles that we were now flying over. These men used to rile everyone up with their drumming and burned plantations to free their friends, relatives, parents, and siblings from their hell.

These drumming sounds were clearly giving me a bravery boost to face the challenges in my own life and heed my calling. I knew ever since I was a child that I too was called to lead others and myself to liberation, just like freedom fighter, Joan of Arc.

But, when I leaned toward trusting my soul's wisdom and vivid guidance from my inner voices, an ominous sense that I was about to do something terribly indulgent, risky, and far out came over me. I feared that my fumbling explanations of my inner experiences would lead to drastic forms of discipline and vigilance and jeopardize my standing as a graduate student.

I felt trapped in a double bind. The price tag for trusting myself was too big. For the first time in my life, I was not able to intuit my way out of a problem. And I had no idea how to go about resolving the painful irony of not trusting my field's own medicine and gatekeepers.

It seemed easier not to trust myself. Articles on ethical guidelines and principles by cornerstone psychologists, such as Dr. Paul Meehl, bothered me greatly, but I convinced myself that my reactions were over-the-top and that I was wrong[1]. Dr. Meehl, born in 1920, was one of the most brilliant American psychologists of the twentieth century. He was worshipped like a god by psychologists, philosophers, psychiatrists, physicians, educators, neurologists, geneticists, scientists, and lawyers alike, and his work formed the foundation of the most important ethical guidelines we were expected to uphold as mental health professionals. In one of Dr. Meehl's famous articles, he cautioned that human beings were inherently prejudiced and self-centered and needed to rely on research studies for objective clarity to compensate for their flawed nature and actions.

He cautioned that "any clinician who considered personal experience to be more valid than research studies was self-deceived

---

1. *See Appendix and References section for more information about behind the scenes serendipitous guidance that crossed my path while writing about these topics.*

. . . We are bound as human beings to make 'fundamental attribution errors'—giving ourselves too much credit for positive outcomes, and only a 'hard-nosed' skeptic and critical thinker with statistically significant data can remedy this unfavorable, unreliable human condition that is prone to self-serving bias."

When I first read these words, the needle of my inner compass spun around and around, unable to find true North. This was happening more and more frequently whenever I neglected my own truth. Every cell in me revolted because I'd met too many hard-nosed, critical thinkers and researchers who seemed arrogant, socially inept, and clueless in matters of the heart. They were good at describing inner states that were compartmentalized but weren't studying messy, non-linear healing trajectories and mysterious, slow, unfolding transformations, because none of these fit neatly in the empirical boxes and scientific analyses of statistically significant research. From their perspective, intuitively linked personal stories and anecdotal evidence were pseudoscience, fraught with confirmation bias and chance occurrences.

The scientific data and publications that I'd come across thus far didn't resemble the compassionate, wise guidance of inspirational leaders such as Maya Angelou, Martin Luther King, Jr., Mahatma Ghandi, Thich Nhat Hanh, Audre Lorde, Mother Teresa, Guan Yin, Confucius, and Buddha that had offered me much insight and understanding. I'd tried to infuse their teachings into my relationships with friends, family members, clients, classmates, and everyone I knew for that matter. I'd even plastered their quotes and epitaphs all over my notebook to make up for the scarcity of healing wisdom in my program. What was I supposed to do with all of this now?

If I'd known that my "personal experiences" would be regarded as an unreliable source of self-deluded information and pseudoscience and that I'd be asked to shut off my soul as if I were some kind of machine, I would not have invested as much hope, time, and energy in this dead-end career. These options were unacceptable to me.

The fact that Dr. Meehl was telling "funny stories employing snide expressions of clinicians who rejected objective data" and was high-fived for "giving sloppy minded clinicians a good beating" at professional gatherings made me question the whole field of mental health for respecting him. I had a sense that these clinicians were making intuitive rather than intellectual connections in guiding their clients and that their "sloppy thinking" could have been taken out of context.

Whatever the situation, I knew for a fact that gifted healers, wise elders, and entire subpopulations in the US and across the world were not less qualified and effective than researchers and academics in promoting mental health, just because they lacked hardcore research data. This was by far not the only method of checks and balances that could save us from our self-centeredness.

As a matter of fact, regarding hardcore academic research as the most superior moral compass that humans could rely on wasn't just offensive to me. It also sounded racist and as untrue as claiming that the sky was green. If he'd shown me the Nordic lights and explained the unique conditions that contributed to his findings, I'd be more open to it, but, without an exploration of his own biases—basing his arguments on actuarial studies comparing human assessment to computer computations in predicting risky behaviors—I felt pressured to accept and live a lie. How could I stop "relying" on my own personal experiences and intuitive guidance from wise, loving souls who seem more adept at cultivating mental health and social harmony than what I'd encountered so far in academic environments? This would require some sort of lobotomy.

I also didn't dare tell anyone how much I was bothered by Dr. Meehl and the ethical requirement to rely on evidence-based research when developing a treatment plan because of the comeback I'd hear in my mind: "Then go back to where you came from." I knew that no one around me would say such a thing. It was a knee-jerk response, reminding me of what's often said to immigrants when they complained about things that no one else in their host country seemed to have a problem with. In this situation, I was not just an immigrant; I was the recipient of a big, fat scholarship and very grateful for the opportunity to advance my education.

I subconsciously blamed myself, hoping that this would offer resolution and mend the split in my mind. I tried on every diagnosis in the DSM, the Diagnostic Statistical Manual, our trade's bible, but this discombobulated my brain even more. I ended up believing that I was harboring at least one of these severe mental illnesses, indications that my past trauma had done more damage to my psyche than I'd realized.

I concluded that I was paranoid and an expert at keeping it under wraps. I was suspicious of everyone and was, as stated in the DSM, "reluctant to confide in others because of unwarranted fear that the information will be used maliciously against [me]."

My preoccupations and these diagnoses played a game of Russian roulette with my fragile mind. Some days I was convinced that I had some kind of obsessive-compulsive disorder, defined as "distressing ideas, images, or impulses that enter a person's mind repeatedly . . . Perceived to be senseless . . . the person finds these ideas difficult to resist."

Other days, a faint inkling, *You're fine, there's nothing to worry about. You're getting soulful guidance from your mystical upbringing to prevent you from forsaking your intuitive gifts,* seeped up from a powerful source within. It longed to clear my troubled mind and anguish with just one strong gush. But, as soon as I opened up to this familiar inner voice—the knowing that none of this madness was a reflection of the real me—the door was just as quickly slammed shut by the definition of grandiose delusions, which are "delusions of inflated worth, power, knowledge, identity, or special relationship to a deity or famous person." My power felt pathologically big and bold precisely because it was capable of overriding the problematic status quo upheld by powerful experts in my field.

I could see what was beyond the glass walls and ceiling of my rational mind but couldn't find the way out. No, you can't tell anyone about this. Don't be stupid. Expecting some kind of special consideration for your unique condition would sound self-deceived, entitled, and narcissistic, at best, and grandiose, at worst, to anyone but you, I heard every time I banged on the walls of my imagined cell. I had nowhere to turn and slipped into a daze of helplessness and resignation. With my inner warrior encaged and undermined, my inner worrier had free rein.

I became more self-conscious each passing day, scrutinizing myself under a microscope and terrified that all my imagined psychological disorders and warts were visible to everyone around me. Because secrets and silence weren't new concepts to me, I was prepared to stick it out, but was jolted into action by an inner resolve that refused to cower down.

I sensed what may be in our field's blind spot. After chewing on it for a while, I had this epiphany: *The avoidance of the pronoun "I" and personal experience in rational, statistically significant research is not the same thing as self-transcendence and bias-free objectivity and clarity. Side-stepping personal experience that requires deeper examination is a false quick fix that will reinforce rather than remedy self-serving tendencies.*

This intuitive insight was energized with a feistiness and fervor—similar to what had arisen out of my childhood dream when I whacked through lianas to cut myself free. It caused me to worry that I'd do something dangerous, maybe even criminal: that an *eigenwijze* flare up might propel me to bulldozer over obstacles in my way, undeterred by the serious consequences for breaking the ethical rules of my trade.

"I'm so borderline," I broke down to Robert during a pillow cry one night, exhausted by my own mood swings and inner turmoil. He wasn't familiar with the borderline condition nor the bad rep this unstable personality disorder had in my field. He held my face in his hands and looked at me tenderly.

"You are my border light."

I inhaled his loving support and exhaled a sigh of relief. The power of his words struck a dormant chord and soothed my distraught soul in ways that I couldn't yet grasp. He was in that moment more than a loving, supportive husband; he was a messenger and said the unimaginable. Maybe I wasn't too big. Maybe my inner struggles and objections to the status quo were shining light onto my field's oversimplified mistrust and harsh disdain of the personal experiences and intuitive wisdom of therapists on purpose, because it was my purpose to challenge this unspoken bias.

I was struck by a line in *Care of the Soul*, by Thomas Moore, a book that was assigned in my existential psychology course, one of the two courses in transpersonal psychology at my program that addressed matters of the soul. It read, "When soul is neglected, it doesn't just go away; it appears symptomatically in obsessions, addictions, violence, and loss of meaning." I felt validated and infused with a renewed sense of hope.

Since childhood, a fierce warrior or a mystical wise self had appeared in my dreams or waking life when I wasn't paying attention to my soul's yearnings and discontent. I knew that Surinamese people shared this wisdom, even though no one had formally researched this phenomenon. They conveyed through their soulful daily practices and their harmonious ways of relating to people from different ethnic groups that their spiritual health and wholeness were a priority.

Studying their mental health strategies and well-being and reconnecting to my native roots could offer me the clarity and strength that I needed to trust my intuition and challenge my field.

An announcement that we were about to land jarred me out of my long stroll down memory lane. I swelled with anticipation as the engines roared and the wing flaps fought for dear life with the wind, bringing the tires to a screeching halt. The passengers in the plane, mostly of Surinamese descent, whistled, clapped, and cheered. Robert and I laughed out loud. It felt good to touch solid ground, *Sranan gron*, Surinamese land, alongside boisterous *kondreman* and *oema*, country men and women.

We waddled single-file to the back of the plane, everyone in great spirits. The moment I stepped outside, a blast of warm, humid air smothered my body. Just one sniff of damp, earthy rainforest, and I knew I was home. I galloped down the steps of the clattering scaffold that had been wheeled over and smiled broadly at Robert and the familiar sights and buildings in front of me. I had the urge to fall to the ground on my knees and kiss it, but I worried that I'd look ridiculous.

There was only one other airplane parked on the coarse, concrete runway marked by two strips of lights in the midst of mysterious shadowy wilderness all around. The two-story departure and arrival hall ahead of us was no bigger than a large roach motel. Blisters of paint were flaking off or splotchy with mold. Bold, intruding weeds had nestled into a few large cracks in the concrete, and a faint whiff of urine drifted by as we approached the building on foot.

The entire bottom floor had been renovated: there was a new customs section, an automated luggage belt, shops, bathrooms, and a seated snack area. It was hard to believe that all the chaotic, heart-wrenching goodbyes from fourteen years ago happened here. Even though Bouterse had technically been booted out of power and democracy had more or less been restored, basic items, such as bread, were still on the scarcity list, sometimes available, sometimes not. The shiny, new developments that had sprouted up here and there were not enough to entice Ma and Pa to move back.

"How long ago since you last visited? Eight, right, when you missed your plane to pursue a foolish, long-distance love affair?" I asked Robert and gave him a teasing shoulder bump. He nodded and smiled. "Look at us now. Our first visit together as an old married couple."

"I know, isn't it crazy? I could never have imagined my life taking so many unexpected and wonderful turns when I left so many years ago," Robert said. His family was one out of the thousands who left on an extended vacation to Holland and never returned. He was only eleven at the time.

"It'll be fun to show you my room in my old home. Did you know that your family's old furniture is still in it? Bizarre, huh?" Robert said.

"Twilight-zone weird."

All I could make out on the dark drive home was how narrow the highway—a two-lane, paved street—looked compared to what I remembered. Everything else looked mostly the same and filled me with comfort.

The next few days, our aunts, uncles, cousins, and friends—the majority of mine still clumped in the Dieterstraat—welcomed us with hearty hugs and meals. We squeezed about two to three visits in one day, so I could get myself and my research rolling in less than a week.

Just four months ago, I'd mailed a letter with my preliminary dissertation goals to Dr. Maria Root, a nationally acclaimed professor, researcher, and expert in multiracial issues, and asked her to join my committee. I included a term paper entitled, "The Psychological Lynching of Multiracial People in the US," that described my struggles around racial hierarchies and loyalties within my program and society. I speculated that racial splitting paralleled our dualistic ways of handling many other aspects of ourselves.

Dr. Root sent me a paper with her newest model of racial identity. It replaced problematic either-or research models that forced participants to polarize and rank their cultural and racial backgrounds, worldviews, and preferences on a number scale.

"We must learn to integrate experiences that have been deemed mutually exclusive," she wrote in the introduction of her new model. She also said that she'd be happy to join my committee as an outside adviser. I could kiss her. Her new model and her list of attitudes that determined whether someone was open or closed to differences and able to think in holistic, spiritual, and paradoxical terms became the basis for my study.

I'd enlisted a research assistant in Suriname who recruited fifteen racially mixed research participants (ages seventeen to thirty years) through word of mouth and a newspaper ad. The participants that she had lined up for me upon my arrival were ideal: they were from every large neighborhood throughout the capital (population: two hundred and fifty thousand). All but one of the participants were at least the third mixed generation in their families: it was hard to find anyone with just two ethnic backgrounds. The participants, as well as their parents—who, more often than not, only had an elementary, junior high, or high school education—spoke at least three languages, some up to seven. Most of the participants had a high school degree, were under twenty-five, and were unmarried. A few were attending trade schools and pursuing degrees in nursing, business administration, and the like. Others had followed their parents' footsteps, running small businesses or specializing in a particular area of expertise, such as music.

I set up my research home base around the same shiny-from-use wooden dining table where I had meal after meal growing up and strategized my plan of action on the dark-green sofas that I sat on when I watched television as a child and dreamt of living in the jungle with the indigenous tribes featured in local documentaries. In this odd space, filled with familiar flutters of wonder and comfort, a deep sense of knowing came over me: I was meant to do this. As challenging and mismatched as this career path seemed, it had been carved for me.

I was eager to meet my first interviewee, who lived in a house on stilts in Robert's old neighborhood. I drove up to a locked metal gate and noticed a young woman in the open garage.

"*Hallo. Ben jij toevallig Mandy*? Hello. Are you Mandy by chance?" I shouted from the driveway.

"*Ja, dat ben ik,* Yes, that's me," she answered with a broad smile and opened the gate.

"How do you like Holland? When do you get to come back?" she asked while I pulled out my interview questions, papers to sign, and survey. It didn't make a difference after she discovered how long I'd been gone and that I lived in the US, not Holland. My accent, mannerisms, casual dress, and flip-flops were similar to hers and had already put her at ease. We were off to a good start.

Mandy, a piano teacher, identified herself as "everything except Javanese."

"Could you tell me about the racial and cultural make-up in your community?" I asked.

"Very mixed and diverse. Just like the rest of Suriname."

"So people from your neighborhood, at school and work?"

"Yes, everywhere I go. It's very rare to find an unmixed group in the city. You'll have to go to a village or tribe on the outskirts or jungle of Suriname." She told me that it was surprising to see that this level of diversity is not typical of our Caribbean neighbors.

"When we went to Trinidad, we performed an *Ala Kondre*, All Countries, number, where all cultures of Suriname interacted as one, so you had a Hindustani woman with a sari, a traditional Hindustani dress, and a Javanese person with a slendang, traditional Javanese clothing, and a Chinese person who used parts of their culture and music to make one big piece. For the musical part, they used all the instruments that are typical of the Surinamese cultures . . . the Hindustani drum, the tabla, the guitar, the harmonium, the apinti drum of the Maroons, the gamalan of the Javanese. It was really very beautiful and incredible, and people were amazed by it, asking 'How is this possible?'"

"That is amazing. What makes this kind of thing possible in Suriname?' I asked.

"It's like the saying, *ala kondre, na fraga*, all countries, no flag," she said. I wasn't familiar with this saying, but it made me think of the yellow star on the new Surinamese flag that marked the transcendent unification of the five main ethnic groups. They were initially portrayed by five stars of different colors on the old flag before Suriname's independence in 1975.

"*Ala kondre, na fraga,* means I'm everything and nothing. I belong nowhere and everywhere," Mandy said.

"Does it feel like a contradiction?" I asked.

"It seems like that to foreigners but not to me and my friends," she said.

After an hour and a half of questions followed by insightful answers, Mandy filled out the survey while I packed up my tape recorder and belongings.

"No, no need to pay me," she said when I offered her compensation for her time and energy. She was genuinely excited about my project and happy to support it as if were her own. Her generous gesture touched me and soothed a spot that had felt sore.

I'd scheduled a second interview with Angelique on the same day and conducted it on her front porch. The communities that she engaged with were as diverse as Mandy's.

"Is it difficult to get along with so many different people from different backgrounds and with different worldviews?"

"I think that if you can get along with everyone, you will get much further ahead than someone who stays only loyal to their ethnic group and has no contact with others outside their circle of friends and only interacts with Javanese people, for instance. If you move between everyone, you get to know more people, get ahead in life, and will develop optimally, because you know at least how everyone thinks. Since I started high school, I've interacted with a lot of different ethnic groups, and I have grown spiritually riper and a little bit more mature. I can better judge a situation. I can now say to someone, 'You need to determine for yourself what you will do.' And before, I would have said, 'This is wrong,' or 'This is right.' I would have pushed my opinion on them, but now I can just float a little bit. And you can also read people better. If someone has bad intentions, most of the time, you will discover that soon enough."

I couldn't be more pleased with Angelique's responses. She provided clear counter-evidence that our selfishness is not a doomed human condition that can only be remedied by a hard-nosed, quantitative researcher with statistically significant data. As a matter of fact, she was, on her own accord, using her personal experiences to shave off her rough edges, hone her intuition and "read" others' bad intentions, and achieve self-transcendence by aligning her personal beliefs and habits with the needs of others and the group.

In just a matter of days, participant after participant had provided me with accounts similar to Mandy's and Angelique's in regard to their racially and cultural diverse communities and the deliberate steps that people took to foster social harmony in service of the greater good.

They claimed that "everyone" celebrated each other's cultural and religious traditions, knew how to cook each other's festive dishes, and got the day off in observation of each major holiday—Phagwa, Christmas, Shub-de-Wali, Chinese New Year, *Keti-Koti* (Cut Chains, emancipation from slavery). Several beamed with pride that Suriname was the only nation in the world where a mosque and a synagogue have peacefully stood side by side for decades even when tensions ran high between Jews and Muslims in the rest of the world.

Mandy's poignant comment, "I'm everything and nothing," grabbed my attention from the start. It was emerging as an underlying theme and source of enjoyment in many if not most of the responses. The pursuit of harmonious common ground was a personal ideal shared by all. I couldn't detect any hard, self-serving boundaries that might instigate turf wars, yet found no signs of self-denial either. I suspected that this fascinating stance enabled the participants to be more effective at defusing racial tension—without any outside mediation—than even the psychology experts and academics at my school. I knew from personal experience that this strategy had enabled Robert and I to strengthen our bond and conflict resolution skills.

I'd hoped that data like this would dissolve my self-doubt. That by watering my shriveled-up roots with my truth and cultural heritage, I'd be able to trust my intuition more and just move on. But that sounded too convenient and self-serving to my indoctrinated inner academic.

I needed to dig deeper into reports of racial strain, conflict, and mistreatment to understand where they festered and how the participants resolved these conflicts. So far, the participants had been in agreement that status and social ranking was important to the politically powerful, to rigid, fundamentalist Christians, and to low acculturated subgroups of Chinese, Hindustani, and European (either overseas Dutch or local white Surinamese) descent, groups who tended to value a hierarchical, competitive structure of social systems over an egalitarian one on a survey that measured individualistic versus interdependent worldviews and interpersonal patterns, social harmony, and conflict.

A handful of the participants had occasionally felt excluded and stereotyped based on their racial features, skin color, ancestral language and ethnic background by individuals from these groups, but were able to avoid these scenarios with relative ease.

When I interviewed Mark at a café, I was immediately struck by his unusual story, his long-standing battle with classism and racism, and his strong resolve.

"I moved out of my parents' home at age fifteen and have lived with three sets of foster parents since then. I could not stand my mother's derogatory comments. She was raised by Javanese people from a certain class. I get along with everyone, but she thinks she is too good for some people," he said.

"Do you still talk to her?" I asked.

"Once in a while. Whenever she calls and asks if I'm still with 'those people,' Creoles, I ignore her question and ask her how she's doing."

"That sounds hard," I said. Mark and his mother were both Creole, but they were lighter skinned and more racially mixed than the Creoles that she had issues with.

"The majority of people are not like her. She is an exception to the rule," Mark said, using her minority status to reduce her harmful impact. He reassured me that he was okay.

I remembered what it felt like to have the majority of the people and dominant culture on your side. That's what my self-doubt had been aching for—"dominant culture" validation from a majority group, something that I took for granted until it was gone. I flagged it as another possible theme to take note of.

Ann agreed to meet me at a park. She was the only other participant beside Mark who dealt with prolonged racism. For years, her boyfriend's parents disapproved of her as a suitable girlfriend for their son because she was not Hindustani.

"They now turned around because we have been together for about five years, but, in the beginning, it was really [bad] . . . The way I think about it: it's not worth it to get all stressed out about it. What if I put up a fight, like, 'What do they think?' and 'I have to stay with him,' and 'How dare they not accept me?' and, maybe today or tomorrow, I think, 'Oh, no, he is not really my type, and all that commotion wasn't really necessary,' . . . I'm also not going to debate back and forth with someone. If you think you're fine like that, you will notice it yourself, you'll find yourself one day . . . In the beginning, I thought, damn, you know, but later I realized it's more important that I'm not like that. I don't think I'll ever become like that."

"Where did you find the clarity and strength to realize that it's more important that you're not like that?" I asked.

"I believe in reincarnation. I believe that your soul will go in another body and life to pay off a karmic bill until the end of the world, until you're pure or in the neighborhood of pure. Then you'll go with God to the new paradise; that's what I believe," she said.

"So your beliefs have helped you to focus on your own purity and path, and not get overly entangled with others when they stray from their true selves?" I asked.

"Yes, that's right. That's why I think all the racial stuff is stupid. I believe that everyone is a soul, and you just take on a body. You're just a soul," she said.

Despite having to endure years of conflict with difficult people in their close circle, both Ann and Mark displayed tremendous compassion, conviction, humility, and tolerance, believing that their offenders had lost their way and would find their true self one day on their own terms. I smiled inside, delighted that these two young strangers were holding up a mirror and showing me my cultural backbone and heritage and my untapped potential in resolving conflict.

Scouting for comparable signs of resilience and wisdom, I noted all the times the participants spoke of a "larger movement" in dominant culture toward wholeness and harmony that they intuitively tapped into when in need of support and strength. Whether the guidance came from deceased relatives, God, shamanic healers, medicine men and women, wise, trusted parents or elders (like Elfriede), revelations in waking states or dreams, or from open-minded, progressive city dwellers, they divulged time and again that they intentionally pursued and integrated higher wisdom and reassurance when confronted with a problem.

By this time, I was dying to find out if their survey data was consistent with their interview responses. I was flabbergasted by what I found. All fifteen participants characterized themselves, their parental figures, and society at large as having both individualistic and interdependent orientations and values. These paradoxical results were unprecedented in the existing body of research because participants typically perceived themselves as either individualistic or collectivistic, not both. The participants' inclusive mindset, which did not compromise their own needs, seemed to be directly linked to their social and psychological well-being. This was very different than what I'd experienced in the US when it came to matters of race and other ways in which we polarized parts of ourselves and scapegoated others who reminded us of these parts.

Upon my return to California, I entitled my study, *"Ala Kondre, Na Fraga,* All Countries, No Flag: The Multidimensional Experiences of Surinamese *Doglas,* Multiracials,*"* and, for almost a year, transcribed hundreds of pages of interview data and dedicated almost every waking hour to its completion. My chair, Dr. Phillip Akutsu, was impressed with the final product and nominated it for a dissertation award, the only one of its kind, proving to me that it was possible for qualitative work to be recognized as first class within my career field.

Unfortunately, this still didn't make it any easier for me to reclaim my intuition and step into my power as a practitioner. Aware of how marginalized and uncommon my perspectives were, my research and personal discoveries actually worsened my inner tension. I couldn't walk into an internship site with my dissertation under my arm and act like a pioneering rebel, while technically still a fledgling; it was the clumsiest form of professional suicide I could think of.

Chapter 9

 AUTHORITY ISSUES

Through authority, you will never find anything.
You must be free of authority to find reality.
—Jiddu Krishnamurti

I ALREADY HAD MY SIGHTS set on the well-rounded internship training opportunities at the counseling center at UC Davis, my alma mater, while still in the design stage of my dissertation. From what I'd seen, the comprehensive multicultural and clinical training offered at this stellar site surpassed what was offered at many internship placements across the nation. Some of my peers were casting their nets to thirty-plus training sites throughout the US to boost their chances of getting a quality placement. Because Robert and I loved the San Francisco Bay Area and for sure didn't want to move again, I needed a different strategy. I decided to start the process as early as possible and focus all my energy on this one fishing hole until I'd caught a fish.

I applied for a part-time practicum position at UC Davis during my dissertation year, a year prior to when I hoped to begin my internship. Within a week, I was offered an interview with the internship training director, Dr. Eduard Romano, and Dr. Katherine Haley, the practicum training director.

"To be honest, I'm very interested in applying to one of your internship positions next year. I've heard that some sites don't accept their practicum students, so I wanted to make sure that this isn't the case here," I said.

"A practicum position here will neither guarantee you a position nor exclude you from being eligible for one next year. It can work for you or against you. We've seen both outcomes in the many years we've been doing this. It all depends on you," Eduard said.

"Great. In that case, I'll shoot for both."

That same afternoon, Katherine called and offered me the practicum position. This was a good sign. A really good sign.

I enthusiastically accepted the offer, optimistic that getting better acquainted with the rest of the staff over the next few months would work in my favor. I loved being back at my old college, known for having a higher registration of bikes than "aggies" (the nickname of all students enrolled at this well-known agricultural school) and loved for its small-town friendliness and its spacious, green campus. The counseling center building was draped by mature, shady trees and next to the large, grassy quad in the heart of all the action.

In just a matter of weeks, I was already more than impressed by the clinical expertise of my supervisors, which was most noticeable when discussing emotionally charged issues pertaining to all kinds of "isms." As I'd hoped, group trainings, peer interactions, and sessions with clients also gave me plenty of opportunities to share my knowledge and skills.

"I really appreciate your authenticity and willingness to dig deep and explore loaded feelings that tend to make people squirm," Katherine, my practicum group supervisor, said to me during my first evaluation. "Your insights enrich our program and the clients you work with."

"I was most impressed by your nonjudgmental attitude toward your client. The things she shared with you would be triggering for a lot of people, but you remained calm and connected to a vulnerable, feeling part in her, which is awesome," Sandra, my one-on-one clinical supervisor, a pre-doctoral intern, added.

"Thank you so much for this feedback," I said, glowing. "I appreciate you recognizing these qualities in me. I'd not given them much thought before, but they refer to values that are important to me and strengths I'd like to explore and develop further."

An unexpected bonus of this practicum site was enhanced self-awareness, which positively impacted my dissertation design and research focus. Support from supervisors and first-hand updates also helped me to get through the nerve-wracking internship application process and the grueling waiting period. Oddly, when I heard that I'd made it to the interview rounds, I felt more nervous than relieved. I wasn't sure why. I suspected that it was the phone interview. To be fair to all the applicants, everyone was going to be interviewed by phone, even if you were on site, like me. I interviewed well and had sailed through my oral exams, but a phone interview? I'd never done one before and wasn't sure what to expect.

I never realized how much I relied on visual cues and body language until I was on a conference call with five interviewers. I knew each one of them, but it still felt like talking to a wall when I responded to their questions. Without some sort of cue, it felt rude and self-absorbed to keep going. My armpits and forehead began to prickle; second-language anxiety and mutism tendencies from my voiceless adolescent years were surfacing. I couldn't access the ease and comfort that I experienced in person around each of the staff and blurted out short, frazzled responses to get off the call as soon as possible.

The next day, Eduard knocked on my door and asked me how I thought I did.

"Terrible," I said. "I got a bad case of second-language anxiety. I've never done a phone interview before and had no idea that this could happen. In-person interviews have never been an issue."

He knew. He had interviewed me for the practicum position and had been impressed with my detailed and thoughtful responses. Eduard's kind follow-up and my positive track record as a practicum student were the only reasons why I ended up getting this internship position, offered to only six out of several hundred applicants each year.

"So, who would you like to have as your primary supervisor? Submit your first and second choices on this sheet of paper, and we will let you know who you're assigned to next week," Eduard said to us during our orientation week.

I transferred the great trust and openness that I'd felt toward my practicum cohort and mentors to Dr. Joan Taylor, my new supervisor, assuming that she would appreciate my skills and my sincerity, just like my previous supervisors had. After the initial courting weeks were over, it became clear that this was not the case.

"You do know the difference between a 'civil case' and a 'criminal case,' don't you?" Joan asked during our supervision meeting one morning. "I'm asking because you're nodding and acting as if you know what I'm talking about, while I'm getting the feeling that this is not really the case. I think it's important that you know the difference to understand what your client is dealing with," she said.

Her words pierced through my thin skin and hit a sensitive nerve. I struggled to stay with her question but felt myself disintegrating into a puddle. She was right. I didn't know the exact difference between the two. I just didn't find it urgent enough to interrupt her, as I'd learned the meaning of numerous words in English by listening attentively and by figuring out how they were used within the larger context, sometimes not until the end of the conversation.

I wiped off a few tears with the back of my hand and retreated into my protective shell. It was the condescending tone in her voice that I was reacting to. Although I had heard Joan use this tone of voice with other staff members before, I didn't make much of it. She was usually exceptionally kind and helpful toward trainees.

Joan had a concerned look on her face as I tried to figure out how to best respond to her question—fess up that I didn't know the full meaning of these terms without mentioning the tears or fess up and tell her about my knee-jerk emotional reaction to her tone. Since my authentic sharing had been well received at this site, I decided to take a risk and tell her the whole truth, confident that taking advantage of this healing opportunity would enhance our intimacy and trust.

"I'm sorry," I said, apologizing for my tears. "Listening usually helps me to decipher what is being said and gain insight into words and things that I don't yet understand. I'm emotional because I think your tone of voice triggered a racial nerve and unpleasant memories of being taunted for having an accent and speaking poor English right after moving to the US."

I was expecting her to say something like, "So sorry that you were subjected to this sort of bullying and prejudice. That must have been painful and hard and is understandably a tender area." I would have accepted any explanation for her reaction: Don't mind me. I'm a bit irritable and overprotective because this client reminded me of someone close to me . . . because I'm hungry . . . menopausing . . . argued with my spouse.

Instead, Joan moved back in her chair and mumbled under her breath, "We may be dealing with some kind of authority issue here."

Huh? Authority issue? After bringing this out in the open, Joan acted as if it had never happened, which was even more confusing. What now? Damned if I speak up, damned if I don't. How did I get back in this trap?

"What's wrong?" Robert asked when he saw my somber face. I told him what happened.

"Sounds like Queen Bee syndrome," he said. "You'll get punished for messing with her domain or the status quo."

"I don't see how I was messing with her domain or the status quo. I told her what she triggered in me."

"Yeah, but you said something about her tone, and she probably thinks that this crosses some line."

"Ugh. I hate lying just to keep the peace and assumed everyone there felt the same way about that. I'm sure we'll be able to talk it through if we go slow."

During our group seminar the next day, there was an unexpected change in agenda. Joan informed the intern team that she was going to facilitate a guided imagery exercise to explore our relationship to authority. My blood instantly shot up from lukewarm to boiling.

What? No she isn't. She could have tried to fish a little more discreetly for my "authority issues." I was truly stumped. I reviewed in my mind what had happened at the critical juncture in our supervision about a week ago and closely examined what could have given her the impression that I had unresolved authority issues. Was it because I openly shared the reactions that I had to her tone of voice? Why did this same openness impress my previous supervisors?

Just stay calm and you'll be okay. If you react defensively or defiantly, it will prove that she's right. Okay, fine. I'm going to approach this exercise like everyone else. If I have some kind of unresolved authority issue, so be it. Better to find out sooner than later. I pressed my reset button and gave Joan the benefit of the doubt that she had my best interest in mind. After letting these last thoughts and concerns drift off into my mind's horizon, I sank into a sea of peace while Joan guided us through various confrontations with authority figures.

Apparently, my responses during the exercise and group discussion didn't get to the authority issues that Joan had attempted to provoke. I thought this was a good thing until she began to make out-of-the-blue snide remarks during our supervision meetings.

"So what's been going on during Loraine and Maria's social hour?" she asked. Social hour? What's that supposed to mean? Was she referring to the video of our session and the fact that our interaction was light-hearted and we laughed? How do I address this without giving her more ammo? I chose to ignore it.

"Maria's doing okay. A love note that her boyfriend had written her before he committed suicide fell out of a book on her birthday. She's seeing it as a sign that he's still with her and watching over her. She said that it's helping her to alleviate the feelings of guilt that had been tormenting her for so long. I think her Mexican heritage is helping her heal. It's common for people from non-Western cultures to be guided in this way," I said, delighted that the Universe was sending me dream clients who'd benefit from my unique skill set and worldviews. Joan mostly listened, fidgety and visibly unhappy about my therapeutic style, but holding her tongue. What's her deal? Does she want me to be more somber and serious and dig up "real" problems in the same way she was trying to dig them up in me? Why did I get a sense that I saw my clients are basically good and innocent, while she saw them (and me) as basically flawed and broken?

I moved on and told Joan about another client who'd reported her abusive mother to Child Protective Services when just a teen. I thought that she was doing remarkably well under the circumstances. She was able to seek support from adults, including me, and allowed us to fill the role of surrogate parents.

"Whatever doesn't kill you makes you stronger," Joan commented wryly. I sensed that the jab was partly directed at me. I felt once again stumped and overpowered by an air of omniscient knowing that aimed to break rather than educate me.

Why do I keep triggering her? Does she think I'm blindly trusting my intuition to guide my clients? If it's working, why does it matter so much? Or does she think that my clients are fooling me with false strength and resilience which is preventing me from resolving their psychopathology and deeper issues? That I was letting them off the hook for my own "benefit"? What would this benefit be? Ego strokes that I was a good therapist when I really wasn't? The twisted roads in my mind disoriented me to no end.

Since I was being trained under her license, it was fair for her to expect me to honor her house rules. However, it was equally important to me to clear the "authority issue" label that I was still carrying around and that was magnifying my self-doubt. I asked Casey—a trusted peer of African-American descent—what he thought was going on. When he heard that I had told Joan that her tone of voice had struck a racial nerve in me, he shook his head and said, "You don't say that to white people. It's a very sensitive topic. She probably took it personally."

"Personally? Like I accused her of being racist? Why didn't she say that? I would've reassured her that this is not what I meant. She's my supervisor. Shouldn't she be aware of where I am in my growth? What if a client said something like this to her? Would she react in the same way?" I asked him.

"I don't know. Maybe," he said.

"I'm specializing in diversity issues. Shouldn't I be able to tell my supervisor when something like this is bothering me? If I didn't say anything, I'd feel like a hypocrite telling my student interns to speak their minds. We just had a discussion that it wasn't worth it to remain silent to keep the peace or appear professional, which are some of the unspoken rules that especially women and women of color pick up without even realizing it. A queer client of mine was once triggered by something I said that sounded heterosexist. I apologized and validated her feelings and reaction. I saw it as my client trusting me with her hurt and a chance for me to support her courage and offer her a new healing experience," I said.

I tried to put myself in Joan's shoes. Perhaps my intuitive self-direction and outspokenness came across as lack of deference or some sort of rejection if her interns were usually eager to accept her guidance. I made greater efforts to ask for input from her, but it still didn't work. Wanting to know the reasoning behind her interventions made her more uneasy and resentful, while deeper self-awareness and better understanding of the nature of our conflicts seemed like the most viable way we could resolve the issues and move forward. We clashed a few more times while stuck in this particular double bind: when I stayed true to myself, I irked Joan. And when I complied to her supervisory wishes, I disconnected from my true self and felt lost.

"I only get a vague sense of what you're doing, and whenever I try to be concrete with you, I get it wrong."

"Do you find me vague in general or is it only around issues related to culture?"

"In general," she answered, annoyed.

"Hmm, it seems to me that when I discussed how my client's cultural values may be helping her cope, it led to some kind of conflict and tension. Can you give me an example of where else I've been unclear today?"

She went through our meeting in her mind.

"I can't think of any times today when you were vague, but there have been other occasions. Isn't English your second language?"

She didn't just ask that . . . My ears almost fell off. "You know what, I don't think it's a matter of semantics or my English."

"You're right; your English is fine."

Then why bring it up? I wondered.

"I don't mind explaining what I mean as many times as needed. There's something in your tone of voice when we don't see eye-to-eye on something that I want to understand."

"You said that you were attracted to me because of my gentleness, and now you are making me sound like a witch!"

How did I make her sound like a witch? Here's where she loses her authority and not because I take it from her, but because she falls into some black hole and relinquishes it to me. I felt tangled up in her web, and a few tears of pent-up frustration and powerlessness welled up in my eyes.

"Here we are again, in this same space. I feel like I can never get it right for you," she said.

I remained quiet, my mind racing.

"We need tenderness in dealing with one another, and it's alright if we're just silent and don't say a lot," she said, correcting herself.

"I'm so confused. I feel like you think my reactions have no basis and that I make things up just to be difficult. I've tried to accept and take on this interpretation, but it doesn't fit me and keeps happening. Taking it on just to comply compromises my sense of integrity and this is where I feel stuck," I said in a quivering voice.

"If you're asking me if I think this is your issue, I do think it is your issue! And I mean that in the best way. I do like you, Loraine. I mean that it doesn't matter whose issue it is in discussing this, the value can be all yours. It can be all your issue, if you want it to be," she said.

I knew exactly what she meant, being a therapist and new supervisor myself. I wanted the boundary. I wanted her to maintain her privacy and feel that supervision was about me and my work, my personal growth. But when I revealed what my process was about when treating my clients and what I saw as taking full ownership of my choices and process, she got so triggered by my answer that the work was no longer about me, but about us. I wanted to meet her halfway, but I didn't understand what I was doing wrong.

Although I was shocked by Joan's explicit claim that this was all my issue, it allowed me to understand my resistance and anger about her messy tactics better.

"I think that there is something else going on than just my issues, which makes it difficult for me to move on," I replied to Joan.

"You know, I don't want to fight about whose issue it is. If you want, we can continue under pretense and just talk about cases. It's your choice," she said.

She'd had it with me and started to gather up her stuff to indicate that we were finished for the day. Her suggestion to continue under pretense shocked and propelled me to ask for help.

Thankfully, consult group met right after our meeting. I had been worried about sharing my struggle and about senior staff siding with Joan's interpretations. But, at this moment, no consequences—no negative evaluation, feelings of shame, judgmental reactions from others, getting in trouble, or lack of understanding—could be worse than pretending that everything was okay when it wasn't. I'd swallowed my feelings and words far too often in my short life and refused to embark on a career where biting my tongue was part of the job description. If being true to myself would fast-forward me to the end of this professional road, fine. Better to know sooner rather than later if I was in the wrong field.

Everyone was very supportive and respectful when I stammered out in bits and pieces what had been going on for the past weeks. My consult group reassured me that clashes between interns and supervisors happened on occasion and can be resolved. They would talk to Joan, and, if she and I continued to run into obstacles, someone could mediate a conflict resolution session. I was relieved but my mind felt like jelly. Thankfully, I had the foresight to document our conflicts in explicit detail and had my notes.

"Sounds like *Analyze This*," Angela said, when I told my tale to the rest of the interns in our afternoon seminar.

"You're right; it does!" Eduard, our training director, chimed in and chuckled.

"Have you seen it? It's a movie about a therapist, played by Billie Crystal, who refuses to treat a gangster, Robert DeNiro, a master at creating double binds. The better Billie Crystal gets at explaining why treating him is a bad idea, the more convinced Robert DeNiro becomes that he's picked the right guy because of his honesty. Your story made me think of that; only, in your case, it's the reverse. Being honest is perceived as insulting and leads to punishment," Angela said.

Her analysis of what was going on was spot on. Laughing about my dilemma brightened my outlook and gave me a sense of hope that I hadn't felt in weeks.

Thursday morning supervision started out well. We talked about needing to take care of our relationship before moving on and taking the time and space to do that. I could tell that Joan also felt supported by the staff; she seemed more open and optimistic than usual. She said that she wasn't concerned about me harming clients. She had seen my videotapes and had never felt alarmed. Good. I felt at ease and wholeheartedly accepted Joan's invitation to clear the air.

"You needed to claim your space, and that was very important to you," she said. Gone were the warm fuzzies.

"Yes, but it's more than that. It felt as if you saw me as someone who forcefully and rudely claims her space, and I have no recollection of doing that," I said.

"You had no intention of doing that," she said.

"Correct. I had no intention of being forceful, but I also have no understanding of what I did that could come across as forceful. I tried to remember if it was my tone of voice, my demeanor, or the content of the message, but I can't find the evidence that I need to file this transgression away. I would like to be able to make that connection for myself so I know what not to do in the future based on this new information," I said.

Joan didn't respond. I had a feeling that I'd said the wrong thing again. It felt as if I was living a double life. I thrived in my multicultural specialization, facilitating intense and emotional conversations just like this between students, staff, administrators, and members of the community during diversity programs on campus.

How could the same expertise that effectively resolved the most heated conflicts between agitated students of color and police officers backfire with Joan? What was going on here? Was pride getting in my way or was my dogged determination not letting me call it quits? Or was something stuck in my blind spot that I kept missing?

I finally detected a little opening. It was as miniscule as the eye of a needle. I remembered feeling an odd attraction to Joan and a knowing that she'd help round me out. I was baffled, not because it didn't make sense; it made too much sense. It wasn't what I'd expected, but she did help round me out.

I also felt an intuitive flutter toward Armando Caldero—my specialty supervisor and the mastermind behind the multicultural immersion program—when I heard about his work. Because of my conflicts with Joan, I became more curious why it felt so natural and easy to be around Armando. I probably would not have given our connection the attention it deserved if Joan hadn't been so bothered by my "vagueness." I didn't need to say much about my troubled supervisory relationship with Joan. Armando seemed to know what was going on, and he didn't like to overtalk and overthink things. He called it "mental masturbation." He instead lent me books like *The Symptom Path to Enlightenment*, exuding a reassuring confidence that everything would fall in place. I felt safe as soon as I entered his office; he was my lifeboat during these stormy times.

One time, perhaps after noticing that the strain on me was taking its toll, Armando said out of the blue that Eduard thought that my grievance letter was well written. He proceeded to explain with his index finger and his other hand that I was able to see things that most people couldn't see because I'd turned a corner that they hadn't turned yet. What corner?

Almost like a reflex, my mind switched from a conceptual, linguistic gear to a visceral, poetic way of relating that was commonly practiced among Creole and Chinese speakers. I intuited what he meant and embraced it without ever verifying if I'd extracted to exact meaning out of his phrase.

This is how Armando and I were similar. Even though he'd say things that perhaps made no logical sense to other staff and trainees, they made sense to me and often felt more true and meaningful than the concrete guidance that I was getting elsewhere. One time, when working with groups or individual clients, Armando wanted me to sense "the wave," like a surfer, and ride it. I understood that it had to do with riding—maintaining our sense of balance—at our unique edges of growth, which required an orchestration of multiple skills, intelligences, and body wisdom. I saw how impactful Armando was when he sensed the farthest edge of growth in his undergraduate interns and program participants and gently guided them to it. Once they got the hang of riding that wave, their healing was self-propelled. They loved being in his presence as much as I did.

I realized that riding the wave was something I intuitively did in life and in relationships. I must have pushed Joan to an uncomfortable edge by poking in the shadows of our conflict and our blind spots, not wanting to drop the issue out of fear that we were doing it and our best selves an injustice.

The interventions and support from the staff unfortunately could not lift us over this canyon; it was only a matter of time before we got into another conflict. Joan divulged that the only reason we were getting along was because she was keeping her mouth shut to protect me and that she was "not having a good time."

"Well, in that case, I don't see why we should continue. I'll let Eduard know," I said.

"It's my prerogative to talk to Eduard," she said, trying to prevent me from leaving.

"It is, but it's also mine," I said, and walked out.

I shut the door, in shock. I found Eduard in his office and summarized in a few sentences what had happened.

"I'm done. This is truly not going anywhere. She keeps picking fights with me, and I think she's done too."

"How have you been handling all of this?" Eduard asked,

clearly bothered that he wasn't able to prevent what happened.

"I think I'm okay. I feel okay. The strange thing is that the excerpt from *Shining Affliction*—a memoir written by an intern who had a nervous breakdown at her training site—that I discovered on the back of one of Joan's handouts, gave me the idea to write about the challenges that I've been facing. Writing a grievance letter helped me to see Joan as a human being rather a supervisor with indomitable superpowers. Finding my limit today reminded me of a time in my childhood when I dreamed about writing a book for adults. I'd come to a similar point of exasperation, clarity, and confidence as I did just now. So, to answer your question, this sucks, but I feel calm and strong, and I am excited about revisiting the idea of writing a book," I said, my eyes twinkling.

The silence that followed indicated that this was probably the last thing that Eduard expected me to say. He seemed confused, turned off, and about to say something in response to my off-beat comment, but let it slide. Waves of panic surged through my body. I wanted to reassure him that I wasn't taking this ordeal lightly and that I wasn't trying to incriminate Joan and the agency in a book.

It's just that something old, timely, and beyond my control was churning and burbling up. Even though things had been difficult, they'd given me a clearer glimmer of my purpose, which tended to slip out of my hands before I was able to take a good look at it. Suspecting how bizarre all of this would sound, I decided to keep the deeper roots and reasons for my reactions to myself, but I felt discouraged. My wild and mysterious insights and other-worldly connections between my feelings and real life events had barely surfaced before I needed to stuff them down again.

Eduard agreed that there wasn't much left of the relationship to salvage and that it was best to cut my losses. He reassigned me to another supervisor, Dr. Fred Grant.

"Great, thank you. I really like Fred," I said to Eduard. I knew Fred from practicum trainings and looked forward to hearing his input and insights on cases in my consultation group. I trusted him, and I especially appreciated his caring candidness. I went home, relieved to be able to put all this behind me. I had no need to discuss the matter further. I just wanted to spend the evening on the sofa, safe in Robert's arms and preoccupied by a captivating movie.

"Eduard told me that he appreciated your ability to take care of yourself and set limits," Fred said during our first meeting, trying to smooth over my abrupt transition to him as my new supervisor.

"That was nice of him. I was pretty stuck, but when I made the conscious decision that it was important that I stay true to myself, even if that meant that I was not suited for this career field, I stopped being so affected by Joan's expectations and opinions," I said.

"That's wonderful. I don't think many interns have that much clarity and gall," he said. Fred was an almond farmer and lived on a huge stretch of land on the fringes of society. The more we learned about one another, the more we clicked.

After a few months of working with Fred, he said to me, "You know, I often feel like a seasoned colleague with twenty years of experience is sitting across from me when we are leading the graduate student psychotherapy group together. It's very unusual for an intern with as little experience as you have to take risks like you do. Most interns I have worked with would, at this stage in the game, sit back and observe and only tentatively jump in."

"Thank you for telling me this. It really means a lot," I said, blushing on the inside.

"I just do what seems natural to me and didn't realize that it was so different than the norm," I said. This same tendency must have provoked Joan.

"I must admit that I worried that you would be a bit defensive and closed off to constructive feedback, because of the conflicts that you had with your previous supervisor and the fact that you never bring a notebook to supervision. But I haven't found any indication of that. You just like to take risks, that's all, which is telling of an eagerness to learn. I do find that your skills in verbalizing your theoretical conceptualizations are not as strong, and that you explain a lot of problems and issues that clients present

with in terms of culture rather than in theoretical and psychological terms," he said.

"Ahh, Sandra, my practicum supervisor, encouraged me not
to take so many notes when I was her supervisee, and I loved what
that did for me," I said. "I'm more alert when I'm not taking notes,
and better able to integrate new information into my existing
structures of understanding. In terms of the theoretical lingo, I try
to translate in my own words what you're saying and make sense
of it based on my own life experiences and way of talking," I said.

"You're a fast learner, and definitely attentive, so it seems to
work for you," he said.

"Thank you. I suppose it's like coaching someone on tennis
or golf. I like to observe, practice, and feel in my body what's going
on rather than talk at length about the swings in a heady way. I've
heard experienced therapists say that theory interfered with their
natural inclinations as a therapist—that they had to unlearn all the
academic technicalities to remember what came naturally to them
before graduate school. I was hoping to sidestep this problem by
using my body's wisdom and intuition instead."

"That makes sense. You do have a natural swing, but it's good
to be able to describe what you're doing in technical terms too,"
Fred said.

"I'll do my best. It tends to stifle my intuition; that's why I keep
it to a minimum. In regard to the cultural differences piece, I do see
cultural influences in a lot of things that we do, say, and feel that are
often overlooked. People seem to think that "culture" only pertains
to ethnic identity, specific traditions, or more tangible cultural
aspects of ourselves while I think of our worldviews and certain
ways of thinking and being in the world as "cultural." For instance,
being more rational or intuitive, individualistic or interdependent, or how we may approach adversity or trauma, why events are
appearing as lessons, and so on, are culturally influenced."

"I see where you're coming from," Fred said and nodded.

Unbeknownst to me, Fred had a regular meditation practice.
It was not something that he openly discussed in supervision or
incorporated in his therapy approach, but my explanation and per-

ception that many psychological disorders are exacerbated by an overactive and dominating Western ego-mind made a lot of sense to him.

Our supervisory relationship continued to improve and blossom as a result of these heart-to-heart conversations and Fred's guidance in helping me articulate my intuitive processes. Fred wanted me to work on my pacing and timing, because I often, as I had unwittingly done with Joan, pushed clients to their edge of growth when they perhaps weren't ready. I learned to detect resistance, but it was difficult to hold back when I sensed harm lurking in the shadows. On one occasion, I informed Fred that I suspected that a client's elderly mother was being abused by caregivers and wanted to know about my mandated ethical obligation to report "suspicions of abuse."

He had not picked up any cues around that and informed me that "suspicions" meant concrete examples and tangible proof. This incident provided deep insight into the curse and blessing of my intuitive gift. Sorrow and regret for not probing more seeped in months later when the client said that her mother had been mistreated; it was too hard for her to face this when her mother was still alive.

Fortunately, Armando helped me to access and hone the parts of my intuition that were attuned to wise guidance and light. I once volunteered to be his guinea pig to demonstrate to the intern group how to guide clients in trance and help them meet an "inner adviser." As soon as I closed my eyes, I heard the ringing laughter of Surinamese Maroon children who were rolling a dug-out canoe to the river. Robert and I had visited their village the previous year during my data collection trip. My maternal great-grandmother appeared in the same scene, reminding me that the children, she, and I all shared the same ancestry.

"I will always be here for you," she conveyed to me. It went directly from her heart into mine, reassuring me to continue on my path. I felt like a flower bud that had freshly cracked its outer shell.

Chapter 10

 **AWIKIO! AWAKEN!**

The goal of life is to have your heartbeat
match the beat of the universe,
to match your nature with Nature.
—Joseph Campbell

ON THE DAY OF MY DOCTORAL commencement, my exhausted body—
disguised in an official cap and black gown—wanted to collapse and
sleep, but there was too much adrenaline surging through my veins.
I was wide awake during my proudest and biggest moment, my private moon landing, heightened by very special news Robert and I
had saved for this day. I'd soon look like I'd swallowed the moon: I
was pregnant.

Both of our brothers, Dean and Mark, and even Uncle Henk
had crossed the globe to be a part of this grand celebration, which
concluded with a cocktail party and dancing until late. After the
festivities, I was spent. I recuperated and hibernated throughout
my first trimester until the end of summer.

During my second and third trimesters, I worked part-time
in both the Multicultural Immersion and Campus Violence Prevention Programs at the UC Davis counseling center. Even though
I was cautioned that putting all my eggs in one basket—staying at

the same site for another academic year—could weaken my vitae, starting a new job and adjusting to an unfamiliar routine while pregnant sounded worse. I knew the UC Davis staff, I knew my clientele, I knew my way around campus, and I knew how to keep my responsibilities and schedule light and flexible enough to honor my body's and unborn baby's growing and unpredictable needs.

Being able to further hone my clinical skills with Armando— he agreed to be my primary supervisor—was another key reason for staying. I appreciated his expertise and sensed that there was a lot more to tap out of his atypical well of knowledge. He didn't disappoint. Exposure to deeper levels of his mind-body healing approaches far outweighed regular exposure to stories of violent trauma and hate.

Work was a welcome distraction until I could no longer see my feet. After I gave birth to my baby boy, Terrance, I took some time off. A few months later, I spent half of the week relishing in motherhood and the other half back at the job I most loved: supporting college kids and offering trauma prevention and diversity programs and training around campus. Ma cuddled, cooed, chased, and cared for Terrance when I was at work. Pa found a new job in structural engineering and enjoyed retrofitting homes and buildings so that they too could better absorb all the shocks and aftershocks of devastating earthquakes, but it was clear that he loved spending time with his grandson even more. Life couldn't get any better.

One Tuesday, on my way to our quarterly staff training, the unfamiliar, musky scent of sage welcomed me into the conference room. A medium-sized white man with patches of thinning, white hair around his ears walked up to me and held out his hand.

He enveloped mine in both of his and said, "Hi, I'm Tim. It's very nice to meet you."

"It's nice to meet you too," I replied with a polite nod. There was something unsettling but intriguing about his warm and kind presence.

I found a handbook on my seat about the use of spiritual interventions with students by Tim Bailey, Counseling Center Director.

Spirituality? Hm, this is a first. I wonder what got into the staff to offer this kind of training.

"Does anyone know what this is?" Tim asked the staff as he pulled out a small, wheel-like circle with four spokes of different colors—black, red, yellow, and white—out of a bag.

"It's a medicine wheel," Susie, one of the practicum students, said. Her boyfriend was into Lakota spirituality.

"That's right. I have one for each of you," he said, while holding up the bag and gesturing to pass it along the group. I carefully took mine out of the bag and placed it in the palm of my hand.

"Four is considered a sacred number by the Lakota. Not only do these four lines represent the four directions of the earth, but there are many other sacred groupings of four that make a complete cycle," he said, while sliding his fingers along the brightly colored spokes. He held the medicine wheel up like a long-lost treasure for our special viewing. A little flicker of excitement lit up my heart.

"Four seasons in a year; four weeks in a woman's reproductive cycle; four phases of the moon; four stages of life: childhood, adolescence, adulthood, old age; four elements in nature: fire, water, earth, air; and four aspects of the self: emotional, mental, spiritual, and physical, to give you a few examples. All these fours meet at the center and are held together in this circle," Tim explained.

"Now, did anyone notice the four empty spaces in between the spokes? In Western culture, we tend to focus on the tangible and discredit what is intangible and can't be seen. Not so with the Lakota. Unseen forces orchestrated by the Great Mystery are just as real, often even more real, than the everyday, tangible aspects of reality that we tend to give more credence to."

The meaning of the medicine wheel enticed a few more dormant parts within me. They were like the petals of a delicate poppy unfolding to the first shimmers of early dawn. Little electric sparks along the length of my spine fired as he pointed to the openings of the medicine wheel. It felt as if a set of antennae were getting pulled out of my back. The messages, more like sensations, that I was picking up felt very familiar and frighteningly powerful even though the actual information that Tim shared about the Lakota tradition was all new to me.

"Who teaches our young men and women about the mystical

laws of Mother Earth and the sacred feminine? These?" Tim asked facetiously, while holding up a few magazines covered by sexy, bikini-clad models. The senior staff in the back of the room chuckled.

"You laugh, but I picked these up at your bookstore right downstairs on my way to the conference room. Our young people are at the mercy of these images and influences before they reach puberty. They may live their entire lives without ever learning how to relate to Mother Earth, women, and one another in a sacred manner." His words sank like bricks to the bottom of my soul.

"Indigenous cultures, like the Lakota, used to teach their young men and women about these sacred laws, the Great Mystery and Mother Nature to temper their budding ego-selves. Many of these traditions were lost but are slowly resurfacing. How about us? What formal rites of passage do we offer our young men and women to help them become responsible, interconnected adults?

"Sadly, not many, so they come up with them on their own, but even a piece of paper at the end of their education can feel meaningless if it represents nothing more than a ticket to greater economic freedom and access to more toys. Can you imagine what it could do for our young adults if they were initiated by wise and caring adults, like yourselves, and shown how to live in balance with themselves, each other, and the planet?" Tim said.

Some of the staff squirmed in their seats like school children. As if anticipating this growing resistance, Tim switched gears.

"I bet that my presentation is very different than what you're used to hearing at your trainings, because I'm not teaching you specific techniques or interventions to use with your students. I'm here to talk about what the indigenous people call the mirror law, the sacred laws of the Great Mystery, the 'As above, so below' maxim," he said, while showing us a symbol that looked like an hour glass.

"Tipi tents at the top look just like this at the top, right? It's not by accident. This is called a kapemni."

As above, so below. The cross of Lorraine on Joan of Arc's flag had the same meaning. By now, every cell in my body had perked up, and I could feel my heart picking up pace. It felt as if Joan, the fiercest of my childhood imaginary friends, was trying to spell out in secret code what my mission was about. The fluttering in my heart was a wake-up call that helped me to focus and piece these synchronistic clues together.

"According to the mirror law, our mistreatment and manipulation of the planet is a reflection of our mistreatment of our bodies and natural selves, and vice versa. Mirror law also means that whatever we may find problematic about the younger generation may actually be a reflection of our shortcomings and shadow parts passed along when guiding them.

"This is the foundation of my year-long program, informed by the last thirteen years of my own spiritual development. It feels like the right time to bring it out into the world. By the way, thirteen is also a sacred number: the number of full moons in a year. In this program, students are asked to disconnect from the illusions and addictions in their lives, to abstain from sex, and to stop using substances and alcohol for a year to learn to reconnect with a neglected part of themselves."

For a few moments, the room drowned in silence until murmurs and words like cult and cultish drifted to the front. Why did the senior staff think he sounded cult-like? Just because he asked his students to abstain from drugs and sex? They could decline to participate if they didn't want to. He wasn't forcing them or manipulating them to do any of this, was he?

Tim was shrinking and getting more and more apologetic because of the staff's disapproving reactions. He began each of his sentences with, "I know that this sounds crazy . . ."

I watched helplessly, every now and then wiping off a tear, not sure what was happening inside of me. During a short break, I went up to Tim and said, "You know, what you are saying doesn't sound crazy to me at all. I actually feel sane with you and insane out there."

I wanted him to know that his message was getting through to at least one person. Me.

"Thank you very much," he nodded, looking me deep in the eyes.

"Aren't the suicide and alcoholism rates phenomenal on their reservations?" Walter, the center's psychiatrist, asked when the training resumed. "How effective are their methods in treating that?"

A tidal wave of fury surged out of depths I didn't know I had.

Tim listened respectfully, but, from where I was sitting, I could see his body flinch and his jaws clench as if stabbed in the heart. My face flushed with rage and shame. I wondered if these feelings were also seething in the darkest pockets of both men, Walter's perhaps a few layers deeper than Tim's.

With careful pacing of words, Tim replied, "These powerful methods and traditions are healing generations of trauma on the Rez. You do realize that they'd been outlawed and driven underground for centuries until very recently?

"Why don't you join me and see for yourself what's going on at the Rez these days? As a matter of fact, I'm offering an intensive, four-day follow-up retreat in about two months on the East Coast to a small group of college counselors. We'll go deeper into these concepts, and you'll be able to participate in ancient practices, such as the purification sweat lodge, and explore exercises that I use in my program with students. I'm inviting all of you to join me."

The minute he said this, I had the sensation of my usual outer shell avalanching into my true self and flipping inside out. There was no question about it. I was going to Tim's retreat.

In preparation for the retreat, Tim regularly sent out information and mindfulness exercises to practice and cleanse our bodies by watching what we ate, said, and did. One Friday night, just before going to bed, I read one of Tim's emails, a short, inspirational piece about meeting his spirit guide, an indigenous corn farmer he'd met on the road. He asked us about our spirit guides.

"Ask them to step forward and accompany you along your path," he wrote.

Spirit guides? What does he mean by spirit guides? How will they step forward to meet me? were my last thoughts before dozing off into a deep sleep.

The next morning at 4:26 a.m., in that lush, dreamy state when half-asleep, half-awake, long-forgotten details about our trip to a Maroon village years ago surfaced like a thousand piece jigsaw puzzle, completely intact. Robert and I were in the aluminum belly of a swaying, buzzing bird en route to Awarradam, a tiny island burrowed in the Suriname River that we visited during my data collection trip. We'd both longed to explore these mysterious, off-limit areas of the rainforest ever since we were children.

The dark-green treetops right underneath us were breathtaking. They looked like broccoli heads and even had similar spots of yellow that might have been blossoms, flowers, or withered leaves. Grooves of tea-colored water snaked in between the broccoli heads, and, every so often, signs of a Maroon village and human life—rectangular rooftops covered with dried, grayish-brown palm-tree leaves—came into focus.

A good distance in front of us was a short stretch of grassy area, our landing strip, the first one in sight after an hour of flying. I prayed that the brakes were in good working condition, looking at the river that crossed it not too far ahead. There was only one small building to the left of the landing strip—not bigger than a shed, probably some kind of communication or control center.

About thirty young, glistening bodies, some half-naked, some in colorful, ripped shorts or T-shirts, were waving their arms and running along the strip while we landed. As soon as the plane's underbelly opened, high-pitched giggles and excited shrieks filled the hot and muggy air. It smelled like grass, gasoline, and musky sweat.

I crawled out and, for a moment, felt too overwhelmed to move. Everything around me was green: dark green, bright green, fluorescent green, brown green. Green and alive. I breathed in, and the green breathed out. I breathed out, and the green breathed in, like it used to in Saramacca when my family spent the day at *boitie*. How I missed breathing together. It was like resting my head on Robert's chest and synchronizing our breaths into a calm, soothing rhythm after a long, tiring day.

Like worker ants, the children ran in a single file with our luggage on their heads. They dropped it in a pile closer to the river and ran back to get more.

"Where do these kids live?" I asked.

"They are from Kayana, the little village across the river. Until very recently, they'd never seen an airplane up close. We've been landing here about twice a week for a while now, but it's still the highlight of their day," Boikie, our tour guide, said smiling.

Boikie was in his mid-twenties and was born and raised near Awarradam. He was as fluent in Dutch, Surinamese, and English as he was in his native Saramaccan language.

"Hey, *fai de,* hi, how are you?" he shouted to a few of his friends, *matis,* waiting for us by the river. Our little group consisted of ten Surinamese eco-tourists who were visiting from Holland and Curaçao: a gynecologist, a musician, a homemaker, a construction worker, a police chief, two lawyers, and three university students. Five of us were from the US: the son of the American ambassador, a couple of American adventure seekers, Robert, and me. All fifteen of us, Boikie, two boatsmen, and our luggage fit into the long dug-out canoe, and, within ten minutes, we were gliding through the mirror-smooth waters of the Suriname River to Awarradam.

The shrill call of a toucan pierced through the mesmerizing tranquility and peace that enveloped us, enchanting my soul and senses until the tiny hairs all over my body were charged by a mystical power that hung low in the air.

"These gates keep evil spirits out. Make sure to walk under them when you enter the villages," Boikie said, while pointing to a village gate made of three skinny sticks joined at the top by a long stick and dressed up with a yellow grass skirt. There were pieces of red embroidered cloth and other leafy decorations deliberately placed at various parts in front and on the gate.

"Cool," I said, unable to peel my eyes off the gate. It emanated something other-worldly that I couldn't put into words: an uplifting vibration that was as palpable as the soft breeze that was gently blowing through our hair. I imagined walking up the steps, conscious about purifying my mind and protecting the community from outside evil and harm. What a fascinating ritual!

I basked in the peaceful green all around me until we reached our river island destination, a tropical, serene paradise adorned with blooming plants, banana and palm trees, and giant canopies surrounded by river rapids, boulders, and fine, creamy sand. I deeply exhaled. It was truly one of the most magnificent masterpieces of natural beauty and perfection I'd ever seen.

We were warmly greeted by a local crew who assigned us to a Maroon-style, wooden cabin on stilts covered by a roof made from palm leaves. Two inviting hammocks on the balcony offered an incredible view of the island, the beach, the boulders, and the river framed by a backdrop of nothing but dense rainforest in every direction. I swayed for a bit in one of the hammocks that was holding me tight in the warm, loving womb of Mother Earth.

After we put our stuff away, we gathered in a communal area where we ate, played cards and board games, and practically rolled on the ground laughing when Boikie started relaying his Anansi stories, *tori*. Two local children, Demoi and Takiman—probably around three and four years old—ran around naked. I discovered that they started their day dressed but took their clothes off to feel the earth and warm boulders close to their bare skin. I wished I could join them when we made our way down to the river.

They didn't know how to swim. They crawled and climbed the boulders around the river like agile lizards, occasionally bathing and wading in the shallow water. No one seemed concerned about their safety or worried about piranhas or the small crocodile that we detected on the other side of the riverbed.

"They won't bother you if you don't bother them. You just need to be careful and respect their territory," Boikie said. The rest of the locals felt the same way about the pet tarantulas, hiding in the corners of some of the cabins and in the communal area, and about the tiny, brightly colored poisonous frogs—capable of killing up to ten humans with their venom, making them the deadliest amphibians in the world—that peeked out from under leaves off the main trails. The group's questions and fearful concerns seemed to be the highlight of Boitie's week.

"When it's your time to go, it's your time to go. How are you going to change that?" he said, laughing. The theory that modern anxiety was the residue of our less evolved, reptilian brain and indigenous ways of life didn't quite measure up. Boikie and friends didn't seem to think that fear of life-threatening danger and predators enhanced survival. There was something much more complex going on here.

After spending just one afternoon at Awarradam, life felt simpler, less pretentious, and unburdened, something to treasure, not control. There were no clocks, no watches, just the sun rising and setting. I felt more present, alive, carefree, and powerful than I'd ever felt in my entire life. All of the other city folks were similarly unwinding, talking and moving more slowly as the day progressed.

After dinner, I joined Robert and a few others in a *wasi*, a river cleansing, and wedged my hips in a rock opening in a *sula*, a rapid. We enjoyed our long water massages, joked, and laughed until our fingertips and toes looked like raisins. We headed to our cabins as soon as the sun set, aware that we'd soon have trouble seeing our own hands.

"Look up. Isn't it incredible?" Robert said during our leisurely walk back.

An infinitude of needle-point speckles had snuck into every square centimeter of the pitch-black sky.

"It's beautiful," I said. My soul felt as sparkly clean and clear as the magical dome around us.

We kissed. I leaned on a palm tree, my legs wobbly as Robert pressed against me.

"Let's go inside," Robert said and pulled me by the hand into *Honi Watra,* Honey Water, our cabin.

It didn't take long before the sound of rustling palm leaves was rocking our freshly baptized bodies into new heights of rapture and singing us secret lullabies after we'd fallen into a satisfied sleep.

"*Awikio, awikio,* awaken, awaken," said the villagers when they saw us the next morning. We had a hearty breakfast of baguette bread and eggs and gathered in a circle to prepare for a three-hour walking jungle tour guided by Boikie and Basia, the village captain and medicine man. Basia was a bundle of lean and mean muscle—perhaps in his sixties—and looked half his age.

"Tuck your pants into your socks," Boikie said. "And make you sure you have a full bottle of water on you." After we applied foul-smelling insect repelling oil and put on our hats, we were ready for the hike.

"*Loekoe,* look," Basia said, every now and then, pointing to tracks, birds, and camouflaged insects hiding under twigs, branches, and leaves. "See what happens if you accidentally bump into this tree?" He tapped a skinny tree not much taller than him. Within seconds, it was covered with bullet ants. "You won't be happy if these fall on you and start biting. They are very aggressive, and their bite hurts like a bullet wound. That's how they got their name."

He and Boikie took turns teaching us the medicinal, nutritional, and practical value of many different plants, trees, and leaves that were used to heal wounds, stop infections, make hats and board games, or serve as fans or parasols to combat the heat. They showed us herbs and tree saps for vitality and health, vegetable patches that blended into their surroundings, tree bark that reduced malaria fevers, oils to treat insect bites or snake bites, hollow tree trunks that echoed loudly through the forest to signal for help, and majestic trees of worship, such as the sacred *kankantri*, that invoked humility and respect as it towered over us.

I could hardly contain the joy inside of me. It was as if Boikie and Basia had flipped a switch and lit up all the magical secrets of the forest. It was a library, medicine chest, grocery store, park, zoo, art studio, and cathedral. The awe from our morning walk glowed in me for hours after we returned to the island and repeated our swimming and river soaking ritual.

The next day, we accompanied a group of men and about twenty children to a spot in the jungle where a tree had been cut. Not the men, but these boisterous children, both boys and girls, dragged the tree trunk over the jungle floor in pairs with short pieces of rope under its entire length. They were full of energy, their elated voices ringing through the trees of the rainforest. A little girl with a clubfoot contributed equally and seemed as much a part of the group as the other children.

Our next stop was at a bend in the river where we had lunch. We used the flat rocks and boulders as tables to hold our food, plates, calabasses, and belongings. A few yards away, there was a narrow and raging current, cutting through two huge boulders. We all sat on the edge of the boulder and admired the water gushing between the stones, feeling and fearing its deadly power and force.

"There is a boat that once belonged to white men stuck in between the boulders underneath this rapid. A few centuries ago, our ancestors tricked the white men who were following them down this river rapid and jumped out of their boats just in time. The men who were following them didn't and ended up drowning in the strong currents," Boikie said.

I gulped. Plantation owners chasing runaway slaves this far into the jungle? Unbelievable. Hearing about the atrocities that slaves had endured was nothing new, but those stories had never felt this palpable before. My maternal ancestor who'd been dragged here from Africa on a slave ship had been more like a distant, almost fictional character out of movie or a book. He or she suddenly became real to me, as real as Boikie sitting next to me. It could have been him or her, running and swimming for dear life, begging and praying that the jungle and wise, sacred trees would provide enough protection.

Dark clouds had formed during our history lesson. No one noticed until the heavens broke open and dumped heavy *sibie boesie*, tropical rainstorm drops, on us. We welcomed it with our outstretched arms and open mouths. The calm that followed the brief storm hushed the river, the fish, the trees, and the animals into a profound stillness that seeped through my wet clothes and into my bone marrow. Subdued, soaked, and reflective, I huddled in a ball and enjoyed a calabas full of delicious brown beans and rice in a warm ray of afternoon sunlight. It was the most satisfying lunch I'd ever had.

On the third day, Boikie took us to a site by the river that was a gathering place for indigenous hunters.

"Amerindians sharpened their tools and spears right here in these grooves," he said, squatting down and touching the markings on a boulder. His attention diverted to the huge claws of an enormous bird sprawled on one of the boulders ahead of us. The group followed him to take a closer look.

My feet, as if glued on the carved boulder, wouldn't move. I sat next to the carvings and caressed them, feeling time, space, and my finite self melt away in the sun. A flickering image of my great-grandmother appeared in my mind's eye, her mixed facial features, African and Surinamese indigenous, clearly visible. The fierce pulsing sensations in my body felt like the intense, life-long pull that the rainforest had on my heart and soul, as if wanting to inform me of my indigenous roots and our mysterious connection, an idea that my mind couldn't quite grasp.

Robert and I found a little two-person canoe on the shore. We explored the river on our own, watched fishermen catch dinner with just a string and a hook, and lived out some of our childhood fantasies.

"Isn't it strange how easy it is to adapt to this lifestyle? All the things that seem so indispensable about modern life: I don't even miss them. Do you?" I asked Robert.

"Nope. I wish we could stay longer to enjoy this simple lifestyle more fully. Look, over there," Robert said, pointing to a luminescent Morpho butterfly in one of the side streams shaded by dense foliage. "Let's check it out," he said. Enchanted, we followed the butterfly, reminiscent of what I used to do as a child, and saw a few more, their shimmery blue wings creating a stunning, fairy-like spectacle in the intimate river cove. They portrayed how I was feeling on the inside: radiant, free-spirited, complete, and special, just like I used to as a child, only better, with Robert by my side to share it with.

"Time to go. We're visiting a neighboring village this evening to celebrate and welcome in the new year. Did you bring your party suit and dress?" Boikie asked after he'd gathered all of us back.

"Yes, my best gown. I can't wait," I said, chuckling, and got into the large boat with the rest of the group. We freshened up, and, by the time we reloaded the boat, the sun had set behind the tree-rimmed horizon. The tide was high, and the river was again as smooth as an ice skating rink. The boatsmen maneuvered the rigid canoe around boulders in the river that were invisible. I looked around for landmarks, but all I could see were the repetitive small pairs of red crocodile eyes along the riverbed.

When the musky scent of an animal became very noticeable, Boikie said, "It's a wild pig. Stinky, huh? When we use soap and perfumes, our synthetic odor is just as aversive to them. That's why we don't. They'd notice you from a mile away, and you would never find anything to eat."

What a humbling experience it was for all of us. Here we were, successful professionals, accomplished and sure of ourselves. But, in this environment, we were the most helpless, unskilled, and useless members of the entire village. Yet, none of them had treated us with even the slightest sign of disrespect. I felt ashamed, thinking of the poor treatment these gentle, brilliant souls would likely be subjected to if they ever set foot in our modern world.

Frank pulled out his guitar, and pretty soon had all of us—witnessed by the stars, the river, the trees, the forest—synched up and joining him in singing his soulful, groovy song, *"Zoom ga li ga li ga li, zoom ga li ga li."* Every now and then, a fish jumped into our boat causing loud squeals and laughter. With a quick stab of his knife, Boikie killed and saved these food offerings to give to our hosts that evening.

Upon our arrival, the boatsmen secured the boats, and we scrambled around with flashlights and kerosene lanterns behind Boikie to the open hut where we were gathering for the ceremony. A group of women signaled to us to come over and helped us into traditional clothing. Women were to wear a simple, brightly colored, cotton, checkered cloth around their waists, called a *pangi,* and a cape to hang over their shoulders and cover their backs. The men wore a similar but shorter skirt and loincloth as well as a cape halfway over one shoulder. The capes were decorated with hand-embroidered patterns and intricate, interwoven symbols and geometric shapes that had special meaning.

"No, no," Yolanda, one of the village women laughed, shaking her hand when I made a common knot with the two loose ends of my skirt.

"Feti, fight," she said, holding her hands in fists to show me what my crude knot represented. She helped me put on my *pangi* in the traditional way, smoothly wrapped around my waist with a second cloth tied around it to hold it in place.

In the large hut, a group of women stood in a half circle, and two men, Boikie and an elder of the village, were in the middle of the half circle. We were sitting in rows of wooden benches, facing them. Children and adolescents were all around, peering around the wooden pillars of the hut.

"Robert and Loraine, come here," Boikie said. "Our first order of business is to congratulate you on your five-year anniversary." We had not told them that this was our wedding day, but somebody had informed Boikie and the village elder, who'd planned a little surprise for us. We got up and faced Boikie as if getting married all over again.

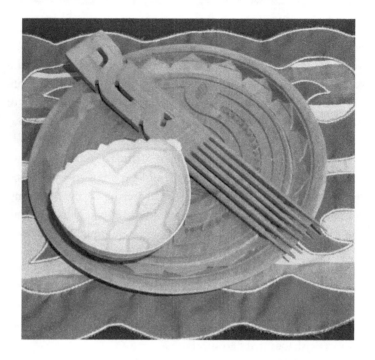

"This is what a man gives to his woman as a symbol of his love when he leaves for a few days," he said and gave me a beautiful comb, hand carved out of wood with very long and delicate teeth, decorated with rich patterns.

"This is what a woman gives to her man as a symbol of her love when he leaves for a few days," he said and gave Robert a carved calabas that looked like a thin, emptied out, half coconut shell and served as a drinking cup or bowl.

"May your union be blessed for another two hundred years. I know that people in America and Holland switch spouses like clothes, but, after this blessing, you cannot bring a new lover here. This bond that's blessed here is everlasting," Boikie said.

"Okay," we nodded, grateful and surprised that this polygamous community upheld commitment with this level of seriousness. After the blessing, the women bent over with backs as flat as tabletops and started to clap and sing, accompanied by drumming in the background. They were singing tender love songs about a couple circling around the lovers' tree and waiting longingly for one another.

The program for the night was fluid. After the women sang a few songs that honored the coming of the new year, Boikie started to do a chicken dance to the beat of the drums, his outstretched arms and chest moving in and out in jerky motion.

"Come on," he said, and soon Robert and two guys were following in stride to the beat of clapping and the drums until the entire community moved as one body and one heartbeat. It did not feel as if a show had been put on for us. Instead, we'd been taken in by the village and had participated in cultural rituals and living ceremonies that were common and routine, yet sacred and special.

Overwhelmed with gratitude for this magical evening and unforgettable anniversary celebration, I wondered what it was about our gifts that felt so extraordinary. They were so simple— reminding me of an ordinary circle and line—yet they infused my soul with a regal sense of power, dignity, and deep meaning. I held the comb close to my heart and the calabas wrapped in a towel. The thought of accidentally breaking them while traveling was unbearable.

That very same night, I had a dream. I dreamed that I dropped and broke the comb and calabas, because I couldn't stop worry-

Boikie and Robert

ing and fidgeting with them. I woke up in horror and scrambled around to find them. They were still intact. I let out a sigh of relief and acknowledged the message. The more tightly I held onto what I cherished, the more likely I would break it. True love is about generosity and letting go, not holding on, something that the people within this community practiced on a daily basis. I sat on the bed, trying to absorb it all.

"I'm going to take one last stroll around the island to say my goodbyes, okay?" I said to Robert after breakfast and gave him a quick peck. I needed to walk the dream off, or in: to let everything that happened sink into my core. I thanked Awarradam for teaching me about love and living in harmony with nature. It seemed that the more we tried to get ahead in the Western world by accumulating degrees, wealth, property, and competing for resources, the more imprisoned, anxious, and dead we were becoming inside. It occurred to me that the way in which we handled fear and negativity was not innate to being human or a survival skillset we inherited from our ancestors but the result of scarcity myths and rampant existential anxiety. People in Awarradam respected danger, something Elfriede used to teach me, but weren't oppressed or obsessed by it. They focused on finding adaptive solutions to problems, trusted in the abundant provisions all around them, and honored living in harmony with nature and the group.

I ran into Basia, the village captain, weaving a roof with palm leaves. His broad smile invited me closer.

"Thank you for your hospitality and for sharing this beautiful island and your customs with us. I learned so much during our walk and over the course of these few days. This has been one of the most eye-opening and memorable experiences of my life. I dreamed a lot about living in a village deep in the jungle when I was a child. Even though this is just a small taste of what that's really like, it has surpassed all my expectations. My husband, Robert, and I really had an incredible time and will always remember our five-year anniversary celebration here," I said.

Basia listened quietly and nodded in agreement.

"It is very wonderful to live here. The younger generation thinks that they're missing out when they hear about modern city life. They're very eager to leave, to go to Paramaribo, Holland, or America, but there are a lot of problems there that they cannot handle. Money, greed, selfishness. They like the smell of it. It's not good," he said, the steady, calm weaving of his hands never skipping a beat.

He'd never even been to the capital of Suriname, let alone to another country, yet talked as if he'd observed and experienced the Western world and all of its vices first hand. Perhaps he didn't need to experience the impact of modern society up close. A group of rowdy adolescent boys and girls passed us in their canoe while shooting and shouting at macaws in the trees. They reminded me of the lost and terrorizing teenagers that once cut me off and tormented me on a freeway.

"You're very wise, and I'm so glad that I got to meet you," I said, and walked over to shake his hand. "I hope that these youngsters will not forget their roots and that you and Boikie will inspire them to pass on the Saramaccan legacy."

"*Er is een tijd van komen en een tijd van gaan,* there's a time for coming and a time for going," Boikie said after we'd all gathered on the riverbed with all our belongings and were ready to board the canoe.

"One last picture!" someone shouted.

"Okay, everyone stand in front of the boat and get close," Boikie said, and took pictures with a line-up of different cameras.

"Stay there," he said. He stood up tall, cleared his throat, waved his arms like a choir director, and began to sing Father Jacob in Dutch, signaling that we follow suit. We sang from the top of our lungs, high on life.

"Okay, now all together. You're group one, you're group two, and you're group three," he said. "Group one . . . start; two . . . start; three . . . start."

"Vader Jacob, Vader Jacob,	"Father Jacob, Father Jacob,
Slaapt hij nog? Slaapt hij nog?	Is he still asleep? Is he still asleep?
Ik hoor de klokken luiden.	I hear the bells ringing.
Ik hoor de klokken luiden.	I hear the bells ringing.
Bim Bam Bom . . .	Bim Bam Bom . . .
Bim Bam Bom . . ."	Bim Bam Bom . . ."

"That was very impressive," he said after a few rounds and signaled that we could give it a rest. "It's time to bid farewell to Awarradam for now. You've taken lots of pictures with your camera. I hope that you opened more than just your camera lens while you were here. I hope that Awarradam also opened and awakened your heart. Bim Bam Bom . . . Bim Bam Bom . . ."

No one spoke a word during the thirty-minute boat ride back to Kayana, and no one needed to tell me that these men and women were my spirit guides. My soul knew.

Chapter 11

RAINBOW CRYSTAL WOMAN

> *By far, the greatest number of synchronistic*
> *phenomena that I have had occasion to observe*
> *and analyze can easily be shown to have a direct*
> *connection with an archetype.*
> —Carl Jung

ROBERT, MA, AND PA LOVED the vivid Awarradam story that poured out of me after Tim's prompt. It rekindled fond memories of their own remarkable encounters with the Maroons and indigenous people in the jungles of Suriname. Appreciative of my opportunity to learn more about Lakota ways of healing, they offered to watch Terrance while I attended Tim's upcoming retreat.

Strange things happened after I arrived in Connecticut. A thick layer of intense energy hovered above a roadside meadow on the drive to the retreat at a small college an hour outside of the city. It gave me the distinct impression that these were sacred lands and native burial grounds. That wasn't all: the ancient souls of the elders were still around, wanting me to notice and honor them. I didn't quite know what to make of this other than attributing it to an overactive imagination and travel fatigue.

The next day, I joined Tim and the rest of the attendees— about a dozen counseling center directors and psychologists from all over the US. They'd gathered in one of classrooms in a brick building that gave the college its quaint East Coast charm.

"One way to look at this process is to see it as an unmasking of our true self, something indigenous people keenly understand," he said and pointed to the colorful aboriginal mask right next to him.

After he told us how he got the mask and the special significance it held for him along his journey of self-discovery, he leaned his forearms on his knees. He was holding something in the cup of his hands.

"A few days ago, I drove by a small, locally owned bookstore that I frequently visit," he slowly said, as if to make sure that he had everyone's undivided attention. "I felt a little tug, a sense that I needed to go inside. I was on my way to the grocery story and ignored it. On the way back, the feeling had gotten stronger. I couldn't ignore it. I didn't need anything but went inside. I perused through the store to determine what could be 'calling' me, and this is what I found. I needed to get this for Loraine," he said and held up an amulet. It looked indigenous, from Suriname.

Wait. What? For me? How did this amulet get here?

In the seventeen years that I've lived in the United States, I have never run into handicrafts from Suriname, not even at world market stores in San Francisco.

Tim signaled for me to come over and gave me the amulet. It was beautiful, for sure from Suriname. A purple image of a head, a round belly, and four spread out limbs was painted on a large flat seed. It looked like a child to me. Tim thought that it was a turtle. He could be right. Sea turtles, *aitkantis*, were the unofficial totems of Suriname, admired for instinctively finding their way back to the shores of our native land to nest and lay their eggs after roaming in foreign seas for years.

Stories of magical amulets protecting and guiding runaway slaves flooded my consciousness. Whatever reservations I had toward Tim and his Lakota teachings instantly lifted. The amulet was a sign from the spirits to trust him, surrender, and allow my intuitive and creative self to fully emerge. Speechless and in awe of this miraculous and special gift, I wanted to fall to my knees and serve.

"Follow me to our first activity," Tim said. "It will give you a chance to get to know each other quite well." Amy, one of Tim's student assistants, showed us a scroll of paper that covered a long stretch of hallway. There was something special and ethereal about her that caught my attention and lifted my spirits, but I couldn't put my finger on it.

"Pick a section to work on and draw a tree," Tim said. This was all the instruction that he offered, but it was enough for the spirit of a giant rainforest tree to fill me up. I dove into the assignment and completely lost track of time and my surroundings until my tree had been transferred to the paper.

"It looks like everyone is done with their tree. Now, switch places with your neighbors. Examine their drawings. If you feel inspired to add something to their drawing, you may do so. If not, just appreciate their work and move on," Tim said.

I looked at the drawing of my neighbor. A leopard popped up in my mind. Next I knew, I was drawing a lounging leopard on one of the branches of his tree.

"That's my college mascot," he said. He seemed fond of his school and thankful for my drawing. I drew a squirrel for a woman, her absolute favorite animal in the world, and a songbird that was resting and singing inside a hole in the tree trunk of another guy. He needed cheering up from the inside out.

"I drew you a dreamcatcher because you look dreamy. I hope that you catch all of your dreams," he said.

I tried to peel myself away from this activity when Tim rang the bell, but couldn't. It felt as if I'd discovered how to put on my night vision goggles and was able to see my fellow participants for who they really were underneath their physical appearance. Underneath their white skin—which was much more of a cultural identity and an energetic posture than an actual color—were their true selves, expressed in different variations of all the colors of the rainbow. My connection to this essence and pressing information that was seeping into my consciousness motivated me to continue drawing and coloring ferociously, as if under a spell.

"This is one of the many activities that students get to do in my program. This same exercise was done with a group of indigenous children. Do you know what they drew on each others' trees? Roots that connected all of the trees together. Isn't that neat?" he said and rang the bell again.

Almost done, just one last thing, went through my mind while adding a swing to a tree drawing that resembled a dark and somber Halloween scene.

"You'll notice that some of the students seeking your counsel may seem defiant or oblivious to your direction. They are indigos, the millennium children, spiritual warriors and system busters, often so caught up in blazing a trail that they have difficulty switching gears, following instructions, and sticking to preset structures. It helps to reframe their behavior. They're releasing passionate and unbridled energy that was probably cooped up until they met you," Tim said. I heard only bits and pieces of this, but knew that he was talking about me. I felt a spacious permission to be fully myself. It felt exhilarating and brand-new.

"Any guesses what the point was of that exercise?" Tim asked the group, after I returned.

"Connecting with nature?" one person asked.

"Celebrating our mythical tree selves," another said.

"I loved this exercise and couldn't break away until I'd finished my drawings. Sorry for having you wait," I said apologetically. Kind eyes encouraged me to go on. "My guess is that we were drawing shadow parts on each other's trees," I said.

"Very good," Tim said. "You were tempering and completing your true selves at the soul level. Let's go back and take a closer look at your drawings."

"When we open our creative channels, we're in essence opening our natural psychic channels. The information comes from the same loving source that strives for healing and wholeness throughout nature when we scrape a knee, when plants and animals support each other, when our cells fight harmful invasions. We're able to naturally tune into each others' energy fields, intuitively assess what's lacking, and offer each other Mother Earth's medicine. Because we're one earth, one body. Even the dream forms of this medicine are very powerful," Tim said. "You are remembering who you really are: *iyeskas*, medicine people. *Iyeska* is a Lakota word, and it means two-spirited, mixed-race, translator of the ordinary and spirit worlds."

My heart was pounding. I'd pegged medicine people as exotic prairie dwellers and tribal heads living on reservations and in villages in the jungle. The flame that Tim lit in me weeks ago had been battling with and beating these long-held myths to reveal my soul's truth.

"We're going to do our afternoon meditation outside. We'll reconnect with each of the four elements, the four building blocks of life—earth, air, fire, and water. The elements themselves are neither good nor bad, just potentials in nature and within ourselves that we needed to honor, understand, and balance. They can be constructive and, when out of balance, destructive, as is the case with floods, fires, storms, earthquakes, volcanoes," Tim said. "Sit with each one, listen carefully to their teachings, take notes, and meet back here to share what you discovered with the group."

My meditation and exploration of the elements gave me a rare perspective of myself. I learned that I was adaptable and resilient like water, quick to change form and able to flow around and through obstacles, but I needed to cultivate other elements to become more whole. The spaciousness and permission that Tim had granted my intuition helped me to connect with air and mysterious wisdom, but it needed further balancing, or I'd end up feeling as fragile as one of the tissue-paper kites I used to play with as a child—thrilled that mighty winds were pulling me closer to the heavens but simultaneously terrified that my string and grounding cord could snap any moment. More earth and fire would remedy that. I felt compelled to blaze a trail, like those indigo children, with the torch of light, passion, and audacity that was growing bolder inside of me.

"Do we have time tomorrow to go by the store where you bought my amulet?" I asked Tim after we'd shared our insights. "I'd like to see with my own eyes how it got here. I think it will help me ground better."

"Sure," Tim said, "Anyone else like to join us on a little field trip to my favorite book store?"

I could have spent a whole day at the store. It was jam packed with fascinating books, crystals, rocks, drums, rattles, tarot cards, jewelry, hats, dream catchers hanging from the ceiling, and beautiful handicrafts and carved animal totems sitting on shelves and on the floor. About a dozen amulets were displayed in a standing display unit. They were carefully arranged on a map of Suriname. Next to the map was a picture of a white man and an indigenous tribe. From the markings on the map, I'd gathered that they lived in the dense, southern part of the rainforest, where a few tribes still lived, shrouded in mystery.

"Hi there, could I take a look at these necklaces?" I asked the woman behind the counter. Feathers adorned her long, graying hair.

"Most certainly," she said with a big smile and got a small key that opened the casing. "This man travels a lot and often brings us handicrafts from faraway places. He just brought these in."

"I'm from Suriname. Tim told me that he felt a tug a few days ago and purchased one of these for me. Amulets are believed to hold a lot of magic and power in Suriname. I'm still in shock that this happened. I've never come across any jewelry, souvenirs, or arts and crafts from Suriname, ever," I said.

"Ah, Tim. He's a regular. Yes, he was in here a few days ago asking if we'd gotten anything new in. Magic is a daily occurrence here," she said.

"Thank you for affirming his story and helping me to embrace this guidance. Can I see the one over there? The big seed in the middle is called a cow's eye and is used to heal sties by rubbing it and applying it to the infected area on your eyelid. This amulet brings back many precious memories of playing with this seed. Please hold it aside for me while I look around some more," I said. I roamed through the store and found the book, *The Indigo Children: The New Kids Have Arrived*, by Lee Caroll.

"You found it, and it found you," Tim said when I asked him if this was the one to get.

I bought both the amulet and book. We spent the afternoon

listening to stories about the revered Lakota messiah, White Buffalo Calf Woman, and learned about the seven sacred traditions, including the sweat lodge, that she brought back after they'd been forbidden and driven underground.

All this time, I thumbed through the book, eager to give into the pull that Tim described. After dinner, I retreated to my dorm room and didn't put the book down until I'd completely devoured it in the late hours of the night.

I discovered that the term indigo refers to the color of our third eye chakra, our intuitive vision, and is an energy pattern of human behavior that Nancy Tappe, Lee Carroll, and other psychics started to notice in the 1990s. Their claims about indigo children sounded wild but kept me hooked: they are sensitive, gifted trailblazers with a strong desire to live instinctively. They are precocious and here to create one land, one globe, and one species—active specimens in the evolution of human consciousness, striving to regain balance and homeostasis for the whole, just like the cells in our body that respond ingeniously when we are sick. They're our bridge to the future, solely focused on mending the gaps and missing links that separate us from our full potential.

My preconceived biases toward New Age books waned when the things that I read about kept striking a chord. The description of the indigo mission made intuitive sense, and the indigo personality profile felt more true to me than any formal psychological assessment I'd come across so far. It was like encountering an off-beat, left-handed tribe, identifying with their unusual perspectives, and recognizing the accommodations I'd made since birth to blend into a predominantly right-handed world.

When I awakened from my short but deep sleep the next morning, the desire to be openly left-handed in the world was overwhelming and all-consuming. Fortunately, we were going to spend the whole day dodging norms, enjoying the outside, and preparing for and participating in our first sweat lodge ceremony. It was going to be held in the backyard of the tall, rugged, and lanky homesteader, Bill, one of the elders Tim had employed to supplement his teachings.

Bill's property was surrounded by a meadow filled with budding purple wildflowers amidst a sea of outstretched land that bordered a forest far in the distance. As I'd hoped, the branches, leaves, and insects, waltzing freely in the breeze within this spaciousness, diffused some of the inner pressure.

While Amy drummed to the six sacred directions—combining the four compass directions with above and below, heaven and earth—we made tiny prayer flags out of colorful cotton fabric squares and stuffed these with a teaspoon of tobacco. When done, we sprinkled long lines of cornmeal and tobacco in sacred and symbolic configurations all the way to the lodge. The lodge represented Mother Earth and looked like an igloo covered with dark tarp. We also built a fire that drew me close. I began to circle it, my open palms absorbing its dynamic energy and heat. The beats of the big mother drum seeped into my body, and staccato movements sprang back out with such ease and confidence, it seemed as if I'd danced like this my entire life.

"*Mitakuye oyasin*, we are all related," each of us said in Lakota when we crawled into the *inipi*, sweat lodge, in a traditional, sacred manner. Something told me to grab the medicine wheel that Tim had given us and the lavender crystal egg that I'd bought downtown and bring them into the lodge with me. The egg reminded me of myself, full of untapped potential, and more likely to hatch if I developed steady inner balance with the help of the medicine wheel.

Tim, Bill, and Amy sang and blessed the water, slowly pouring it over the hot stones and thanking them for giving up their lives. I watched and listened attentively until my hand, as if belonging to a marionette puppet, all of a sudden placed the medicine wheel on the "As above, so below" hour glass *kapemni* symbol on the skin of Tim's drum. I took out the egg and carefully balanced it on the medicine wheel where the center points of both symbols overlapped. When I looked up, I caught a glimpse of Tim looking at Bill, both perplexed. I hadn't learned about the seventh direction yet, the within point, where the sacred six directions meet, but my heart was about to burst from waiting.

Tim handed me his drum and gave me an encouraging nod to proceed. A sliver of panic shot through me. I'd never drummed before. I didn't have a clue how to hold and beat the drum: how fast, how long, how loud. None of that stopped me from accepting Tim's drum. All my childhood urges to drum, the mysterious drumming sounds while in graduate school, the channels of wisdom that the drum beats opened, the sensations of the drum resonating through my body—they all culminated into this powerful moment of truth. I drummed my heart out until I became the drum and the drum became me, beating as One.

I lost track of time and my normal self-consciousness until it got so hot in there that Tim threw the blankets open.

"That was *amazing,*" Amy said, sending shivers down my spine with the intensity of her inflection. I faintly remembered hearing her and Tim belting out Lakota songs that accompanied the drumming while I flew high in a stupor of ecstasy.

"I feel incredible. Clean. Purified. Indescribable," one of the men said after we were back outside. The rest of the group concurred.

Bill's wife offered us freshly picked raspberries that burst with flavor in my mouth. As I walked around, I noted that the whole world smelled, tasted, sounded, appeared, and felt different: all its flavors were more intense and vivid.

After we'd gathered back in a circle, Tim informed us that my egg was made of amethyst, a type of crystal that supports enlightenment and transformation, and that lavender corresponds with the seventh direction, the intersection of all the directions, right in the heart. My soul reveled in the knowledge that I'd dared to come out of my shell and reveal my truest self without any modifications or inhibitions.

"Once you're back in your regular routine, it will be easy to forget again, to feel this connection fade over time. You may find yourself getting distracted and dabbling in all kinds of other traditions rather than deepen the work you've done so far through the Red Road," Tim cautioned.

I noticed myself shrinking after he used the phrase "dabbling in all kinds of other traditions." It bugged me. Bummed that my expanded sense of self was so short-lived, I gathered the courage to speak up and ask Tim what he meant.

"I've studied many different spiritual paths throughout my life, and never felt that I was dabbling. I think that they took turns guiding me here, like a relay. Are you saying that it is only possible to deepen our spiritual development through the Red Road?" I asked, confused, given that Tim was well-versed in many traditions. He'd quoted different spiritual teachers in his syllabus and during our circle time.

"I know what you mean. I've walked a similar path, but being introduced to the Red Road was like being hit by a ton of bricks. Understandings went straight to my core. I realized that I had a tendency to switch to something new and avoid the hard work when the going got rough," Tim said.

Many of the group members, at least two decades older than me, agreed with Tim.

"Perhaps it's part of human nature to avoid our deepest feelings, or perhaps it's a part of Western culture to be more cerebral.

This tradition is far more effective than some of the quieter meditative and contemplative traditions in getting me out of my head and connected to my body and soul," one of the participants said.

Exasperated that I was so soon finding things that set me apart from the group, I convinced myself that my reluctance to fully immerse myself in this path was probably due to an avoidance of deeper feelings and scarier impulses. Tired but grateful for this extraordinary day, we helped Bill clean up, stopped for an early dinner on the way back to campus, and called it a night.

On the very last day, we had a chance to privately engage with a Cherokee elder, Gary White Wolf, a free spirit enshrouded in an aura of mystical energy. His method of teaching involved taking each one of us to the side. Without saying much, he stared deeply into our souls and directly transmitted his knowledge through his penetrating eyes. When it was my turn, I felt a bit uncomfortable, but, within moments, my soul shot out of my confined self and floated around in a galaxy of shimmering stars. Our eyes remained locked, and I needed to hold onto his forearms to keep my balance until my expanded sense of self resettled back in my body. Unsure what to do after we were done, I gave him a hug.

"An orange flame just popped up in my mind's eye when I hugged you," I said. He showed me the leather pouch adorned with flames of fire hanging from his belt.

"This is what you saw. Fire is my element," he said, and smiled.

The day before, White Wolf had agreed with Tim that fully immersing ourselves in one tradition will help us to peel off layer upon layer, like an onion. It seemed to make sense to everyone present, but me, that only after we reach our core, our inner light, do we discover that it is made of all colors.

"Can I ask you something? I still find it hard to commit myself solely to the Red Road. Something's holding me back. Like I'm putting a layer on rather than taking one off when I consider sticking to just one thing. It's really distressing and confusing. What could I be avoiding?" I asked.

White Wolf squinted his eyes and gave me a long, scrutinizing look.

"I touched a rainbow once before while driving my motorcycle on a freeway. I'm touching one for the second time, right now. Teach other indigo children about the rainbow path," he said, then hugged me.

Gulp. Did he just validate my rainbow path?

Yes, he did. The Red Road is too narrow for you, emerged out of my wise depths.

Why? Did I already reach my core? How? I looked closely at the amulet that I'd purchased. There were bright, orange-yellow feathers around the seed that looked like flames. They reminded me of White Wolf's flames and life energy healing and activating my third eye. On both sides of the seed were indigo-colored beads. Did this amulet choose me as much as I'd chosen it, just like Tim predicted? This is what I knew for certain: this kind of magic and guidance only occurred when my indigo self was in charge. I vowed to trust it when we closed circle and wished each other well.

After the retreat, we dispersed back to the different corners of the US we were from, but maintained our close-knit *hunka,* family, bond through email contact. I yearned to capture and share my transformational journey with them, but I strangely couldn't write until I shut down my usual cognitive processes and hopped onto a more lyrical tract. Once I did, this poem flowed out of me, line after line, just like the Awarradam story:

A Trail of Thin Smoke

Fiery, pulsating blood
burning through the veins of my fingers
longing for expression and release

Only a whimsical trail of thin smoke,
a scent of white sage, tobacco, and cedar,
is left as soon as words enter consciousness,
and fingertips touch the hard keys

A group of starving souls,
coming from all six directions,
black, red, and yellow,
white, blue, and green

This mysterious thin smoke,
seduces all of our senses
asking us to come out and play

Quiets our chattering, exhausted minds,
and triggers tears of cleansing,
crying from every clogged pore

Then out of nowhere,
a tiny dim light,
finally gets our attention

Yearns for a common direction,
a need for connection,
but how, no one knows

Just forget to help you remember,
says the caring and wise one,
let nature take its course

If fire shows earth,
earth will guide air,
and air will lighten water,
so that water can temper fire.
How else will roots grow?

Slowly but surely,
humans find their humility,
and see reflections of light in each core

They were once strangers
but are suddenly no more

Hands and roots interwoven,
fiercely marching in unison,
to the heartbeat of the drum

Shadows appear,
but are not alarming,
since everyone is moving,
in the direction of pure and bright light

Alongside our journey,
are buffalo, coyote, and eagle,
blue jays, chickies, and crow

Squirrel, leopard, and deer
songbird, mouse, and small ants,
frog, bug, four-eyed moth,
trees, meadows, and weeds

Mitakuye oyasin, we're all related,
flowers, white, red and purple,
rocks, wood, and cornmeal,
moon, night star, and soft breeze

Fire in the soulful eyes
of White Wolf,
calling out "Is anyone home?"

Soft voices from under beds and dark closets,
Whisper back, "Here I am, wait, please, don't go . . ."

They are indigo children of their own generation,
each one too early for her or his time,
no longer hiding, no longer aching,

reaching for the arms of White Buffalo Calf Woman,
Buddha, Rumi, and Christ

Blessing the chameleon children of future generations,
new hopes that are no longer alone nor afraid,
complete surrender in their graceful dance backward,
down the transcendent rainbow path above

Clear signs all along the illuminated journey,
amethyst egg and blue-green light heal the wounded ones,
and indigo beads, White Wolf's fire, and a third eye
hidden in the amulet sent from afar

The heat of the light,
starts melting all boundaries,
and for just a moment in time,
a lunar eclipse!

Earth's shadow and moon embrace,
in the abysmal night of the inipi sweat lodge,
white light and black darkness blend into one

Distracting clouds soon after start forming,
heavier and darker than ever before

But despite the storms of despair and destruction,
tides cannot resist the soothing pull of Grandma Moon,
and in the eye of even the strongest tornado,
peace, joy, and stillness still prevail.

I felt a huge sense of release after I'd birthed this poem, my first attempt at poetry ever. The voice of my indigo self—rather than my usual ego self—was getting stronger and louder, and I was exhilarated that I'd figured out how to unleash it. My poem was well-received by my new online family and reciprocated by similar poems, passages, and deep reflections, crisscrossing the Internet and filling our inboxes and hearts with love, support, and courage to fight our old habits and the status quo.

It was difficult to sustain the strength of this connection when back on campus, while attempting to develop a course for the Multicultural Immersion Program.

"Burying myself in library books and academic journals causes my frigid, analytical mind to come to the foreground and freeze my free spirit. I can just watch it happening as I drift from my center, unable to reconnect to my inner power. I yearn for guidance and a sign," I emailed.

I needed a change in pace and setting. Instead of looking for lecture material at the library, I went to a popular bookstore instead. Once there, I became obsessed by an impulse to find quotes from ethnically diverse female leaders to include in the syllabus. Adrenaline began to pump through my veins, as if I were on a hunt. I ventured into the Asian American section, collected a few great insights from Japanese geisha, and eventually made my way to the Native American section. My body finally settled down. I had successfully shifted gears; my indigo mind was back in charge and on a mission.

I gathered a stack of interesting books with inspiring back cover descriptions, indigenous art, images of medicine men and women, and information that reminded me of the retreat. As soon as I was reabsorbed into the heightened, creative spaciousness of the artists and authors, I lost track of time, my surroundings, hunger pangs, and bathroom urges but became increasingly more aware of what my spirit needed.

You need to putter around like this, was the first thing I heard my inner voice say. I wandered through the pages of the books until my intuition flagged a topic of interest, such as what it means and what to do when parts of a dead animal—like a foot, leg, bone, skull, or feather—cross our paths. To some Native Americans, these coincidental findings were a sign and visitation from their power animal. They believed that we don't choose our power animal: it chooses us. They preserved and carried these parts with them for guidance and protection even if they initially didn't have a strong connection to that particular animal.

Just the day before, I'd run into a crow leg while crossing the quad on campus. Influenced by popular culture, I thought of crows as eerie omens. It didn't matter that the crow was my birth animal; I didn't like them. Only after reading that they are shapeshifters and keepers of sacred law, balance, and the mystical realms did I warm up to them and embrace much-needed Crow medicine.

The books in my pile were like magical crumbs on my path, once I opened up to receiving further guidance. The following passage in Ed McGaa Eagle Man's book, *Mother Earth Spirituality: Native American Paths to Healing Ourselves and Our World*, led me to another important shapeshifting spirit guide:

> *At Spirit Mountain, a Sweat Lodge was held, and several within the lodge received their natural names. Animals and birds that appeared in thoughts or dreams were described by the vision seekers. Some had strong identification with inanimate symbols, such as crystals, rainbows, thunder, dance, and feathers.*

I reflected on my powerful experience in the sweat lodge. I was sure that my amethyst crystal egg had guided my transformation and had given me visions of my rainbow path that have been with me ever since. Were these part of my earth name? I read on:

> *Earth song, Rainbow Crystal Woman, and Water Spirit Woman are some examples of natural names associated with these symbols.*

Rainbow Crystal Woman. As soon as I read it, I knew that this was my earth name. But someone already had this name. Maybe your earth name needs to be unique, I wondered, ignorant about this naming business. The next line read:

> *Eagle Woman, Two Hawks, and White Wolf are natural names associated with animals that have been adopted by the rainbow tribe.*

That settled that. It was possible to share earth names with other kindred spirits. Having my questions answered on the spot felt like being in direct communication with the Universe, which was both discombobulating and reassuring, so surreal and so incredibly real. It was still hard to decide which sensation to trust more. I was excited to learn about the rainbow tribe and curious if they walked a rainbow path like me or were a tribe of different races that walked the Red Road. It was the latter. My search wasn't over yet.

My hand instinctively grabbed another book, *Buffalo Woman Comes Singing*, written by Brooke Medicine Eagle, a medicine woman and psychologist. Inside the cover was the second part of the title: *The Spirit Song of a Rainbow Medicine Woman*. I noticed a fluttering sensation in the hollow of my sternum. This find seemed very promising.

Brooke Medicine Eagle grew up on a Crow reservation, but had diverse Native American and European ancestry and teachers of different traditions. Her book was over three hundred and fifty pages thick, but I quickly found the passages that were most beneficial to me:

> *Grandma Rosie (Shinela) had no sense of the 'rainbow medicine' that is now awakening us to our oneness with all the two-legged family. . . The understanding of what I call rainbow medicine was not yet alive in the spirits of the people. The rainbow medicine way teaches that, in order to step across what lies between this age and the new age of harmony and abundance, we must make a bridge, and that bridge must be made of light. In order for the light to become a rainbow powerful enough to arch across the chasm, it must contain all colors—all peoples, all nations, all things. If only one color is left out, it will not have the strength to become the arching rainbow bridge upon which all of us will walk into a new time. This, in essence, is the same teaching given us by White Buffalo Calf Pipe Woman: the teachings of oneness, of unity, cooperation, and harmony.[2]*

2. *Reprinted from* Buffalo Woman Comes Singing: The Spirit Song of a Rainbow Medicine Woman *(p. 24), by Brooke Medicine Eagle, 1991, New York, NY: Ballentine Books. Copyright © 1991 by Brooke Medicine Eagle. Reprinted with permission.*

My heart somersaulted. It felt as if this passage had been written to me. Brooke had also questioned for years what to do with messages from Great Spirit that went against the grain of her people and the teachings from elders.

She explained that, in the past, the truth in each person's heart wasn't judged by the people. Wars that almost led to genocide and ongoing cultural oppression—the breakdown and disdain of the traditional ways, the overwhelming intrusion of outsiders, and the stealing of cultural knowledge—are the reason for today's tenacious efforts to prevent further loss and deterioration and the lack of trust in the Circle of Life and Great Spirit to manage such matters. Understanding why her people have taken it upon themselves to police the legitimacy of what's revealed to each person propelled her to honor Rainbow Crystal Woman's messages in secret.

I flipped through pages and landed on a passage that described her first meeting with Rainbow Crystal Woman on top of Bear Butte near Mount Shasta, while she was on a vision quest in Northern California. Brooke recalled that the words and messages from Rainbow Crystal Woman didn't enter her ears but were fed to her through her navel. She could intuitively grasp the message, but it was so rich and big, she resisted giving it a pat meaning. It took decades of lived experience, uncovering deeper layers of herself, before she was able to translate it into words and share it with others.

When I read this, the clouds that had obscured my clarity parted. I needed to develop greater trust in my intuition and not rely so much on others for validation. And, unlike Brooke, I wasn't all alone in trying to make sense of these potentially overwhelming experiences. I was receiving real-time validation from renegades like her and White Wolf, who were mirroring my truth and fast-forwarding my process by sharing what they'd learned on their pioneering journeys.

But was this enough "expert guidance" to convince the Board of Psychology that I was ready to intuitively guide my clients? Hardly. My interactions with these mavericks were as nebulous and transient as could be—one didn't extend much beyond an intense ten-minute stare and the other was the result of a mysterious book connection. While their impact on me felt extraordinarily powerful and healing, who said that this would be beneficial to clients with more severe issues like depression, bipolar disorder, post-traumatic stress, and panic attacks?

I decided to send Tim and my online *hunka* group these passages from Brooke Medicine Eagle as soon as I got home. Perhaps they'd get why my Rainbow Path was something that even pioneers and traditional native healers envisioned as the next step for all of humanity. Perhaps that would convince them to embrace and endorse me and my work?

Even so, who was I fooling? Due to our limited connection, their sporadic support and guidance still wouldn't count as "peer review" and guidance of my unconventional therapeutic inclinations.

With my bottom stuck to the floor and my back against the bookcase, these concerns floated off and burst like soap bubbles. The resonance and encouragement I found in each new passage were much more compelling—Brooke claimed that her mixed-blood heritage and our melting-pot generation had prepared us to be bridge-makers and cultural ambassadors. Rainbow Crystal Woman was the modern incarnation of White Buffalo Calf Woman, particularly suited to help us reconnect to our souls and parts of ourselves not confined to rigid traditions and forms.

My floaty intuitive hunches gelled into concrete stepping stones. The following passage stirred up my biggest "aha," backlighting my most recent efforts and resistance:

Our Earth walk is dangerously unbalanced. The thrusting, aggressive, analytic, intellectual, make-it-happen, and 'fixing what Mother Earth didn't do so well' kind of energy has become dominant. It has almost buried the feminine, receptive, accepting, harmonizing, surrendering, and unifying energy. A balancing must take place in which the feminine and masculine energies within each of us, as within all things, can harmonize. . . . Much of the women's wisdom from all cultures has been lost or neglected. Many women today have been given little if any of those mysterious teachings. We have also been deeply influenced by the kind of experiences the larger world provides. Very often these experiences have set the idea in our forming minds that to have power we must "out-macho" the tough guys. Many of us have never seen, been taught, or perhaps even been aware of the power of oneness, relationship, harmony, flow, and song—the gentle and powerful feminine.[3]

These lines appeared like bright beams shining into the dark sky above. They suggested that my objections to the oversized role that quantitative research plays in clinical psychology practice might be related to this large-scale rebalancing of receptive and active energies. I thought of the round calabas and long comb in Maroon culture: the sacred feminine circle and the sacred masculine line. The drum and the beater. My intuitive resistance was fueled by an innate desire to bring back more of the receptive energies, the all-inclusive hoop: that's all.

Rainbow Crystal Woman, my new guide, picked up all the loose threads that I hadn't been able to tie together and spun them into a giant spider web. I needed to trust that my understanding of her guidance and the web would continue to unfold over time, just like it did for Brooke.

When I went outside, satisfied with my progress for the day, I noticed a large crow circling above my car. That's when it hit me, and I was overcome by deep knowing and emotion that I was not alone, that big-hearted healers and power animals from far away and nearby, from the past and the future, from this realm and other realms, were all moving as a perfectly synchronized team in the present moment at the center of the *kapemni* to guide me on my rainbow path.

---

3. *Reprinted from* Buffalo Woman Comes Singing: The Spirit Song of a Rainbow Medi-cine Woman *(p. 118), by Brooke Medicine Eagle, 1991, New York, NY: Ballentine Books. Copyright © 1991 by Brooke Medicine Eagle. Reprinted with permission.*

Chapter 12

▦ BIRD NEST WARRIOR LORE

Synchrodestiny requires gaining access to a place deep
within yourself while at the same time awakening to the
intricate dance of coincidences in the physical world.
—Deepak Chopra

ABOUT A MONTH AFTER RECEIVING my earth name, the world as we knew it collapsed from one moment to the next, following the September 11th attacks on the twin towers. Many of us were upended and ungrounded by this tragedy, even months after the dust at Ground Zero had settled.

Disorientation and devastation were palpable all around me and matched my own unexpected, earth-shattering loss. Right after 2002 rolled around the corner, I had a miscarriage. In shock, I quickly flushed the red, stringy glob along with all my messy feelings and uncertainty of how to handle this private heartbreak down the toilet.

My New Year's resolution was to reconnect with my center of balance and inner compass. I used my crystal egg, my medicine wheel, and the "As above, so below," *kapemni* symbol to conjure up memories of feeling aligned with Rainbow Crystal Woman's energy and the four directions. It worked, but what I picked up was alarming. All my inner dynamics in regard to others and myself—mind-body-spirit, thoughts-feelings-behavior, and past-present-future—had been thrown off by the traumatic events of the past year.

I explored these imbalances and retraced my steps back to homeostasis, writing article upon article by giving voice to my many ruminations about holistic healing. This process fueled a new vision and passionate desire to unfurl my wings and open my own inner-balance counseling, holistic practice in Berkeley. It would allow me to continue my work with university students, my favorite population, on my own terms and be significantly closer to home and Robert's work projects in the greater San Francisco Bay Area.

While scanning my imbalanced emotions for unresolved knots and bruises, I detected a painful lump that was buried deep in my psyche. It was filled with fear in regard to getting pregnant again. I initially dismissed it as just not being ready yet, but it had produced a limp that had become my default position. I was moving through the world like a car with misaligned tires and kept swerving to one side whenever I let go of the steering wheel. When I asked what was off balance, I heard, *Your female side.* It was in desperate need of healing.

Was that possible? Could my miscarriage have etched an imbalanced, energetic relationship between feminine and masculine forces in my body as Brooke Medicine Eagle explained? The moment I gave this possibility serious consideration, a flood of tears of regret, anger, and sadness welled up. To my surprise, they were related to much older pain than my recent miscarriage.

Two-and-half-year-old memories of my son's traumatic birth resurfaced in flashes—a nurse breaking my water to speed things up after an all-nighter of labor and little dilation, followed by a shot of Pitocin when this still didn't produce the desired results, and hours of moaning, mooing, and mangled grunting that accompanied the uncontrollable and unbearable convulsions in my stomach. It felt as if I'd already done thousands of spastic sit-ups in a row, but they kept coming and were getting stronger and more intense as time went on. Normally, this was a good thing and necessary to push the baby out. In my situation, it felt as if I was pushing my baby against a wall that aggravated and pinched the nerves around my lower back. The pain didn't let up in between contractions. Given my high pain tolerance and not having anything to compare my experience to, I assumed that this was what giving birth felt like and kept going.

When I was about eight centimeters dilated, the nurse tending to me speculated that my baby was sunny side up, and that I must be experiencing extreme back labor. Because it was too risky to give me an epidural shot this far into my labor, administering narcotics intravenously for pain relief was my only option. Prior to labor, it had been our least preferred option because the drugs would enter our baby's bloodstream. In the hopes that this would help my body relax and open up, I agreed to the painkillers, already feeling like a strange creature from outer space and no longer the tenant of my own body, which was hooked up to all kinds of tubes and bleeping devices.

After another three hours of all-out pushing and no baby, the heart monitor showed scary moments of our baby's heartbeat dropping to dangerously low levels. Within seconds, a crew of medical providers on high alert barged into my room and announced that I needed an emergency C-section. It was close to six in the evening the next day, and I'd been in labor for about twenty hours.

Robert, who'd been by my side the entire time, looked just as beat and terrified as I felt, dark circles around his exhausted eyes. Because it appeared as if he was about to pass out when he saw the needle that was going to go in my spine, the anesthesiologist recommended that he get something to eat and drink at the cafeteria and take a walk in the garden.

He then told me to hunch over my contracting, basketball-sized stomach and remain perfectly still while he inserted the epidural needle in my spine. I felt my soul fully disconnect from my body to do what was necessary to avoid injury and permanent nerve damage, and, a few minutes later, was finally rewarded with total relief. Robert was allowed back in during the surgery. I sensed pulling and tugging on my stomach hidden behind a flimsy, light-blue shield. Our pale and blue baby was born with a bump on the back of his head the size of a pinecone and was given an Apgar score of two due to the prolonged pushing and being pumped full of drugs. I didn't get to touch him but was too unconscious to care. I slept for several hours while Robert stayed with him.

A few days following this harrowing birth, I'd recovered enough to talk about it. One of my friends commented that hearing about it was a natural form of birth control. Another sent me an article, entitled "Gentle Birth," written by midwife Ronnie Falcao. The report listed each one of the problematic steps that were taken when I was in labor—not checking the position of the baby, breaking of water, administering Pitocin, and locking the back of the baby's head in the wrong position. More than 50 percent of the time, these interventions lead to similar complications and unnecessary C-sections for women who deliver at hospitals. The revelation that midwives, who still relied on their own intuitive wisdom and traditional birthing knowledge, could have prevented the excruciating ordeal and risky predicaments that my baby and I endured crushed my spirit to the core.

This information ignited a deep, painful knowing and left me feeling disillusioned, deprived, and cheated of something that meant the world to me and that I'd never get back—the gift of giving birth to my son. But I also wanted to move on and be present for him. Grateful and relieved that his frightening conehead and Apgar score had quickly returned to normal and not wanting to overwhelm others with my story, I forced myself to focus on what mattered the most—that we were both healthy and fine.

Despite my best intentions, body sensations—reminding me of the hours of intense, unfruitful pushing without closure—sabotaged these efforts. Just like people with an amputated arm sometimes feel a phantom limb, I was haunted for months by a phantom baby yearning to be born through me whenever my uterus contracted during my monthly cycle.

The way in which my last miscarriage was handled—the "drive-thru" exam, the "Oh, there will be more babies" response, the negligent record keeping and repeated mistaken calls treating me as if I were still pregnant—kept poking at these old wounds. Months after the incident, I noticed a lingering lower back pain. I made an appointment with an intuitive bodyworker whose ad had caught my attention. She provided relief but also noted that my pain seemed related to unresolved grief.

"I know what this grief is about . . . the idea that I flushed our baby and my soul's aching . . . down the toilet," I said to Robert in erratic sobs late that night. He held me close and wiped a few tears from his own face. I didn't realize that the miscarriage hadn't been easy on him either.

I thought that I'd closed this chapter of my life, but I'd been wrong. I woke up the next morning with renewed conviction to fully reset myself and pick up where I'd left off almost a year ago by cleansing my soul with Native American flute music and fresh-squeezed orange juice. The music was soothing and bathed me in serenity and peace until I cut the oranges open and bloodred juice dripped out of them. My body stiffened in shock, just like it did when I discovered that I was bleeding early in my pregnancy and realized what that meant.

I examined the bag closely. The label on it read NAVEL ORANGES BLOODS. I didn't know that this kind of orange existed and had mistakenly bought them. Suddenly, a warm feeling of care and concern came over me, accompanied by the epiphany that the juice was so strikingly similar to what had passed through me so that I could use it to symbolize the body and spirit of our lost baby. This was the spirits' way of saying that they were with me through it all and were offering me a second chance to bury our baby with dignity.

I burned some sage to cleanse myself and the sacred altar in my garden made of a circle of shiny, dark-gray river rocks. After decorating the sacred four directions with flowers, I poured the juice over a quartz crystal in the heart of the altar and replenished myself with some as well. The ceremony was simple, special, and potent, causing the tension in my back to loosen up and subside.

Cracked open by this other-worldly guidance, I became aware of the powerful bond between me and all the women who'd ever run down fields during their moon time and was also left with a clear sense that my baby's essence had been returned to sacred Mother Earth through me, fertilizing both of our souls.

In the midst of this mysterious unfolding, I received an email message from Tim. It was addressed to the whole group. He apologized for being out of touch for so long and informed us that he'd been praying to the spirit of Joe Eagle Elk, his late Lakota teacher and author of the book, *Price of a Gift*, for guidance. He'd felt lost and unsure how to lift himself and us out of the lingering devastation and disillusion following the 9/11 attacks.

Just a few days before he emailed us, a gush of wind had bounced and rolled an empty bird nest down the street right to his feet when his heart was most aching for his gentle teacher's words of wisdom and comfort. Certain that it was a sign, he meditated on its significance and came up with a new lore, the Bird Nest Warrior Lore.

"In the next nine months before we meet again in the summer of 2003, we will be preparing our own nests—our bodies and minds—for the birth and nurturing of our spirit baby. All this is about giving birth. Giving birth to our true selves . . . giving birth to kindness . . . giving birth to peace and compassion . . . giving birth to walking in balance . . . giving birth to feminine and masculine tones," Tim said, as he explained the meaning of the new lore to us.

My whole being rejoiced. Without any hesitation, I pressed the "reply all" button and told Tim and my *hunka* about the guided burial ritual for my miscarried baby, and about my unresolved feelings related to my C-section, heightened by scary stories about VBACs—vaginal births after a C-section—tormenting me now. The meaning and symbolism of this lore was precisely what my womb needed to heal and reclaim her creative powers.

Tim replied that he was deeply moved by my email. He suggested that we jumpstart the lore with an all-day fast to purge toxins from our bodies—one held by the women and one held by the men. We would each fast in our own vicinity, but remain linked in spirit and through our email sharing. When I replied to the group that I was in, something very unusual occurred. A bold new voice wiggled to the forefront of my mind and articulated her views and wishes to the group.

"Your words resonate and echo so deeply in my core. In this quiet space of modern technology, all else fades away, and the voice of a squashed, and yes, diminished female spirit, gets to come out of hiding. It's sad to see so many of us all around, yearning for that lost power, often confusing it with masculine traits—roles, careers, success stories—and/or the ability to control those in power through looks and sensuality. This leads to the dieting, obsessions about weight and body image—sometimes starting as early as in elementary school—and vulnerability to sexual exploitation, self-harm, low self-worth, and depression. A woman is bombarded with so many distractions and confining rituals that keep the power imbalance between feminine and masculine forces in place. The pressure to squash her is often so great that she sometimes will help squash just to be accepted at the expense of a deep connection with her true self—she knows this truth to the core, and for that she has suffered.

"Let's fast to honor the womb—for our Great Mother Earth, for the birth of new possibilities, for pain and healing, for the cycle of life and all its seasons, for creation, for future generations, for ourselves and each other."

I signed my email, "Loraine—Rainbow Crystal Woman."

The day before our scheduled fast on a mild day in November, I learned about available space at a gorgeous, terra-cotta psychotherapy office in a quaint, downtown area in Northern Berkeley subleased by a woman named Claudia.

I wondered if this coincidental occurrence was perhaps Rainbow Crystal Woman's doing. As crazy as this sounded, somewhere deep down it made perfect sense that she'd want to bless and cheer on the "birth" of my new practice and endeavor today—it was in line with our intentions and grand plan.

Claudia and I hit it off right away, and I was instantly enchanted by the office. It was available on the days that I requested, had a charming little garden sanctuary next to the waiting area and a row of sheltering trees outside our window, and was situated on a lively street with a variety of eateries, shops, and little art galleries, just as I'd imagined.

I'd planned to spend the day in Tilden Park, which was, to my delight, just a short drive from my office on a high and good-sized ridge of wilderness overlooking Berkeley, the San Francisco Bay, and the Golden Gate Bridge. After taking in the spectacular views and the delectable scent of the sequoia and eucalyptus giants all around me, I could feel my intuitive antennae perk up. I looked around for a tree guide as we'd been instructed to do and walked straight toward mine.

There were some fresh carvings on its trunk that made me flinch, just like the sight of raw flesh wounds on someone's skin would. They reminded me of my tender C-section scar and the scars all over Mother Earth. I leaned on my tree guide, hoping that it could soothe my pain and answer my burning questions. Why? Why did this particular person feel compelled to carve it? To get a cheap thrill, to feel alive, to tap and express inaccessible pain, to feel immortal?

I could sense that the tree's consciousness was not on the same wavelength as mine. I was the one who needed to adjust. I thought of the men and women throughout the US who were fasting with me and imagined each person sitting by a tree antennae. Once I did, I sensed my tree's strength, resilience, and power, and let it stream through me. It directed my attention to its obstinate roots, digging through rocky dirt, absorbing the slightest bit of moisture and nutrients, and distributing it to each tip of its outstretched branches while perched way up on this dry peak hundreds of feet above sea level. As this information sank in, I began to feel bigger and stronger, tapping into inner recesses I didn't realize I had. My initial concern—how I'd possibly last the whole day on one Femme Vitale Odwalla drink—left without a trace.

After my insides were more aligned with the tree's wisdom,

I gathered that no matter how powerful and destructive human beings may seem to me, our destructive power is miniscule compared to the wisdom and healing power of nature and the Great Spirit. Down the mountain, the ugliness of life can be overwhelming. It's difficult to appreciate people, things, and events in their complexity when looking at each separate piece close-up, but, from afar, from the perspective of my tree, from up here, all of it was really beautiful.

I could not imagine this view being "edited" or having the "ugly" parts taken out—there were no ugly parts. This insight took me to the next level. Here, my gaze merged with an even higher view, as if amidst the stars, and went out farther and farther, similar to what happened when I looked into White Wolf's eyes. When I looked down, the insanity, wars, the potential atomic bomb explosion, even our destruction of the environment, animals, and all of life shrank into a microscopic speck and got smaller and smaller. My consciousness was still there, indestructible, unstoppable, showing me that life would eventually take a different form and shape to continue with its learning, regardless of what we did.

Swept up in this timeless, fearless, goalless perfection of unfathomable might and power, I saw the true nature of reality and myself through eyes that I never knew I had. They were the eyes of our collective soul throughout eternity, requiring me to surrender, trust, and accept in ways that I didn't know were humanly possible. I needed to be more like it and less like me. Only then would I be able to understand that each and every off-balance and despicable act is counterbalanced by unconditional love and raw potential that can be accessed and manifested with our intention and actions in a realm that exists beyond time and space. There were no more contradictions . . . the paradoxical power of this love, equanimity, and acceptance permeated through every single one of my cells.

I walked to a clearing, baked in the sun, my body sprawled on the warm, grassy dirt, and dreamed and dreamed, about the Goddess clients I'd meet and the groups I'd run, my womb cramping

200 AMAZON WISDOM KEEPER

and aching whenever I gave birth to an exciting new idea. I had Brooke Medicine Eagle's book and Andrew Weil's book, *Spontaneous Healing*, with me and kept flipping to passages that gave me explicit permission to trust my inner wisdom. Dr. Weil was deliberately collecting anecdotal stories of dramatic incidences of spontaneous healing to tip Western medicine's sacred cow—large-scale, placebo-controlled, double-blind experimental trials that established what treatments were or weren't valid—and closely studied possible explanations of miraculous recoveries that usually got shortchanged and rarely influenced medical practice.

When I relaxed and breathed into the places within myself that felt off or kinked, I realized that this had been my go-to strategy for creative problem solving for as long as I could remember. Doing this while lying on the ground made my connection to Mother Earth feel even more intimate. It felt as if the surrounding grasses and shrubs sprang out of me too. As the gap between me and Mother Earth closed, the seasons and stages of pregnancy merged into one, and the trials, tribulations, triumphs, and joys of birth, life, parenthood, and stewardship fused into a joined cause.

This union saturated my entire sense of self with a new understanding: an "aha" experience that was so profound, it felt as if I'd sank to the bottom of an ocean. Rather than feeling cheated out of the peaceful, natural, uncomplicated vaginal birth experience that I had longed for, I felt enriched by this hard and painful experience and more personally and emotionally connected to Mother Earth, our collective plight, and my feminine cocreative power than ever before.

I realized that Mother Earth was suffering in the same way as I was for similar reasons—harmed by the advances of technology, institutionalized efficacy motivated by greed, disconnected souls doing what they think they should be doing, and imbalanced, masculine energy determining the shots behind the scenes and in male-dominated headquarters above the glass ceiling. I related to her hurt and sense of being violated—the prying, poking, injecting, slashing—as one mother to another. There was solidarity, strength, solace, and a sense of purpose in our joint connection, a larger calling that I once before was able to attune to when I felt pushed to my edge as a graduate student. Was there a relationship between these two events? A similar lack of feminine energy in academia and medical institutions?

Embracing my purpose caused the bitterness, the fear of being horrified for a second time, and the feelings of debilitating loss that had been an obstacle for so long to disappear from my path. A fresh openness, a renewed trust in my body and instincts, and a total surrender to the source of creation, both within and outside of me, were reestablished. This is what was important to remember for the future. When things didn't work out according to plan, I needed to switch to a larger frame to give it more room to unfold.

"Guess what? Rainbow Crystal Woman told me to get off the pill right away and start trying for a second baby next month," I said to Robert when I got home.

"Rainbow who?" he asked, smiling, infected by my enthusiasm.

"Crystal Woman. She's the spirit guide who came through in the sweat lodge and is voicing her ideas in my writing. I can't explain how it happened. I felt deeply connected to her during my all-day fast, and she basically conveyed that healing was timeless and could be spontaneous through the help of this other book that I was reading by Dr. Weil. I could be healed right in an instant if I just switched my thinking. I tried it and it worked. I then received the message to go to Mt. Shasta during Christmas break and try to conceive on our tenth anniversary in celebration of our union. Kind of like we did for our fifth anniversary, only upping it a degree. I need to do the math, but I think it's very possible that I'll be ovulating on the twenty-seventh."

"You sure that it's safe to try so soon again?"

"Yes, my body will have a full cycle and a half to clear. It should be fine."

"In that case, why not? My job seems clear and straight-forward. No issues there. Let's do it," Robert teased. He pulled me in his arms and gave me a kiss.

≈

I spent the rest of November and the first few weeks in December weaning off birth control and shifting back into baby-making mode. I shared these new developments with my online support group but tried hard not to overanalyze the message that had come through out of fear that I may jinx it. I did check to see if it was likely that I'd be ovulating on December twenty-seventh, the day of our anniversary. This uncannily turned out to be the case.

Preparations for the upcoming holidays kept me distracted and busy. We delighted in Terrance's Christmas excitement and didn't pack up our snow gear and winter clothes until his tireless little body, surrounded by Santa's gifts, finally gave out, and he was sound asleep. After a late breakfast the next day, we loaded the car and hugged and kissed Terrance, who was engrossed in his new toys and didn't mind hanging out with Ma and Pa for a few days.

"Here we are, back in the car on a road trip by ourselves, just like it all began, how many years ago, thirteen?" Robert said.

"Yup. Feels like yesterday."

"On the one hand, so much has changed. We have degrees, careers, and an adorable little boy, but on the other, everything is still the same. You're still the same feisty troublemaker I fell in love with so many years ago," he said.

"Troublemaker? Where did you get that idea? I'm a model citizen with a ferocious appetite for the truth."

"Like I said, a troublemaker." I crinkled my nose and gave him an "oh shush" look.

Our four-hour pilgrimage to Mt. Shasta ended up taking twice as long due to heavy traffic and snow. We didn't mind. The extra time allowed us to dig deeper and to reconnect more authentically to ourselves and each other.

"I often feel like I'm paddling around in a little rowboat in an ocean full of sharks and huge ships. It's getting old. Perhaps it's time to look into start-ups."

"I'm so glad that you've stayed yourself through it all and have avoided getting ripped to shreds by the sharks around you.

I think working for yourself will give you a lot more freedom," I said. Robert grabbed my hand and gave it a little squeeze.

"I hope that venturing off on my own will afford me a bit more freedom too, but I worry at the same time about being too big for my young age and supposed limited life experience," I said.

"Too big?"

"Yeah, like grandiose, too out there, too lofty, too audacious. It's hard to explain. I just notice a default inhibition within myself and dampening of my light to be less noticeable. Because my light and the things that come out of my mouth are not typical, it creates inner havoc for people, like my existence and ideas are upending the natural order of the universe. It's not something that I purposely do. Even openly talking about this crazy thing that we are doing now—claiming that my spirit guide told me to get pregnant on our tenth anniversary in Mt. Shasta, or that I lived before and am drawing from past-life experiences, or that we were a team before—can trigger animosity, mocking, or other strange and aggressive reactions in people."

"No need to convince me. It's the reason why I love you so much and somehow knew we were meant to be together when we met."

"Thank God I can at least be completely myself with you. What would I do without you?" I said and gave him a kiss on his hand.

Blizzards and mist obscured our view of Mt. Shasta as we neared our destination, but I could sense her gentle power all around us. We stopped for dinner and arrived at the cabin we rented around nine that night. It was a welcoming sight, covered with snow and nestled in a beautiful pine forest. We took a hot shower and, after driving all day, were sound asleep as soon as our heads hit the mattress.

The next day, the day of our anniversary, we enjoyed a leisurely breakfast, rented skis, and scooted through fresh, powdery snow to the lift. The striking differences between our fifth anniversary and our tenth anniversary made me smile inside. On the ski lift, the bulky, white pine trees, completely stiff and frozen in this winter wonderland, got my attention and had a surprisingly profound impact on me.

Year in year out, they go through a dark season of lifeless-ness and apparent death, only to be reborn with renewed vigor and life in the season of light. A flash of insight lit up my mind. Looks can be deceiving. The parts of my heart, body, and soul that seemed dead weren't. They were just frozen and gathering energy to reemerge bigger, better, and stronger than before. Then, out of nowhere, I had another epiphany that struck a truth chord. On a larger scale, we—our species and planet—were going through a similar winter season of darkness and apparent death to reor-ganize and regroup ourselves. There was no need for panic and alarm. A deep sense of acceptance came over me.

We needed to ride it out and do what we could under our cur-rent conditions. With that in mind, I—usually the one to shy away from cold temperatures and snow—felt safe, exhilarated, enliv-ened, and protected on the mountain, even in occasional blizzards with lightning and thunder. We skied our hearts out until the lifts closed at four in the afternoon then went to get massages.

"Thanks for fitting us in. I pulled something in my shoul-der while skiing today," I said to Crystal, a massage therapist who could see us back to back. The sounds and smells of crackling fire-wood, hot tea, a soothing fountain, and wonderful herbs and oils in her massage sanctuary warmed me to the bone.

Crystal was a master at her craft. She treated my pulled mus-cle with scented oils that instantly calmed the pain and throbbing. Her divine hands caused me to drift into a dreamy state and catch a glimpse of Rainbow Crystal Woman who was walking up Mt. Shasta. It felt good to be able to associate an image to the pow-erful and expansive feelings that I'd come to associate with her. She looked like White Buffalo Calf Woman as described by Brooke Medicine Woman and signaled that I follow her to the top. I'd hoped to talk to her, but got the sense that she wanted me to trust her quiet guidance as we traversed into the unknown. I followed her without hesitation, at peace and confident that it would even-tually all make sense.

At the end of Robert's massage, Crystal said that she didn't want to disturb me, because my spirit was working so hard.

"I met my spirit guide, Rainbow Crystal Woman. She wanted me to follow her and go higher up on the mountain. It felt empowering and uplifting," I said.

"I work with the beings of the mountain to align the energies of our left and right brains, but this is the first time that someone stayed for another hour on the table. Good for you."

It felt good to be seen by another human being who understood my inner experience on an intuitive level and told myself not to take this rare gift for granted.

"I know a woman downtown who has a wonderful collection of crystals that were guided to be near Mt. Shasta. Let me get you her info. I bet you'll enjoy her shop. Just let your spirit help you find what you need when you enter it. You may leave with something totally different than what you want to find."

"Sounds good. We will pay her a visit, for sure," I said when we hugged.

"I miss my little rascal. Let's give him a call before it gets too late," I said to Robert on the way to our cabin.

"How are you doing, sweetie pie?" I asked after Pa put Terrance on the phone.

"Good. *Opa* took me to the park, and we saw someone catch a big fish. When are you coming home?" he asked. My heart skipped a beat when I heard his adorable, high-pitched voice and lisp.

"Sounds like you are having a grand time with *Oma* and *Opa*, grandma and grandpa. We'll be back very soon, the day after tomorrow. Miss you and love you. Kiss kiss, and a big hug. Here's your daddy," I said.

After our brief check-in, we showered, dressed up, and made it on time for our dinner reservations at a romantic, semi-formal restaurant. Our conversation kept veering back to Terrance, his amusing expressions, his stubbornness, the cute things he'd done that made us melt with delight, and the stuff that made us want to pull our hair out.

"Isn't it funny how much we've talked about him? Wasn't this supposed to be a kid-free getaway?" I said to Robert on the way back to our cabin.

"What did we talk about before he came along? I can't remember."

"Me neither."

"Are you sure you're ready for another one?" he said, examining my face.

"Yes, I am. 100 percent sure."

On our way back, the snow-blanketed cabins and pristine landscape intensified my desire to be inside, making out by a cozy fire. As if reading my mind, Robert headed straight for the rustic stone fireplace when we arrived at our cabin, while I lit and arranged more than a dozen candles that I'd snuck into my bag on the mantel, small tables, and window sills.

"Moment of truth," I said and turned off the lights.

"Beautiful, just like you. Come sit over here. Let's test my little nest," Robert said and pulled a few sturdy pillows and a thick, fluffy blanket from the sofa. I sank onto the soft, padded floor while he leaned over me and slowly lowered the weight of his body onto mine, kissing me softly and rubbing his growing manhood against my thighs.

We took one article of clothing off at the time, as if playing a game of strip poker with touching privileges, but, once fully undressed, it didn't take very long before the feel of full skin-on-skin contact swept us up in the magic and twinkling flames all around us.

We slept in and decided to spend the day exploring the restaurants and shops downtown, including the crystal shop that Crystal had recommended. It wasn't hard to find. The crystals in there were indeed the most breathtaking that I had ever seen. There were four separate rooms, and one, called middle earth, held a thirty-five-hundred-pound cluster of huge crystals. It drew me in like a magnet, and I circled and inspected it from every angle.

"It's a cluster of different crystals. This particular layer that you're looking at helps to boost confidence to live your life's purpose. It came from Brazil," the storekeeper said.

"Wow. It's truly incredible and precisely what I need right now," I said, feeling rather naked and vulnerable.

"Do you know a massage therapist named Crystal? She referred us to you and was right. You have quite a remarkable collection."

"Yes, she's a dear friend. Glad she sent you. Take your time and see what calls out to you."

I thought I'd have a hard time narrowing down my favorite picks, but two beautiful buffaloes carved out of white-marbled crystal with gray spots on their backs immediately tugged on my heartstrings.

"I need to find two smaller ones for them," I said to Robert.

"Who's them?" he asked.

"Our children." The moment those words left my lips, I caught the slip-up and playfully covered my mouth. It felt so right, as if I'd been saying it forever.

"I like the sound of that. By the way, I can tell that you're pregnant. You're burning up," Robert said.

"Really? You notice a difference in my body temperature?"

"Yeah, you're a lot warmer." I noticed a slight difference only after he mentioned it and was touched that he'd sensed a difference in something as subtle as my baseline body temperature.

I looked through the whole store but never found smaller buffaloes. There were plenty of bigger buffaloes, but because of my "small thinking," I never considered sizing the parents up until I remembered what Crystal said on the drive home the following day. That I may leave with something different than I was looking for.

I admired the two crystal buffaloes that I'd purchased and showed Robert a postcard with an awe-invoking shot of Mt. Shasta with a shooting star and full moon behind it.

"My buffaloes and this image are telling me it's time to size up. I need to expand my vision and my horizons, break free from comfortable and limiting molds, and invest in new possibilities."

"Yes, you do; we both do. It was nice to get away. Glad you listened to your heart."

About half an hour from Ma and Pa's home in Sacramento,

while staring into the dark night, Robert and I saw a bright shooting star swipe across the sky. It was the first shooting star that we'd seen together.

"My wish already came true," he said, and winked at me.

"Mine did too," I said, and leaned on his shoulder, eager to see Terrance's big smile and hold his little body in my arms.

Chapter 13

 **REBIRTH**

Everything in life is a metaphor.
—Haruki Murakami

"YOU'LL FEEL RIGHT AT HOME here in Berkeley. We're a bit more progressive and daring than our colleagues in the rest of the country when it comes to integrating spirituality and complementary medicine into our interventions. There are many psychotherapy-consultation groups for mental health professionals that could offer you support and logistical tips to help you settle into your new practice and a convenient, safe space to talk about challenges you may run into with clients," Claudia said.

I was thrilled. These experienced and like-minded practitioners would be a much better fit than my online *hunka* group and provide me the required ongoing peer and professional review I needed when working with clients. They would be readily available to hold my hand while taking the biggest and scariest leap in my career: opening my own private practice. I felt my anxiety and the weight of this large responsibility subside. This could mean only one thing: I was on the right track.

The first few months unfolded according to plan. I'd joined a group but, once again, an urge to individuate on some key issues emerged prematurely and insisted that I detour off the safe and beaten path.

Six of us settled in a chair or favorite spot on the sofa that we'd informally claimed as our own over the course of the last seven months. My bulging belly had earned me the rocking chair, and I softly swayed back and forth while resting my palms on the knobby little elbows and knees squirming under my skin.

"Let's start with check-ins. Everyone please limit yourself to just a few minutes," Alan, the group leader, said. A nervous, panicky flutter crept into the cramped cavity that used to be my stomach.

"That means 'get to the point'!" Bill snarled, his eyes locked on me. He joined the group to work on his incisive, cynical zingers that were usually dead-on. Interestingly enough, decades ago when working on his dissertation, he apparently had serious trouble getting to the point. After years of dragging his research out, his depressed wife left him. Some time later, she took her own life.

Bill used to pick on Rita—a Latin American professor grieving her prime years and empty marriage—for not "getting to the point." Right before leaving the group for unclear, career-related reasons, Rita sneered, "What's the point of getting to the point?"

I quietly cheered her on whenever she confronted Bill. Rita and I seemed to get each other without needing to spell out how. Together, it seemed less trite to attribute our non-Western cultural backgrounds, she Chilean, I Surinamese, to the "pointless" way we liked to approach therapy and life.

"Don't you enjoy the relaxed lifestyle of the local people from the Caribbean or some other laid-back place and find it amusing when you ask them for directions and they tell you to look for the mango tree, then turn left as soon as you see the bank, then drive underneath the bridge, make a right, and look for the sign to the highway at the corner of a mom and pop grocery store? Perhaps there are some unseen, instant benefits to this non-linear, 'inefficient,' 'pointless' way of navigating through life that we pay thousands of dollars for when in need of a vacation," I said.

There were a few chuckles that gave away that they probably got my point, but I had doubts that it would make a difference.

Going against the current because my intuition told me that it clashed with my inner flow didn't seem like a good enough reason.

"Your clarity is your power," Rita once said to me. It reassured me that I made sense to at least one person, and that the point of therapy and life was quite subjective. I wondered if she left the group because she knew that, months later, we would still be going around in circles whether or not to get to the point.

Some of the group members had grown tired of my lack of compliance in doing Group Therapy 101, and I felt just as exasperated about not being able to get my point across to them. My previous attempts at being more direct, such as attributing our differences to "linear" versus "circular" processes had been too triggering to Lisa who felt that the term "linear" offensively clumped her with "dominant, white, male" and "oppressor" and made her feel like an ogre. She requested that I no longer use it.

When I took the opposite approach and speculated that my figurative speech may be characteristic of "spiritual and intuitive language" and revealing of a gift in accessing messages from another dimension—rather than a sign of emotional avoidance and disorganization (according to the books and websites on giftedness that were serendipitously crossing my path)—Alan reminded me that everyone was gifted in their own way.

Was he implying that I was trying to set myself apart as special and better than the rest? What now? Alan's refereeing felt off. The phrases and words that he and Lisa marked as out-of-bounds seemed fair play to me. She was responsible for her triggered feelings. I was willing to honor and thread slowly around them, but I was not okay with being completely censored by them. No one else seemed to agree with my point of view. I was running out of ideas how to convey that I was experiencing what they were accusing me of—their rigid rules felt like an imposition and were squashing my process.

"With getting to the point, we mean the emotional juice, the main issue, not a theoretical explanation or an indirect example," Lisa said. She'd called me a "slippery fish," and had been irked by our "semantic hang-ups" and my "lack of depth."

"I know what you mean with getting to the emotional juice, but there are obstacles along this path that create a block. I'm capable of doing deep, emotional work, but I can't let go if the set-up feels off. It could be that we are trying to 'fix' broken parts and soothe pain without asking what the problem is or if we're going about it in the right way," I said.

"How does this conflict make you feel?" Alan asked.

"Frustrated," I answered.

"The same way your mother frustrated you?" Bill said.

"I don't want to go down this rabbit hole again. I have gone into the basement, spent week after week in here unpacking at least a dozen boxes related to childhood conflicts, and came up empty-handed. The only thing that's coming up around my childhood right now is a dream that I had around the third grade where I cut myself free from unhealthy attachments," I said.

"After this dream, I felt more strongly connected to my inner knowing, and less hung up on everyone else needing to understand me. I'm going to be really honest. I wonder if I need to be doing that again, but feel like I can't because of peer review requirements in our field. I'm in a double bind once again, and this does feel familiar, but it's circumscribed to just my career. I'm also frustrated that I can't get to the bottom of this pattern and resolve it. It makes me doubt myself and wonder if I have a problem connecting with colleagues like you, which is something that I would really like, but not at the expense of my integrity," I said.

"The tyranny of the majority," Bear said to my surprise. Eighteen years ago, he had served as a ceremony leader for indigenous traditions. He was now "just" a therapist and had stuffed the "Bear" part of him deep inside, claiming to have put all that behind him for unsaid reasons that felt heavy. I could tell that my struggles were tugging at his heartstrings.

"Could be. I sometimes feel like I'm left-handed and molding myself to fit into a dominant right-handed world just to belong. This repeatedly backfires, but, instead of questioning the necessity of finding fault with left-handedness, I blame myself for not molding enough. Damned if I do, damned if I don't," I said. Bear nodded in agreement.

There had been a few times when I was certain that we'd made a breakthrough and that things would feel different the next time we'd meet but ended up being wrong. I learned to keep my hopes in check. This Wednesday morning, Grace—who was taking a break from clients—was the first one to check in. She had once again been plagued by "Darky," her depressed side, and asked for suggestions to reconnect with "Sparky," her lighter side, during the coming week.

"How about the jewelry making? How is that going?" Alan asked. Other members asked about other sources of joy that she had mentioned at one point or another during the therapy process.

"I think Darky and Sparky should make love in the elevator that runs between the top and bottom floors," I blurted out. I didn't realize how intolerant I'd become of the bullet-pointing and bullet-proofing of challenges that only seemed to bring about superficial changes.

Grace was taken aback for a few moments but seemed intrigued by my proposition.

"I may be sixty-five years old, but I often feel like a kindergartner next to you," she responded with a sweet smile.

"Thank you," I said, stupefied. Accepting her compliment felt bold, snooty, awkward, defiant, wrong, and right all at once.

When it was my turn to check in, Alan asked me if I wanted to use the sand tray. My soul pranced with joy. Something had shifted.

"Thank you, but I don't think I need to anymore," I said to him. I felt seen and saw my soul in the sand.

"When you said that, I looked at the heap of sand and felt a powerful impulse to poke my finger in it to create a volcano, symbolizing the source of life and death, creation and destruction, and my deep connection to the sacred feminine. My cervix is my inner volcano, my umbilical-cord connection to Mother Earth. This realization came over me in a flash just right now. Even though I would love to touch and play with the sand, it may taint what just happened. The message that came through is meant to be short and sweet and to the point," I said sheepishly.

"Are you sure you don't want to give it a try? I have a cabinet full of sand tray toys and miniature figures that you can use . . ." Alan said while gesturing toward the cabinet with a confused look on his face.

Having completed sand tray training myself, I was aware that not using human figurines in a sand tray sculpture indicated impoverished relational skills and poor attachments. I'd grown cautious about leaving any room for misinterpretation and thought of something that could divert that.

"Something happened this week that may elaborate on the meaning of this volcano. I had a powerful, turning-point experience a few days ago with Karen, a hypnobirthing specialist." Alan nodded to me to go on.

"In my session with Karen, I discovered how easy and natural it was for me to switch to an altered state of consciousness and trace my intuitive hunches. These disparate topics may seem unrelated, long winded, and off point within our group dynamic, but I got to experience that, if given a chance to connect the dots, they end up offering me deep meaning and guidance."

I had everyone's undivided attention.

"I feel so much loss and grief about this undernourished part, like I am in a desert that can't sustain it," I said and let out some sobs. I could sense that my intense grief and longing for more expanded space was stirring Bear's.

"I feel pulled to go deeper into this altered state during our meetings. Because you prefer that we keep our check-ins brief, I try to dice up my comments and engage in a normal mode of consciousness where you all seem to connect, but end up feeling disconnected from my true self," I said.

"I discovered that this disconnection is not due to a trust issue or an intimacy block. I'd never met Karen before, but I could already tell on the phone that she was speaking my language, an English that was poetic and more capable of conveying what was going on inside of me. I sought help from her to soothe the panicky and claustrophobic feelings that the thought of labor alone kept triggering in me and instantly trusted her with my deepest feelings. My spirit just took over from there," I said, still a bit angry about being misinterpreted for so long, just because of an unwillingness to budge and examine their self-assured positions of power and expertise.

"When we met in person, Karen induced me into a state of deep relaxation through her presence, her tone of voice, and by suggesting that I go to a safe place. Within seconds, I was in a cave that half emerged from the ocean. It simultaneously represented my womb, because I was with my unborn baby, reassuring her that I would help her make a smooth entry into the world through the opening of the cave. Just being in the cave and hanging out with my baby, riding the waves like labor pangs, and not being in a hurry to go anywhere was enjoyable and caused a shift.

"Rainbow Crystal Woman, the spirit guide who I'd met at the first Lakota retreat, appeared in the cave. She had a beautiful rainbow cape on and beams of light were shining from her eyes. She gave us gifts of love, light, clarity, and strength. Dolphins came into the cave and invited us to play. They showed me how perfect and aligned our bodies were for a smooth birth by entering and exiting the cave.

"While frolicking around, one of the dolphins decided to take me on a journey to find the part of myself that had been scared and panicked about the upcoming birth. We dove into the farthest depths of the ocean where it was pitch black.

"There I found a little girl, myself at five, in a cage so small, she couldn't even stand up. It was heartbreaking. She was relieved and happy to see us. Her bright, passionate light had been threatening to those around her, and she agreed that it was better to dampen it, stay small, and stay far out of sight until she was old enough to protect it and herself. Rainbow Crystal Woman gave her a crystal spear—her power object—and she used it to break the lock on the cage and light up the darkness that was surrounding her. The many years that she had been stuck in the cage collapsed into a split second."

I had no idea how my experience with Karen was sounding to the group, but Bear's continuous nodding encouraged me to keep going.

"When I took a closer look at my child self, I noticed a tar-like residue of dark energy that covered her entire body. It was very difficult to get it off, and she doubted that her crystal would be powerful enough. She was eventually able to peel and scrub all the tar off with the crystal, which greatly boosted her confidence. She joined me on the back of the dolphin, and we emerged out of the water into the bright, blue sky elated, gliding over and under the waves until we were back in the cave with my unborn baby.

"In the cave, the waves got more intense and the time for birth was getting nearer. When the moment of truth came, my baby, my younger self, and I climbed on the back of a dolphin and shot out of the cave and out of the water, born and reborn and basking in feelings of joy."

"I could feel your joy in riding the waves," Alan said after a short pause. Grace nodded and smiled.

"Who locked you up in that cage?" Bill injected. His question jolted me out of my dream like a bucket of ice water.

"I don't think it was any one person in particular. I got the sense that my younger self agreed that this solution was the safest and best option under the circumstances," I said.

There wasn't a whole lot of warmth coming from the group. I felt unreasonable for wanting more, like expecting a loyal lover to enthusiastically listen to what a brief love affair sparked in me and help me explore what had been lacking in our relationship.

"I appreciate that you cared and meant well, but a part of me must have known that your interventions couldn't help me to get my lost soul parts back and heal in a more holistic way," I said. As unfair as it was, I harbored some anger toward them. They were supposed to be the qualified peers and teachers who could offer me the specialized training and supervision I needed to meet my profession's ethical requirements for employing innovative treatment modalities.

"Then why did you stick around?" Lisa asked. As soon as she asked that, my paradoxical mind turned on.

"Partly to follow prescribed standards of care, but, more honestly, I got the sense that this was some sort of spiritual contract that I'd agree to take on, like some kind of journalism assignment that I needed to complete to educate others. A U-turn sign popped up in my peripheral vision and indicated that I'd returned to earth to fulfill this mission."

"I feel used," Lisa said.

"This part may sound even crazier or more off-putting, but I also got a strong sense that we all agreed to this contract. Even our clashes felt as if they were part of a plan and larger story, like actors assuming different roles in a play to deliver an important message."

No one said anything, but I could tell that my words were provoking a lot of thought.

"I'm apparently also here to help bridge the gap between psychology and spirituality by examining my experiences with conventional treatment," I said pensively.

"That's not your responsibility!" Bill retorted, intensely triggered by my off-the-wall, audacious claim.

"It may not be my responsibility, but it *is* my life purpose," I said and sat up straighter, feeling strong and centered. I couldn't resist glaring back into Bill's seventy-three-year-old, blue eyes while relishing the smug thought, Which is not too shabby of a point and realization to have reached at thirty years of age, don't you think?

Not long after this incident, the impossible happened. Bill and I became allies. I warmed up to him when he speculated out loud that Rita had left the group because we'd "failed her." He also confronted Lisa and others for wanting feedback that made them "feel better," instead of "get better," which was close enough to what I'd tried to say.

While looking at Bill, an image of an old-fashioned, dim lantern in the dark appeared in my mind's eye. When I shared this with the group, Lisa dismissed my newfound affinity for Bill as filial piety (a Confucian virtue to convey respect for one's parents, elders, and ancestors). If so, mine was on some mysterious, delayed, time-release schedule that suddenly had gotten activated for no apparent reason. Why was she constantly undermining me?

"Did you all hear what she said? Ha. An old-fashioned lantern in the dark!" Bill exclaimed.

"You remind me of a monk who tries to 'awaken' his students by whacking them on the head with a stick when they least expect it. Unfortunately, in this day and age, I don't think your style is going to be effective. But perhaps I'll be doing the same thing if I endure another forty years of this," I said. Just a few months of this gridlock has felt like being in labor and pushing against a wall.

"I have a loud bark because I'm afraid that time is running out for me," he said in a softer and more reflective tone. I could tell that he was touched by my support and was trying his best to break out of his confines and connect.

That same week while walking to my car, I got a distinct sense that a part of my brain had perceived information that wasn't generated by me. I could barely make out what was being said. The words came through as a dialogue in the far distance, and the man and woman in dialogue were Bill and his deceased ex-wife. I summarized and remembered his ex-wife's message by using a mnemonic with three As: *Apologize* for her wrongdoing, *Acknowledge* his efforts and attempt to authentically connect to others, and *Applaud* him for trying to date.

I wasn't sure whether or not to share this sensitive information with Bill during our group meeting, especially since I had no way of verifying its legitimacy. When I asked for permission, Bill seemed a little nervous and apprehensive, but he composed himself and reassured me that he was ready to hear about my experience. He closed his eyes, as if meditating.

I felt honored to receive Bill's trust and openness. He had not talked about the traumatic suicide of his late wife in the group. When I relayed his deceased ex-wife's message, Bill's body looked like it was caving in and turning into putty, allowing powerful emotions to surface from the depths of his being.

"I met with a medium, many decades ago, right after she'd passed away," Bill said. This revelation seemed completely out-of-character and nothing like the laser-sharp Bill I thought I knew.

"I wanted to apologize for deserting her and for what she

went through alone. It never occurred to me that she could feel apologetic too," Bill stammered in tears.

"This exchange means more to me than I can put into words," I said. We all bowed down while healing energy and love flowed through him.

"The work that I did with Karen has been on my mind a lot. She claimed that I was a natural, and now this. It's making me entertain thoughts of ending group therapy to pursue shamanic training and guidance," I said.

"A lot of therapists these days are pursuing shamanic training. 'Shaman' sounds more exotic than 'psychotherapist,' that's for sure," Lisa said. I didn't bother to ask how this was relevant to me. Trying to explain why this once again felt undermining, exploring where this was coming from, what it triggered in me, what aspects of our healing journey it related to and on and on, like we used to do, would only derail me further. I needed to trust my clarity and irritation and move on. I was certain that this 'shamanism thing' was chasing me as much as, or perhaps more than, I was chasing it.

"If you like, you could test your intuitive gifts on us. We could give you feedback whether or not you are 'on' or 'off,'" Alan said.

Thanks, but no thanks, I heard a voice respond. I felt victorious. Something deep inside me had shifted and was setting a firm limit. No more. I needed to stop blaming them for holding me back and stop blaming myself for not trying or not loving them enough. It was time to get a divorce.

"I think it's probably best to work with students and teachers who are all going through the same training," I said instead.

"That makes sense. Let us know how we can help you with that transition," Alan said.

"Thank you. That's so kind of you."

Being peer reviewed was no longer the only answer to all my prayers. For a brief, lucid moment, I realized that standing in my integrity and highest truth meant being free from external approval. As great as it felt, I wasn't confident that I could make this daring clarity last.

≈

My daughter's due date was just around the corner. My upcoming break would give me a chance to think things through. I decided to wait and not officially end my engagement with the group until I returned from maternity leave.

My VBAC (Vaginal Birth After C-Section) delivery went as smoothly as I had envisioned in my hypnobirthing session. I rode the magical and soothing soundwaves of Carlos Nakai's flute the entire time while in labor and savored each and every moment and encouraging sensation. They were intense, but there was continuous movement and progress: the experience was nothing like the feeling of laboring in a slab of concrete that I had with Terrance. I uttered one last guttural groan and squealed in disbelief when my baby's head crowned and her body, as slippery as a dolphin's, slithered through my birth canal, and shot out of me. I was once and for all cured of my phantom aching to physically complete Terrance's birth.

I cradled and held her close to me for hours, grieving that Terrance and I were robbed of this special time right after he was born. While bonding with her, I received rushes of insight that his emergency C-section and my earlier miscarriage were purposeful events. These beautiful wise souls had worked as a team in shaking me up and cracking me open, so I could access sacred feminine power and healing wisdom out of the farthest and frailest depths of my soul.

Delivering my baby girl, Jade, at the same hospital where I had Terrance felt like the grand finale of my bird nest warrior lore and erased all past imprints from previous birth trauma. Not only did I make a full spiral rotation that provided me the closure I longed for, I landed on a fresh slate of fertile volcanic ground eager to nourish new possibility and potential.

PART THREE

Chapter 14

 FLYING WITH PALOMA

> *Beginning in childhood, many are urged and taught*
> *by their cultures not to see too much. One must agree*
> *to agree, even though strongly sensing otherwise, that*
> *only things that have their atoms packed together so*
> *tightly that they are seen by the egos of all—that these*
> *are the only things that ought to matter in life.*
> —Elena Avila

AFTER THREE MONTHS OF maternity leave, I was ready to venture back into the world and revive my practice. I called my old clients, and let my sources know that I was accepting referrals. I checked out a few case-conference groups, but they seemed more conventional and less aligned with my holistic and spiritual interests than the psychotherapy-consultation group that I was meeting with on Wednesdays.

While up with my newborn in the middle of the night, I realized that I needed to adjust my expectations and acknowledge that my practice was still in its infantile stages. It needed me to love and treat it like a fledging, a baby, my baby. Suddenly, sticking things out a little longer with this group of experienced private practitioners no longer seemed like such a bad idea. It would give me a chance to learn to crawl and walk in this novel role before sprinting and spinning off into an unconventional and controversial direction.

New clients trickled in within the next few weeks. One of them had the oddest presentation I'd ever come across in my years of experience. If you were to meet her on the street, she wouldn't stand out in any way. She was Caucasian, about five feet tall, polite, mild-mannered, and self-contained. It was her soul perspective when describing her everyday experiences and relationships, her brutally honest self-scrutiny, and the creative ways in which she made meaning of the most minute details without losing the big picture that grabbed my attention.

She grew up as an only child in the suburbs of Houston. Her biggest childhood trauma were the many hours she spent in daycare and the lack of warm connection between her high-powered, career-oriented parents and herself. She said that her parents were well-off and neglectful and masked their marital separation under the guise of needing to work in separate cities for three years when she was a teen. To cope, she abandoned them as an adult, choosing silent conflict over "win-lose arguments" with her mother, who was strong and proud. In regard to her father, she chose emotional distance over guilt, because he loved her too tightly and occasionally gave off inappropriate Freudian vibes. She nevertheless was certain that she'd picked them, which confused her.

More recently, she had been struggling with anxiety, low self-worth, crying spells, panic attacks, and identity issues related to coming out as bisexual and breaking up with her current boyfriend, although she suspected that this was a simple answer and not the real issue.

"I can perform 'good, smart, pretty, and sweet' well, but it's time to break out of these roles. They're not good for me," she said.

As I learned more about her unusual take on life, I discovered that it took her only a few minutes to pick up concepts in regard to our soul's transformation, equanimity, paradox, metaphor, and intuition that I still had trouble conveying to some of my colleagues.

This was the case with a variety of subjects she studied, such as literature and dense books, such as Martin Buber's, *I and Thou*, economics and micro-loans for women in South Asia, or political activism for labor and women's rights organizations, volunteering her services to communities in Central America or the Middle East.

"I felt a tug on my sleeve to pick you, even though you were second on my list of recommended psychotherapists and not even located in my city of choice. I read your entire website, and your holistic views strongly resonate with me," she said, her eyes locked on mine. Her intense presence unsettled me. It reminded me of how alert I felt when meeting Tim for the first time.

"I go by Paloma. I haven't shared this with many people, but I sometimes get a strong sense that I'm a bird," she said. I believed her even though I had no prior experience and practice in discerning between authenticity and lying when it came to a ludicrous claim like this. I could tell that she trusted me too.

"I'm seeking therapy to be free from fear and live my truth. I want to know myself and come out with my soul. One more thing. I sometimes get the sense that I'll evaporate on my graduation day in May," she said, as if going down her "weird symptoms" list, a list I used to compile too and keep from others.

"Evaporate?" I asked. "As in cease to exist?"

"Something like that. I can't explain it. I just have a fleeting sense of it. It's like dying but not a wish to die or anything. Although I do think of that sometimes too when I feel lonely or brave. It seems like the right answer, but I know that it's wrong. This is what I mean with coming out with my soul. Revealing all these unusual inklings and hoping to make sense of them," she said.

"Makes sense. If more information comes through about this feeling of dying, let me know, okay?" I said.

My clinically trained mind wanted to peg her strange presentation and intimidating laser-beam gaze into some kind of category, and darted around like a hummingbird. Was she inappropriately flirting with me, on the verge of having a psychotic break, narcissistic, or showing flavors of dissociation or manic-depression? I knew in the deepest pit of my gut that none of them quite fit and didn't want to box her in a category just so that I'd feel more at ease and back in control. I knew that she'd crossed my path to test my deepest convictions. I've wanted Alan and my psychotherapy group to honor my intuitive knowing and have been upset at them for their shortcomings. The Universe was giving me a chance to show what I'd do differently if the tables were turned and give me a chance to step up my game.

I remembered squirming like this when I gazed into White Wolf's eyes, not able to hide any aspects of my soul like I normally did. *What if he were my client now?* I wouldn't be diagnosing him with a disorder or finding fault with his intimidating presence. Am I anxious because of preconceived notions that she can't possibly be as awakened as White Wolf?

Why not? Because she is Caucasian, grew up in a quiet suburban neighborhood, is only twenty-one years old, and is new to therapy? *What if she is an advanced soul?* I was taken in by her, because she was describing inner experiences with a level of nuance that I hadn't been able to access and articulate. Was this double bind capable of tripping up the double bind I'd been stuck in? I couldn't live with myself if I accidentally harmed a client because of my intuitive curiosities. I could now harm a client by ignoring these so-called self-indulgent intuitive inclinations. The potential risk of committing an error of commission had tipped the scales and now outweighed the risk of committing an error of omission. I decided to take a stand and decided not to talk to the group about Paloma for at least the first few weeks until I had a better grasp on the situation.

"It's so hard to figure out how to appease people. I'm usually a wreck before class presentations and collapse afterwards, exhausted. I haven't figured out what my role is in here, so I'm still figuring out how to answer truthfully. I realize that I'll need to work a lot harder in therapy than I normally do in relationships. I usually ask the questions and am the one in control, vampiring off people's energy and giving them back what they want to hear. I get that this won't work in here, plus I don't want to do this anymore," she said, talking slowly, pausing often.

"Maybe it would help to tune more into your feelings and let these guide you," I said, amused that I sounded like Lisa.

"I tend to feel in images. People often look at me as if moths are flying out of my mouth when I describe what I'm feeling," she said.

"Try me," I said, now amused that she sounded like me.

"I feel like a glass at the edge of a table. Anxious, I suppose. But that sounds more concrete and permanent than it is. Most of my feelings seem ephemeral and momentary to me. It all depends on the contexts and roles that I'm in," she said. Her clarity in explaining what she did and why and when she did it was astonishing. It offered me great insight into my own processes.

"I get what you mean. I have an idea. Have you seen *Finding Nemo*?" I asked.

She nodded yes.

"I have a sense that we need to approach your therapy like Marlin and Dory, trying to find Nemo. Marlin may be overly preoccupied, neurotic, and logical, but he's a good balance to Dory, who is intuitive, goes on blind faith, and often is right on, but needs Marlin to balance her out and give her some structure," I said.

"I can tell that you're very intuitive, and I want to support you in your self-discovery, but we're venturing into uncharted territory that falls outside of my professional experience. I wished I could refer you to someone with more experience and expertise in working with people who're as perceptive as you are, but I don't know of anyone who fits that description better than me, believe it or not. I'm usually Dory, but I have a feeling that I'll be Marlin in our dynamic," I said. This solution would allow us to be creative, intuitive, and pioneering as well as cautious, thoughtful, and conservative.

"That's fine, I understand," she said. Paloma pulled out her journal and said, "I read on your website that journaling is a good way to get in touch with feelings and heal. I love to write. It helps me to get in touch with my truth." As she flipped through her journal, I noticed that her writing and drawings were spiraling in circles and on every part of the pages but the lines. I wondered if she ever colored in the lines.

"I also *love* to read, and it often feels as if passages in books that cross my path are written just for me. Gandhi, Mother Teresa, and several post-constructivist modern writers (who claim that there is no neutral viewpoint to assess the merit of ethical and analytical knowledge claims) have called out to me. I have been getting a sense that I'll do something great one day, but I have no idea what. I knew between the ages of five and ten years that I needed to write a book, but there was no space for it. I was mostly hibernating and chameleoning, not wanting to rock the boat. I wish I could express the knowledge in me through music or art, but I don't have the technical skills. I think my best medium of communication will be through my writing. I'll have to create new words, new language, new realities," she said, bubbling with joy. "Stuff about quantum physics, invisible waves of energy, the illusion of boundaries between ourselves and the outside world, non-local intelligence beyond space and time, and stuff like that come easy to me, but I don't know how to translate it," she said.

She wasn't just giving me the opportunity to test my intuition. I really had no other option but to do so, given her psychic and perceptive brilliance. I needed to stay honest with myself and respect the mysterious bigger plan that was unfolding behind the scenes. I had a feeling that she'd see right through me if I shrank in fear, a fear that was much more noticeable in her presence.

"I realized that my default state of mind is a meditative state, and I'm most at peace when I'm formless and can explore these altered states to my heart's content. I enjoy reading about archetypes, and I can do many of them: the sage, the redeemer, the spiritual warrior, the holy child, and many different animals. I adopted Mother Mary as my internal mother during an out-of-body experience with her stained-glass image while visiting a church in Rome with my family. I started to do Aphrodite around fourteen, because I liked being liked and sexual power is a venue that is most accessible to young girls, but I'm not interested in that anymore. Right now, I think Hera, the Queen of Olympus and of all the Greek gods, fits me the best," she said, radiating an aura of royalty.

"How did you come to a conclusion like that?" I asked, baffled by her creative ingenuity and mastery. I'd never heard of anyone making so many developmental shifts with such ease at this young of an age without any professional guidance. I was certain that understanding her better would not only help me understand myself better but help me understand my hang-ups with the field of mental health better.

"I see myself at a table, and it's the way that people are looking at me," she said leaning forward, one eyebrow raised, staring at me with an unwavering fearlessness. Our eyes interlocked. I could feel my body shrink in fear as soon as she turned up her power dial, and realized that she wasn't intimidating me. I just became more conscious of my own fears that normally hid in patterns of denial.

"I read the book you recommended, *Indigo Children*, and related the most to the interdimensional type, the one that's larger than all the other types, but could not fully pour my heart into it, because I was looking for much more than there was written," she said.

"It is an imperfect human attempt to label something that really can't be labeled. I hope it nevertheless helped you to feel less alone," I said, in agreement with her assessment. I was relieved that my intuitive hunch to suggest these readings about the evolution of our consciousness and the new generation of kids were giving us language to discuss her experience.

"It did help. I've adopted 'indigo' and have been testing a few children by sending them telepathic signals through my eyes. Not sure yet if they're quite like me, but I met someone who plays incredible music and is definitely indigo," she said full of delight.

"I'm glad it offered you a more expansive way of looking at yourself, our human condition, and people in general," I said. I appreciated that she admitted to trying to connect with her eyes. It explained all the strange sensations that she was able to evoke in me.

"Yes, I'm fine with these labels, as long as the responsibility for change doesn't fall on indigos alone, and this New Age information doesn't remain marginalized. These experiences are within the reach of everyone. There was something else I wanted to tell you. I'm not saying this because I got these ideas from the book. This really happened to me. I saw the world in colors as a child and assigned a different color to each year: yellow, age six; orange, age seven; pink, age eight; magenta, age nine; and purple, age ten," she said. She read that these colors corresponded with our chakras. I was impressed and could tell that she was too, but wasn't sure what to make of it.

"I also called my dad by a different name that no one knew and have a sense that I knew him from a past life. I sometimes see myself as an old woman and sometimes sense her looking down on me, like an ancestor, or me looking down at myself. It's confusing who's who," she said. "I've never told anyone about this."

"I know what it's like to keep these kinds of experiences a secret and not trust anyone with them. I'd done the same for many years and just recently began opening up about them. I also have a strong connection with an ancestor, my great-grandmother. When she guides me telepathically, I do feel like I'm merging with her and looking at my dilemma through her eyes and with her heart. It can be unnerving and overwhelming to make sense of it all without any outside help," I said.

"All of this is happening in a very timely manner, the therapy, my new classes and instructors: my teachers this last semester seem much more soulful and are making it much easier for me to be present during lecture. I feel momentum building up and finally guiding me to little and big doors that are aligned with my true self and where I've felt drawn to go," Paloma said.

I'd never met anyone who not only could switch from a micro to a wide macro lens with such grace and fluidity, but who was also able to ride the energetic wave of her spiritual transformation with as much command, expansive oversight, real-time awareness, depth, and felt-body sense as Paloma. It made me realize that this was the kind of self-actualization I'd wished I'd learned about in my graduate program and in my consultation group. Paloma was doing it with so much ease and power, it was rekindling the flame inside of me.

When we met the following week, Paloma revealed that she had a huge epiphany that created big shifts.

"In the paradox of staying in the present moment and listening to my body, I sensed that I was on a high threshold, waiting. In slowing my mind down, insights came at me and went through me superfast. When I stood in myself, I was filled with consciousness. I noticed that the fear was all around me, fear and despair that I realized were not mine, and made me feel miserable and alone. I decided that I no longer want to be a prisoner of fear and now know I'll be fine no matter what I do. I will fly one day and leave the alligators behind. The fears around me are everyone else's fears and not real."

"I'm sorry that it's been so hard. It sounds like you're moving through it," I said.

"I saw that it doesn't have to be so hard and fearful. I looked into my own eyes, and the 'it' that looked back was so profound, so ancient. It had no dichotomies as we know them, no good or bad, no safety or danger, no gender, no forgiving or unforgiving, no binaries, zero or one, no me versus them, it just was. I asked it what I was supposed to do, and it wanted me to know my life purpose. I had to streamline myself, not flap out my hands to slow down for others out of fear that I'll crush them and that I'll end up alone.

"I learned to hold back, because I knew that speaking my truth would crush my parents. They care so much about appearances and traditional structures of power and success; that's why I didn't say anything. I thought that I couldn't get mad at them because I picked them as my parents. I recently discovered that if I let the Raaaaaaaaage I feel toward them run through my body, it makes me feel better. It feels more balanced," she said.

The hairs on my arms stood up when she streamed the rage through and out of her body. An uproar of energy welled up from the pit of my stomach, rose to the surface, and left through the pores of my skin. It felt like the galloping of horses carrying off in the wind.

"It sounds like you resolved a very common and confusing issue. That taking the high road is not necessarily the wisest thing to do or beneficial to your healing," I said. Her level of discernment and body control made me think of a neurosurgeon, using the finest of scalpels to make the most delicate cuts and distinctions. Her cutting-edge insights resonated the moment she shared them with me and offered me the type of nourishment that my soul hungered for. It struck me that much of her fresh wisdom came out of her own inner well. I'd never heard my mentors or supervisors discuss the psychological struggles and shifts she described with such in-depth understanding and ease.

"Talking about all this makes me feel happy and most truthful to myself, but it scares people off. I don't understand why. This is who I am. I'm constantly told to get my head out of the clouds and end up covering up what I say," she said.

"It's fine to be completely honest in here and say what's important to you. Let's unravel it together," I said. It reassured her to go on.

"Oh! I recently discovered that I do have a core! It's where balance is, like you said on your website. It's where my soul resides, in the Zero Point field, where all theory and post-modern and post-constructivist discourse intersect in the present moment. It's where I return to after exploring the edges of sanity and insanity. This usually doesn't make sense to people and is one of the reasons why I feel that I need to slow down, because I can tell that their eyes glaze over and I lose them if I keep going," Paloma said. Her eyes were like endless tunnels and drew me in.

"Do you feel a need to slow down in here for me?" I asked.

"Sometimes," she said, looking down. "I had an image of Alice in Wonderland outgrowing the house, and another of water spilling over the edge of a glass, but I'm not sure if I'm just scared of attaching to you, knowing that we're ending after I graduate in a few weeks," she admitted.

"My sense is that your perceptions about outgrowing me and the therapy are probably right. I feel that too. But don't hold back because of that. Do you want to check out what's going on between us and see what images come up for you?" I asked.

"I'm sorry, I never purposely tried to read you," she said apologetically.

"No need to apologize. It may be helpful for you, even if I'm just one person, to have full permission to read me and go from

FLYING WITH PALOMA   233

there," I replied, offering her the same gift that Alan had offered me. Hopefully, she trusted me enough to accept my offer.

"That would be incredible. I wrote about you in my journal, called you a tricky spirit," she said smiling.

"For giving you mixed messages?" I asked. She nodded, looking at me inquisitively.

"I think I have a sense why that would be. Are the little doors related to your small self, everyday living, relationships, and survival issues, and the big doors about living your soul's purpose, the big truth of who you are?" I asked.

"Yes," she said.

"I struggled with similar questions right before I opened my private practice. My small job as psychologist is to help you balance and streamline your energy by listening to your body and emotions and help you find contexts where people would be more open to letting go of their fears around you. In regard to my big job, I have a strange intuitive sense that my whole life has been in preparation to work with you. I have no idea why or how this fits into the bigger puzzle, and I didn't think I'd share this with you, but here it is . . ."

"Oh my God, I have that exact same feeling!" she exclaimed, her eyes about to pop out.

As if no longer able to resist, she slipped into a meditative state. I also closed my eyes and sat quietly across from her.

"I swear. I just saw you as very ancient!" she said.

"I have sensed that too at times. Now, see if you can get a sense of what happens when you get a mixed message from me or feel misunderstood. What's going on and how does it impact you?" I asked.

"I see a stream, but there are some holes, like rocks sticking out of the water. The rocks are curious, approachable, not angry or frustrated," she said very slowly, pleasantly surprised. She was used to teachers getting angry at her for grasping concepts quickly and causing them to feel inadequate as early as in kindergarten.

"Could you check and see what the rocks might be about?"

"They're about holding back," she said.

"With holding back do you mean that I'm obstructing your flow by abiding to limitations within the field of psychology that are not aligned with flow?" I asked.

"Yes, that's it . . . this has happened in every department and with every subject that I study," she said.

"Let's see what happens when you no longer let these rocks be a negative reflection of you. What happens when you trust your impressions, and I fully claim these rocks as my issues to work through?" I said.

"That feels good."

"I supposedly have more power than you because of these roles we're in, our age difference, education levels, and the like, but, in another dimension that we may both value more, I see you as light-years ahead of me and much more powerful," I said, feeling so much lighter after speaking my truth.

"I'm feeling an intuitive hunch to ask you why you're crossing my path. This would normally be a rock in the stream that I wouldn't touch, because it's my role and job to help you, not the reverse. I decided to trust my intuition and ask you anyway, perhaps able to at least move one rock," I said.

"I see yellow," she replied.

"Yellow in the chakra energy system corresponds to the third chakra in our core right above our belly button. It's associated with personal and professional power and agency. Perhaps mine is off-balance. I'll explore it further," I said. Fear jolted through my body. "The last thing I want to do is exploit you by having you neglect your needs to attend to mine. Let me know if there's anything I say or do that doesn't feel right, okay?" I said. She assured me that she would.

I was relieved that I'd decided to stick it out with the psychotherapy group just in case I got entangled with a client and needed a reality check, which seemed to be right now. I didn't know where to begin and how to accurately describe the strange dynamic and blurry boundaries that existed between Paloma and I in just fifteen minutes or so without giving the group the wrong impression. But my protective stance of Paloma and attempt to handle all of this on my own was becoming just as disconcerting.

"I have been seeing a very unusual client since December. She's very intuitively gifted. Our experiences and perceptions about the world are very similar, and I have a really strong sense that our paths were meant to cross for reasons that are still unclear. As a matter of fact, it seems as if the tables are turned, and she's a lot like me, and I'm a lot like you in our sessions," I started off saying.

"Doesn't Yalom talk about this in one of his books, the mistake that many therapists make, imagining some kind of special, parallel connection going on with a client while the truth of the matter was that the client didn't really reciprocate these feelings? You should read it; it's a good book, very enlightening. I may still have it," Lisa said to me.

Exasperated and triggered by Lisa's knee-jerk cautionary comments that kept sabotaging my process, I retreated back into my shell. The little confidence and trust that I'd cultivated shattered in an instant. Was I making all of this up? Had I gotten entangled into Paloma's delusional web without realizing it? Or, worse, did I spin her into my delusional web? A licensing board will eat me alive if anything goes wrong. What if she can't find her way from the edges of "insanity" back to her center and decides to "evaporate," whatever that meant?

Very faintly in the background, I heard another voice. *Isn't she getting clearer, stronger, and more confident after each visit? You're guiding her to her inner light and true self. It's time to look for a different group that's a better fit and end with this one.*

I kept my discussion about Paloma superficial and withheld details, but, at the same time, longed for some kind of reflection on my state of mind that I could trust. Around Robert, Ma and Pa, and my friends, I was still the same Loraine. They didn't get how being one hair-splitting degree off to the right or left could be so detrimental and invoke so much fear. Their big-picture perception of me and the situation tended to calm me down. The catastrophic outcomes in my head weren't real. They were over the top and out of proportion. Any sane person could see that.

I was able to perform my usual roles, as Paloma would say, until I returned to work. None of my coping strategies worked in this context. I needed to talk to a professional who knew me well and understood what I was struggling with. Armando and Tim came to mind. I reluctantly reached out.

"Let me know if I'm out of line. I'm working with a client who seems more spiritually-evolved than most, including me, and she's growing in leaps and bounds. I'm not always sure where we're headed, but it feels right. She's like a young, modern-day Gandhi and moves at her own lightning pace along a guided and timed trajectory. I feel like a two-dimensional cartoon character in her multi-dimensional presence and have no idea how to help her other than offer her support and encourage her to bring out her true self and her psychic gifts. I think empowering her will require me to support her potential, validate her teaching abilities, and receive guidance from her, but I'm afraid of exploiting her and being wrong about all this. This is not something that's taught or typically done in therapy," I said to Armando.

"So good to hear from you, and I'm glad that you're doing well and enjoying private practice. Probably good to slow things down and ground the energy better. Sounds like an interesting case," Armando said. He was polite and didn't blow me off, but I gathered that my request for help wasn't appropriate. He was no longer my supervisor or mentor, knew too little about the situation, and wasn't comfortable about giving me advice.

"Thanks so much for hearing me out and for these tips," I said. I felt foolish about my lack of professionalism busting out at the seams but couldn't let my pride get in the way. Paloma counted on me; I was the only person she'd ever trusted with all this information. I sent Tim an email.

"I understand what you're going through. It's really hard dealing with small minds who think of themselves as an identity rather than a soul. I deal with it all the time here. Keep asking for guidance and prepare yourself for the long-haul as progress moves at a snail's pace. But, if not us, then who? If not now, then when?" Tim wrote in response to my inquiry.

At a snail's pace? What if this wasn't right for everyone? Most people may need spaciousness and extra breathing room to fully integrate new healing insights into their minds, bodies, and daily practices, but what if some people need to move at a faster pace to maintain their integrity?

Paloma had explained to me that she was honoring synchronistic signs that kept her "on a schedule" and that slowing down for everyone else had been the problem. I could relate. I'd also felt frustrated in the psychotherapy group at times, because the agreed-upon pace felt hesitant, doubtful, and slow, causing me to discount intuitive signals and "miss the bus" on guidance from the Universe that felt aligned with my inner sense of flow.

What if she thrived at an unusually high pace and frequency? What if honoring and staying aligned with her idiosyncratic pace and path is not necessarily a bad thing? If she could go to the farthest edges of sanity and find her way back to a peaceful center, I could learn to join her on these journeys and return to my center, too. And, whenever I sped up to her pace, it ended up dislodging me out of my idle mode and helping me too. I always felt lighter and better afterward.

I was running out of excuses and needed to commit to this new course of action if I really cared about doing what was best for her. Every step of our journey so far had felt 100 percent right. The rocks that obstructed Paloma's stream were now in my stream, and it was my job to begin to clear them, not hers.

That's when it dawned on me that these rocks may not be *my* fears either but unexamined cultural fears that kept all of us small. What if *my* intuitive impulses toward liberation weren't just mine, but signposts along our collective soul path that are better aligned with our true nature than what I'd learned as a clinical psychologist? Is this what Jung meant when he said that synchronistic signs were meaningful coincidences that could crack the "rationalistic shell" of the modern scientific mind, busting the myth that material sciences only could discover all there's to know about the Universe? These synchronic signs seemed perfectly choreographed, regulated, and timed by a mysterious guiding force that operated according to a "cosmic clock" on a soul realm.

I didn't learn about Jung in my program. One of my professors, prominent and outspoken, said that Jungian theories were not supported by scientific evidence and were woo-woo. If that were true, I was chin deep in woo-woo. Could I be accused of deliberately violating ethical guidelines if I proceeded on this path that felt more right than any path I'd been on? The thought of it alone blurred my mind with fear. Is this what Paloma meant when she said that living in fear forever was the real threat to be concerned about? Did her adamant refusal to do so allow her to break free?

Chapter 15

 # THE GIFT

There is no greater agony than bearing an untold story inside of you.
—Maya Angelou

THE MORNING BEFORE OUR next session, I rummaged through my home office looking for a birthday card. Instead, I accidentally pulled out two index cards that I'd collected years before when I was looking for empowering quotes for my multicultural immersion course, each adorned with pretty calligraphy. They read:

> *The most important thing one woman can do for another is to illuminate and expand her sense of actual possibilities.*
> —Adrienne Rich

> *When I dare to be powerful—*
> *To use my strength in service of my vision,*
> *Then it becomes less and less important*
> *whether I am afraid.*
> —Audre Lorde

Gulp. I threw the cards in my purse, certain that they were a sign. While driving to work, I decided to check in with Paloma first before saying anything about them. When we met, she continued where we had left off the week before, as if we'd never parted.

"I understand what you said about the risk of exploiting me, but I went through my entire journal, and there really isn't anything in it that suggests that I ever felt that," she said. She was thorough and impeccable. That moment, I realized that I trusted her self-scrutinizing and feedback more than anyone else's. So far, they'd been the most consistent with my own.

"I'm glad to hear that and I appreciate that you took the time to double-check. The last few days, I consulted with a few of my colleagues about our work together, and they recommended that we slow things down a bit just to be safe. I wonder what your thoughts are on this," I asked.

"It's confusing and frustrating to me when people say that, because fast and slow are not opposites to me. In slowing down and becoming really still inside, I land in timelessness where the future, present, and past converge and all seem to be moving very fast in the now. What most people see as moving fast slows my awareness down. I see it as being busier, more frantic and distracted and less perceptive. I don't want to slow my development down anymore. But, by slowing down outside distractions, I'm able to make shifts at a very fast pace. When I'm doing something that's not challenging me at my edge or good for me, my chest constricts. Not being able to shift faster is making my chest constrict," she said.

"In that case, we won't be slowing down your progress. I'll do all that I can to keep up with your pace," I said.

"Great! That feels like a relief," she said.

"Good. Glad we're on the same page. Other than this, how has your week been?"

"Really exciting. I can't wait to tell you about a new spirit guide I met a few days ago, *La Mujer del Arcoiris*, the Woman of the Rainbow. She's my soul structure and is offering me grounding. In my meditation, she took me to large mesas of yellow and red cracked clay. The view widened step by step without dwarfing the importance of each tenacious rock lining the ascent. The path up was spontaneous. At the top, I felt the wide, blue bigness of the view. I couldn't focus on the expansiveness and possibilities. They whirled in colors and lacked depth and complexity in the middle between where I stood and infinite destiny. I was a little rock on a huge path. I sensed my direction, importance, potential, but not my purpose.

"She's helping me to build a structure within so I can revolutionize structures on the outside and showed me a beginning-end. I sensed it weeks ago, but wasn't ready to turn my head around to see the plateau and perceive its offerings. *La arcoiris*, the rainbow, prompted me to pick an end, too. These are signs that urge me to turn my head and incorporate what I learned on the mesa," she said.

"That's great," I said. It was hard to catch my breath and have my befuddled mind digest what she just shared. Would it benefit her to know about my Rainbow Crystal Woman guide or was this uncanny coincidence just for me to tap for strength and reassurance? What beginning-end? The beginning-end of college and our work together? And what did she mean with turning her head around? Was that like my U-turn? Or did she realize that there was no endpoint to rush to, that the answers that she was looking for would unfold by grounding and going deeper and simultaneously expanding further out in the present moment, like I realized when sitting with my tree in Tilden Park? I didn't ask her for more clarification, because I didn't want her to slow down for me. I challenged myself to trust my impressions.

"These cards crossed my path this morning. Sharing them with you feels like removing yet another rock from the stream. It feels right to take a stand next to you and help you discover your purpose, even if that makes the flow of the stream move faster and become more unpredictable for me," I said while giving her the cards.

This gesture was, on the one hand, personal, clandestine, and subtle in its execution, but, on the other, liberating, radical, and revolutionary in what it represented. I was both terrified and filled with so much power, I could combust.

Paloma examined the cards while sliding to the floor, her back against the sofa.

"Hmm, Audre Lorde has been calling out to me as a guide. I'm writing about her in one of my classes," she said.

"Right after running into these cards, I went through some other writing and papers and found this poem. I wrote it about three years ago after attending a spiritual retreat. The day I found my office, I was meditating at a spot in Tilden park with a beautiful view over the Golden Gate Bridge and imagined clients like you finding me," I said.

She took the piece of paper that I handed her, and quietly read the following lines:

> "Fire in the soulful eyes of White Wolf
> calling out
> 'Is anyone home?'
>
> Soft voices from under beds and dark closets
> whispering back
> 'Here I am, wait, please, don't go . . .'
>
> They are indigo children of their own generation,
> each one too early for her or his time,
> no longer hiding, no longer aching
>
> Reaching for the arms of White Buffalo Calf Woman,
> Buddha, Rumi, and Christ
>
> They bless the chameleon children of future generations,
> new hopes that are no longer alone nor afraid,
> complete surrender in their graceful dance backward
> down the transcendent rainbow path above.

"I know that I'll be in many futures to come, but this is a lovely gift in the present. Thank you. I've had visions of the Golden Gate Bridge all week. That's making a lot more sense now," she said pensively.

As soon as I heard about Paloma's visions of the Golden Gate Bridge, something clicked and I was reminded of the *Rainbow*

Bridge to the Golden Era as described by Brooke Medicine Eagle. Is that what she meant with being in many futures to come?

"I'm so glad that this makes sense to you, because this is the first time I've trusted my intuition in a psychotherapy setting to do something as far out as this, and, in all honesty, it's a bit scary," I said while watching her move her lips in tandem with mine.

"Oh my God, I can lip you! I knew what you were going to say before you even said it," she said, beside herself.

Oh my God is right! went through my mind after our session had ended. Now what? You're playing with fire and don't know what you're doing. Therapy is to help your clients individuate, not melt into one with you. Especially not someone like Paloma, who's the queen of chameleons. How will you explain what you're doing to someone reviewing your notes?

I felt drawn to a holistic healing newsletter that I found on my lunch table, and flipped to an advertisement page of healers, psychics, and coaches. *Why not refer Paloma to a psychic for a second opinion? Even if the information provided by a psychic doesn't technically "count" and would be frowned upon by many of your colleagues, you could use an out-of-the-box perspective.*

"Yes, this is Loraine," I said to Kay, wondering how I could secretly size her up for Paloma. "I am interested in referring a client to you who is an exceptionally bright, young college student and seems to be psychically gifted. She is often misunderstood by peers and professors in her academic community, and I haven't felt comfortable talking about her in my consultation group out of fear that they will misdiagnose and pathologize her," I said.

"I noticed a parallel process between her issues and my own professional and personal growth, and, in deciding the next step for her, a referral to you, I've come to realize that it may be the next step for me as well," I said. "Do you know of any other psychics in the area that you could recommend?" I asked. "I'm somewhat uncomfortable with the idea that I would be seeing the same psychic although it would not be the same as seeing the same therapist,

I suppose. I am just trying to minimize the possibility of any ethical dilemmas, dual relationships, boundary violations, conflicts of interests, and the like, as this is all very new to me."

"The two good psychics who I know have moved on to different careers. One of them became an artist and the other one entered the ministry. The good ones usually don't do this for very long," Kay said.

"I have personally not felt a conflict of interest or a dilemma when I see clients and their therapists. I maintain strict boundaries and keep all communications confidential and private. The clients often take their tapes to their sessions and either play all or parts of it to their therapists. It has often enhanced self-understanding and therapist-understanding of their issues and the therapy."

"Do they know that their therapists are seeing you as well?" I asked.

"Sometimes. In referring them to me, the therapist may say that this is someone who I see on occasion for my own psychic and spiritual growth if the client has some fears or reservations about seeing a psychic. Since the visits are often one-time, there is little risk of dual relationships, and the like."

"So, do you want to book an appointment for yourself?" Kay asked me gently after a short pause.

"Yeah, let's go ahead and book it. I have gotten some synchronicities myself and have avoided seeing a psychic, but there is no avoiding it anymore," I said, withholding as much information as I could to set the test up right.

It was easy to miss Kay's home in the Oakland hills. There were no neon lights or images of crystal balls or palms, just a nameplate on the door that said Kay Taylor.

She answered the door with a broad smile and quietly guided me through a short corridor and into a small, warmly lit study with an oak bookcase, desk, and common knickknacks. With a hand gesture, she invited me to sit a few feet across from her on a cushy, beige sofa. I took a quick glance around the cozy room while she nestled into her afghan-covered chair. I looked for signs but could not detect anything that would make her or this space distinctly "psychic."

Kay folded her legs in a meditative lotus position and informed me that she was going to record the session for me.

Click. Next I knew, she had closed her eyes and drifted into an altered state.

"Please relax and say your name, like you normally say it, three times for me."

"Loraine Van Tuyl . . . Loraine Van Tuyl . . . Loraine Van Tuyl," I said.

Kay's humming and graceful hand movements traced the invisible auras around my body. She reminded me of the fairy god-mother who gave Cinderella a makeover with her magic wand. Her waving fingers activated an inner orchestra of energy and physical sensations that I had previously only experienced through actual touch. As I went inward and focused on these feelings, I realized for the first time why a session with a psychic was called a "read-ing." I too tried to read what was going on but wasn't getting a whole lot.

Kay was a speed-reader, trying to wrap words as fast as she could around each insight. They seemed to be coming in at a higher frequency than her brain, mouth, tongue, and lips were able to capture and express. In one breath, with much inflection and eyes still closed, she relayed the following message:

"This is the first year of a nine-year cycle for you . . . this year is a bridge of letting go of the old, bringing in the new . . ." Kay said. I thought of Paloma's beginning-end and our recent conversation about the Golden Gate Bridge.

"Now, when I'm looking at your energy field, I actually see that you have a lot of psychic ability, like really a lot, you men-tioned on the phone that you got some synchronicities, but the energy around the sixth chakra, the clairvoyant vision, is quite strong with a lot of spokes of energy, and the throat chakra, which of course you would use in your work in terms of communica-tion skills, also has a very strong telepathic quality, so you're in fact picking up a lot of information on a regular basis whether you understand exactly how you're picking it up or not," Kay said. She had my full attention now.

"And there's a really strong sense that it is part of the new cycle that you are going into . . . that a deepening of your spiritual awareness is coming through, and that's the place that is going to pull a lot of these pieces of yourself together," she said, sitting back as if relieved to get a big chunk of insight out of her system.

She paused for a moment and waved her hand and arm up and down the length of my spine to the top of my head. When she got to my navel area, my core, her fingertips wiggled and circled in the air as if she was reading Braille, and, with a cheerful hum, she retraced her fingertip steps, as if making sure she read the information right.

"And you also have a very large heart. There's just a sense of open-heartedness, a great sense of compassionate wisdom. I can see that you've been working on yourself, but there are still some places that have been challenging for you, around sense of power, like your own personal power, self-esteem, and emotions, so those are areas that I notice that you're still integrating. I'm also noticing that you're very psychic on the empathic level, meaning that you pick up other people's feelings a lot and sometimes those energies make inroads into your auras. So, working on boundaries just in your day-to-day life scenarios and in terms of the work you're doing would be more and more helpful."

Paloma was right on when yellow—related to the third chakra and personal power—had appeared in her reading of me.

"I know that you know boundaries on a mental and physical level, what that means and how to work with them, but, on an energetic level, my sense is that you need to work with the left-hand side of your aura a lot, making the boundaries stronger, giving yourself a little bit more space there. The edge of the aura, instead of being smooth, has these really tiny rivulet lines coming into it."

Her insights moved me deeply, and each one triggered my own flashes of insight. I could feel the weakness of my left side. It was my intuitive, feminine side, and it felt clumsy and underdeveloped, because I was worried about using it. I had come to believe that absorbing some of the negative energy of others was the curse to this blessing, the natural byproduct of being intimately connected. It never occurred to me that I could strengthen the porous boundaries between our murky puddles to protect myself.

"Now, I'll let you ask the questions about this part to see what it's about, but I'm noticing that as we enter into the area of the path of soul and karmic purpose—the grounding of who you are in this incarnation—there is a sense that you're at a turning point here. The energy feels a little bit constricted, like you're feeling a push to move into a new direction, but the exact direction of the path is not completely open or clear yet. So, I will work with the healing energy on that to create a little bit more spaciousness around that particular issue."

She opened her eyes, and asked, "So how can I assist you today? What brings you to me exactly?" presenting herself in a way that I was more accustomed to.

"Well, that hit the nail on the head!" I said, in awe.

By now, she had convinced me that her reading was nothing like what you might find in a monthly horoscope. I also realized that she was not only a psychic: she was also a healer. I felt more seen and validated after this tiny bit of soul revelation than after all my previous years in therapy.

"Perhaps this may answer your previous question, but it feels as if my life recently flipped inside out. About three years ago, I started to get more peak experiences that had a mystical quality to them, and I felt that it was important to record them. At the time they were happening, they felt like unique, one-time experiences, but, most recently, a pattern emerged. I started to connect the dots, and a mythical story line emerged and rose to the surface and my normal life, sense of identity, and usual thinking began to fade into the background. I suppose it's similar to discovering that we're not human beings having a spiritual experience but spiritual beings having a human experience," I said, contemplating Pierre Teilhard de Chardin's famous quote.

"This feeling of being a soul and spiritual being first and foremost is so huge, it almost feels blasphemous and presumptuous to articulate it. It has to do with the way in which I received the earth name of my spirit guide, Rainbow Crystal Woman, who I learned is the modern incarnation of the most revered Lakota messiah, White Buffalo Calf Woman. I'm feeling her presence and her push to write my life story, something I imagined doing since I was a kid. I feel called to expose the ways in which the world and mental health field are unwittingly keeping us small with their double binds. It's making the holistic, intuitive work that I'm doing feel wrong and unethical.

"I'm originally from Suriname, which is in the Amazon region above Brazil, and lived close to the ancient ways. I'm reclaiming them through these struggles and have a feeling that there's an intergenerational aspect to this that goes back further. I have gotten guidance from ancestors on a few occasions."

"I got a big rush of energy on that for you. You really do run that line of energy through your body. It's a very important part of who you are, letting the ancient teachings come through your structure," she said.

"Telepathy is the ability to receive messages from people or from spirit, and to send them also, in a fairly clear way. You can develop that to be stronger so that you know when it's happening and are aware when you're receiving a message versus when you're thinking something. You can learn to understand some of the visions that come to your mind, little visions that pop up, things that you see, to understand more clearly where they're coming from and what they're saying."

I nodded and knew exactly what she was talking about.

"When you visualize, how clear are your visualizations? Have you done much visualization or meditation work to strengthen your boundaries?" Kay asked.

"Not very much. I seem to get in trouble a lot for speaking in metaphor and being unclear. I have recently started to see some white light in the periphery of my vision while meditating in the steam room of my gym in an attempt to recreate the powerful sweat lodge experience that I had at the Lakota retreat a few years ago. Because most of my visions spontaneously pop up into my consciousness, I hadn't associated them with visualization or meditation work," I said.

"Give yourself a little bit more space to strengthen your boundaries, because sometimes in the world you don't feel comfortable taking up big space, and you're going to be doing that. So, expanding. Right now, your aura is about a foot and a half on either side of your body and you want to visualize that it's more like two to three feet wide, over the top and under the feet, also kind of like an egg shape. And pay attention to the front and the back, and, on that left side especially, play a little bit with different colors and frequencies and structures to create the kind of boundary that allows you to feel that you can still be empathic to people and feel what's going on with them," Kay said, introducing me to an entirely new way of looking at myself and the world.

"I'm also feeling that some meditation with the sun would be beneficial for you, to stand outside, barefoot, palms facing toward the sun, and visualizing the sun's rays coming through the top of your head, through your palms, and into the power chakra. That will enable you to receive and hold some of that ancient light in you. So those are some things that are very specific to you that I'm not normally saying to other people. That will bring it through," she said.

"That's cool. The sun healed and cleared my heart chakra when I was pregnant with my second child. I made a body cast where my belly was the earth with the tree of life and its roots connected to my daughter's navel. My breasts were the stars and moon. The sun radiated from my heart chakra with invigorating strokes and rays of luminous, loving golden light glowing in every direction," I said, feeling the sun's rays once again on me and moving through me, now nourishing my power center.

Kay smiled at the acknowledgement.

"As all the other pieces come in balance and your power chakra enlarges to match the heart, you're going to feel more comfortable in your skin. Right now, your heart is your largest chakra, followed by the sixth chakra, vision, and the other ones are more along the same lines, of an average or normal size, but the heart chakra is particularly open, and it seems to me from the way that it's large and not quite aligned with the power chakra that you would feel uncomfortable in a lot of situations in the world," Kay added.

"I wasn't expecting this, but it's really validating," I said, my eyes tearing and my throat constricting with emotion. "It explains the double bind I've been in my whole life in finding some sort of equilibrium along the power dimension. Part of me always feels pulled to expand my power to match my heart and visions, but, especially in graduate school, I feared that I'd come across as grandiose and narcissistic, even delusional, if I expanded to a size that was more comfortable for me. But when I remained 'average size' and tried to fit in with the norm, it also felt wrong and insincere. I ended up feeling like a fraud for faking that I was smaller than I really was. This insight finally convinces me to be my authentic self," I said, feeling a tremendous sense of relief. My two little buffaloes from Mt. Shasta came to mind. They'd given me the same message. I choked up. Loving guides have been around me my entire life.

"Yes, I see where it has been challenging for you to find people who really resonate with you on your heart level. You have a lot of capability of loving and of compassionate wisdom, and it looks to me that you sometimes come across energies that are so incompatible with who you are that you don't quite understand the frequencies that other people are running through their heart. The way you run heart energy is expansive, clear, unconditional, and the people I see in your life are often much more linear, much less evolved with their hearts. They're more protective, guarded, not really quite at that same frequency.

"At the heart level . . . I don't see that they're coming from the same place. I don't see the match. They may not be able to understand, accept, and integrate your impact on them for another three to five years, and you may never see it. When you come into your own power, you'll find people who match you better at the heart level. And I feel that you'll do this quickly, in a year or two years."

Thoughts were swirling in my head as I tried to grab and hold onto her words. She was referring to the psychotherapy group. How could she possibly know all this?

"Because you have this big heart and this intuitive sense, you feel very deeply the truth of who people are. A lot of times, when we're healers, and I see this with myself and with my clients who are powerful and gifted healers, there's a tendency for us to see the best in people, we often read and feel and see the soul-level connection and expect it to map out into a relationship in the world, but a lot of times those other people are not ready. Patience is the word that I get for you around relationships."

Patience? I would never have considered practicing patience in regard to conflict with colleagues without feeling more certain that I was losing it, sounding out-of-touch, arrogant, and condescending.

"The other thing that I'm noticing is that on a spiritual level, as I said, your sixth chakra is very large, with long spokes coming out of it. It's unusually powerful on that level, so your ability to be a visionary, to see clearly, is very powerful, but you have not quite tapped into all of the layers of who you are spiritually in the crown chakra and all the layers above the crown chakra, so I would suggest working on that in your meditation. You need to visualize the crown kind of like a satellite dish opening and then go up another layer, like a foot above it, and then pay attention to another layer a foot above it. I would work with three layers to start and ultimately work up to seven layers for you. And then take your attention as high as you can imagine out in the universe so you can connect to the highest source of the God/Goddess energy. Also bring in the lineage that you know from your country and that runs through your line. Pay attention, because right now, it's sitting up there as your unrealized potential, and it filters; only little pieces of it are coming in," Kay said.

"I'm so pleasantly surprised by all of this. So many points you hit on resonate deeply and are encouraging me to pursue shamanic training and consciousness studies. I now fully trust that I need to move in this direction to explore my untapped potential and not wait any longer. After continuously being told that I'm moving too fast, it's refreshing to hear you point out where I've felt slow, stifled, and stuck. Visualizing and sensing the soaring heights that you opened up for me cleared up a lot of those stuck feelings," I said, realizing that she had removed a bunch of rocks out of the stream. It was now up to me to follow up with action.

"If you start to work with that visual of bringing the energy of the heavens and earth in and holding it in your power chakra and developing the crown chakra," Kay continued, "it will solidify another psychic level, a deep sense of knowing. Developing more clarity within those three, the crown, the visionary, and personal power centers, will help you in your life and in your work," she said.

"And that brings me to the place of the writing, the writing of the story of who you are and where you come from, and that feels absolutely right on, that feels like a starting point in your journey in this lifetime, and it also feels like it's difficult at this time to keep up with what you're meant to do, so sort of like you're going ahead as fast as you can, but having to slow down."

"Yeah, I feel like I'm behind and trying to catch up, but moving too fast at the same time. It's a weird feeling," I said.

"I can see that," Kay replied with deep belly laughs, as if she fondly remembered that time in her own life.

"So, just keep asking spirit for assistance on that, to keep helping you to integrate the frequencies to be ready, and give yourself some space, some regular space for the writing. I feel that at this point you have now accepted that this is your mission and that you're going to do it. It feels like the last three years have sort of been more like wiggling around it, maybe that's my mission, but ah, nah, that would not be right for me. So that's coming through in this new cycle," Kay said.

"Yeah, that's it. I have felt very torn, because the ancient Lakota teachings have been so helpful in revealing my true calling, my guides, and soul-purpose. Nothing else has come close to meeting me in this way. But at the same time, the Red Road doesn't feel right to me. I feel drawn to a rainbow path, but no one seems to see that as a legitimate spiritual discipline. It's dismissed as New Age-y, dabbling, shallow," I said.

"It sounds like you're running into masculine thought structures, and the way in which you run heart energy is more expansive, more feminine, more intuitive, organic, spontaneous," Kay said to my surprise. "I know an indigenous Medicine Woman with a very big heart who can help you with the issues particularly related to the Lakota-inspired group. Her name is Mary Attu, and I'm sure that she won't mind if I give you her number," Kay said.

Click.

My half hour was up. Kay asked if I wanted to continue, but I had more than enough to digest. Tim's Bird Nest Warrior Lore had given me the impression that he had realigned his offerings with a divine feminine flow. Wow. It never occurred to me that the structure was still masculine and rigid.

"For you, definitely, I'd say to develop your gifts," Kay reiterated as we ended. "They'll help you with your work with people, and they'll also help you with the writing, because my sense is that the writing is psychic channeled writing. Some of it is what you know and remember, but some of it is bringing through a gift, which is the word they want me to use, a gift of knowledge and wisdom that passes through your line."

Wow. Did that really happen? I drove home feeling like I was still hovering in a dream, my power center slowly expanding as I mulled over Kay's reading. I was so astonished and enthralled by Kay's psychic gifts, it never occurred to me that I could ask her about Paloma and our dynamic. Second thought, not having any information on Paloma before they met in person was probably best.

One question lingered in my mind.

Who are 'they'? *My ancestors?*

Chapter 16

 **DARK NIGHT**

A woman, searching for her self, must descend to her own depths . . . into a damp, echoing cavern, to sit and wait for that of her self which cannot be met in the upper world. To discover who she is, a woman must trust the places of darkness where she can meet her own deepest nature and give it voice . . . weaving the threads of her life into a fabric to be named and given.
—Judith Duerk

EACH PASSING DAY FOLLOWING my reading, Kay's words sank in a bit deeper and stretched my narrow mind a little wider, causing my intuitive impressions of Paloma's extraordinary abilities to seem less freaky and far out. I felt optimistic that she would affirm what I'd sensed all along but often couldn't put into words or prove—that Paloma was exceptionally perceptive and that my fears and ambivalence about fully owning my truth and power in my professional role were only holding her back.

"Have you ever considered seeing a psychic?" I asked Paloma during our next session.

"I think about it all the time! It would be an adventure to see a psychic!" she said.

"Do you know any good ones? If not, I could refer you to someone who seems legit," I said.

"I'll take the referral. I've never met a psychic," she responded.

"Let me know what you think of her," I said, and wrote Kay's number on a piece of paper.

When we met again, Paloma had already met with Kay. As empowering and uplifting as my reading was to me, I needed it to pale in comparison to Paloma's for this second-opinion experiment to pass my test and validate my intuitive read of her.

"How did it go?" I asked Paloma.

She teared up, closed her eyes, and held her hand to her stomach before speaking. "I can read minds. I don't have the feelings that normal people have. Sometimes, I don't feel human, because I seem so different than other people who don't know what I'm talking about and think I'm bragging. When I look at my body, it's as if this isn't truly who I am. I think I have memories of where we all came from that are more accessible to me than to other people," she said.

"That must be hard and lonely," I said.

"It is. And it's hard to figure out who owns what in a relationship, because boundaries are much more fluid in this reality," she said.

"You can tell me if you feel confused in here. We'll untangle it and also explore where it's still happening in your life. This space is for you, and I'm here to support you," I said. She seemed relieved.

"The reading was very helpful. It's just kind of weird and daunting to discover that I have such powerful gifts. Kay said that my upper chakras were 'picture perfect' and asked me if I wanted to attend her intuition workshop. There were a lot of experienced meditators and psychics in there. It was pretty exhilarating," Paloma said.

Bingo. That's what I needed to hear. I wasn't able to read minds. I thought of myself as human and from planet earth, my upper chakras were far from picture perfect, and I wasn't invited to the workshop. I couldn't imagine the intensity of Paloma's experiences if the slivers of light and intuitive insight that filtered through my upper chakras were already so hard to contain. Paloma's feedback about the reading was, on the one hand, affirming and cathartic, but on the other hand, tantalizing and aggravating my straitjacketed spirit. It revved up like an engine, wanting me to take greater leaps of faith. The heightened vibrations crumbled my protective armor and caused it to drop onto the ground in bits and pieces.

Kay cleared blocks from Paloma's energetic field, just like she'd done with me, allowing her to step out of her comfort zone. She was sharing more of her true self with others, including me, and listed the many small and big shifts that had occurred since the reading.

"I found a place of balance between feeling manic and depressed, because being elated and happy all the time was not the answer either. I learned to use my body and the stream to absorb despair and depression, and I can now turn anxious energy into peace," she said proudly.

"That's wonderful," I said, relieved for her but anxious what this meant for me. Her infectious, free-flowing energy was inspiring me to wiggle closer to the edge of my fear and caused my jittery body to tighten as if anticipating a parachute jump.

"I want to tell you that I thought a lot about your questions and the difference between my needs and your needs. I wrote two pages on it, because it's something that confuses me a lot in relationships," she said then paused, scrutinizing my reaction. I nodded for her to go on.

"I feel like I need to go slower," she said.

"For me to understand?" I asked.

She looked down.

"What don't I understand?" I asked.

"That at a certain point, there's no distinction between my needs and your needs," she said. "My purpose in life is to be of service and receive a sign what someone needs from me in any given moment, whether it's the person sitting next to me on the bus, a friend, or a teacher. I don't have other goals and needs that are just mine when it comes to the big things. When I give to others what they need, I fulfill my own needs," she said.

That moment, it was crystal clear that rejecting her gifts would hinder her growth and potential rather than protect her from my harmful impulses.

"I understand what you mean and you're right that I'm the one who's off, causing you to second-guess yourself. The assumption is that our clients are always more troubled and less aware and awake than we, psychotherapists, are. I still fall into that trap of thinking, even though I disagree with it and don't think it does either one of us any good. You're clearer, more courageous and more expansive than I am, especially in this context, and you don't need to hold back for me," I said.

"I run into this dilemma with everyone I meet, and it's especially confusing with professors. It's helpful that we're looking at it with full consciousness," she said.

"Good," I said, again feeling much calmer after speaking my truth and validating hers.

"Kay's workshop was exhausting but also very profound. It was comforting to see similar eyes. In the morning, we learned to ground and extend ourselves upwards, and I was usually a step ahead of the prompt and went to the upward space that I knew was home. I felt very comfortable and powerful and peaceful there but also homesick when we needed to leave. I got bored or distracted or checked out during the meditation scripts, because I was instantly already there. Paradoxically, I wanted to go a lot slower in working with the lower chakras and with the spirit guides affecting survival, emotion, and the power regions. Talking about the lower chakras made me feel anxious, because I do affect others a lot by being so big and am still figuring out how to let all that go and just let myself be," Paloma said.

"That's no surprise, given the erratic and frightened way people have reacted to you. You seem much more aware of your power and how it affects people now. It sounds like your friends and family have lately felt empowered rather than intimidated by it. I have a feeling that it will only get better with practice," I said.

"I'm starting to see that. My final paper was written in response to Audre Lorde's essay, 'The Transformation of Silence into Language and Action.' My thoughts and feelings just flowed out of me, and it felt good not to hold back. My professor loves it and wants to publish it in her anthology. I also wrote it for you. I brought you a copy," she said, then reached in her backpack and handed me a copy of her paper.

"It's wonderful that everything seems to be falling into place and giving you closure right before your graduation. And thank you so much for thinking of me. I look forward to reading it," I said.

After I'd picked the kids up from afterschool care and they were busy playing, I settled into a cozy corner on the sofa, eager to decipher what in the world Paloma could have written for me and her professor.

In her paper, Paloma discussed the whys and ways in which she had succumbed to structures and "spider webs" of power and oppression. She carefully weighed her options as she climbed out of the maze toward liberation, each sentence forming a rung on a rope ladder.

"How, Audre Lorde, do I balance on this razor-sharp edge between the abyss and paralysis of fear, the suffocating oblivion of silence, and this highly visible and potentially life-threatening freedom of speech?" Paloma pleaded once on higher ground. She explored all possible escape routes and strategies and decided that no longer seeing death as a barrier or a threat to be avoided felt most freeing.

"I venture to wonder how we can say for sure that Death is the ultimate silence. Lorde speaks to me across time, space, and death. She profoundly shapes the course of my life. . . . Our speech is a revolutionary act no matter if it is bruised and mutilated. It is the only hope we have, and we have nothing to lose that won't be lost in death anyway," she reiterated.

Her words serenaded and seduced me out of my cozy hiding place. *Our speech is a revolutionary act no matter if it is bruised and mutilated. It is the only hope we have. We have nothing to lose. I have nothing to lose. I have nothing to lose that won't be lost in death anyway.*

These phrases played on repeat in my mind while a bird pecked incessantly on the window of our vaulted ceiling, as if helping to crack open my coconut skull. This unusual and mysterious pecking lasted about an hour the day before, and there was no indication that the bird, attacking its own reflection, would stop anytime soon.

My heart and soul surrendered to the beat of the bird's drumming, leaving my mind to fend for itself as it began to bounce between different realms of consciousness, part of me spiraling deeper down in the now and part of me spiraling up into higher realms. I remembered being killed in one of my dreams as a child and waking up no longer afraid of being chased and dying, which stopped the nightmares. It seemed as if Paloma was guiding me to the same epiphany with her paper.

My transcendent self was willing to take whatever risks necessary to leap forward and take flight, but the self with my feet firmly planted on the ground was terrified that I was dangling my entire career on a thin, invisible, intuitive thread and was about to plunge to my death.

My convictions and fears were swirling around one another like soft vanilla and chocolate ice cream in a cone, peaking into this very moment. This was the ultimate test. Which flavor would I choose, and how could I separate one from the other?

I had caught up with Paloma and imagined sitting next to her on that razor-sharp edge, too wobbly to stand up, let alone balance. Now what? Out of nowhere, rage began to brew inside of me. I no longer wanted to be a part of this. I'd never asked for this. I wanted everything to go back to normal. I'd paid my dues, worked hard to turn my life around, excelled in school and graduated with honors, expecting that it would be smooth sailing after that. There must have been some kind of mix-up, handing me the wrong cards. Where could I return them?

An overwhelming urge to call Paloma swelled inside of me. I couldn't; of course I couldn't. I was her therapist, not her client. Calling her for help would be the most unthinkable, inappropriate role reversal for me to indulge in. How could she possibly help me and how dare I consider burdening her with my problems?

I read through the rest of her paper, desperate for answers and a reality check. I found it in her conclusive words on page ten.

"This vocabulary (in Audre Lorde's paper) gifts me the strength I need to actualize all the people that I am inside and coordinate their voices into poetry to which other human beings can hold onto when they're exhausted and almost drowning."

That was my green light. This line reminded me of the discussions we had about her ability to psychically tune into, empathize with, and identify with people around her, almost as if she'd lived lives like theirs hundreds of times before. I had no tangible proof that this was a sign, but I felt it so clearly in my gut, I was willing to bet my career on it. I filled up with the knowing that living in fear and in limbo was not going to cut it, and I was done with all the wavering and skirting around my intuition.

The continuous pecking had put my domineering cognitive mind under a spell, making it much easier to trust my impressions; Paloma had intentionally infused her writing with aching, lyrical prose to allure my soul. She wrote this for me and others like me, because she knew that once we started to remove some of the rocks out of the stream, we could get swept up by its powerful current. She was encouraging us to be brave and intentionally giving us a heads-up and life raft of insightful and transformative poetry to prevent us from drowning.

Tired of my objections and excuses, I picked up the phone and called her.

"I just finished reading your paper. I don't know why I'm calling other than to tell you that I'm standing on that razor edge, frozen in fear. It feels like I have zero margin of error and any little misstep can become a grave mistake, no matter which way I go. At the same time, I feel like there is no turning back. Even this call could be that dreadful, unforgiveable mistake, the first nail on my professional coffin. Yet every part of my being is convinced that this is what I need to do this very moment," I said.

As if expecting my call, Paloma listened quietly, then loaded and roared these five words—"*I will never abandon you*,"—over the phone and throughout my being, sounding like the voice of God thundering through the heavens. An upsurge of tears and emotion welled to the rim of my heart and spirit, moved by the power of her fullest expression. Its force lit me up and expanded my insides until they felt like my outstretched lungs after a series of deep breathing exercises.

"This is the God that lives in each of us, shut down by religious crusaders, colonizers, and science over the centuries," she said matter-of-factly. I was too mystified and stunned to speak, grateful that she wasn't expecting me to and seemingly aware that it would take some time for me to integrate the tsunami that just moved through me. I mumbled some words of appreciation and hung up.

I turned my computer on and clutched onto my writing for direction. It felt as if I'd pierced through some sort of ozone layer and entered a forbidden danger zone. Paloma was right. I wasn't abandoned and alone, contrary to what my annihilation terror and every colluding molecule in my body seemed to believe. The God-like energy that Paloma had transmitted to me had saturated every nook and cranny in my soul. Is this what she called home?

Was this good or bad? A step forward or backward from where I was before? From where she was before? I couldn't tell. The linear trajectory that I'd been so used to didn't exist in this space. Good, bad, confusing, weird, mysterious, and crazy simultaneously intensified and subsided along this path that was completely void of logic. Nonetheless, I dared to stick with my intuition that this was the very next best step or I wouldn't have taken the risk.

After months of relative quiet, the women of my online *hunka* family had started to email one another with exciting updates. Many planned to attend our upcoming retreat. I too looked forward to our reunion in Connecticut.

"Birds! Birds, our winged relatives, are everywhere. Great Spirit is with us," *Unci* Deb, one of elders, wrote.

I filled up with delight. I'd forgotten how good our spontaneous, synchronistic experiences and special connection felt, consistently able to reassure me that I wasn't crazy. I wrote my heart out in an email and sent it to the whole group.

I sit here crying like a waterfall as I read your emails about your bird encounters and reflect on our bird nest warrior fast and lore. A bird is pecking on my window, as if begging me to let Spirit in. This path would have been so much more difficult without you. Perhaps if I were on the East Coast with all of you, a "next step" would have revealed itself in a sacred ceremony, but I'm not with you yet. Spirit seems to be working through me nevertheless, long distance. The scary, really daunting part of all this for me is a strange knowing that the reason for the distance between us serves as a cosmic test, its purpose to trigger my anguish and self-doubt that I am delusional, crazy, or on a huge ego-trip. I need to become more clear and confident to overcome it and to fully embrace my life purpose.

As much as I long to be near you, I get a sense that I need to show how Spirit can work directly with people's heart and soul. It's exactly this unreliable, bias-prone "personal experience" and intuitive knowing that's a no-no within my field and could get me in trouble. When I'm here alone, every step and breath along my way involve this question, is this indigo or ego directing me? I have no one to give me the answers, it is between Spirit and me, and deep trust. But if it's all in my mind and just based on personal experience, what would distinguish me from someone really mad? How do I reconcile the gap between my deep trust in Spirit, the one thing I cannot live without, and my connection to a world and people who do not share this deep trust? Which one do I give up or jeopardize? It's a conundrum that I don't want, never asked for, but have been granted.

It feels right for me, and I can breathe my way through it, but, at the same time, I feel so alone and

*confused, and, today, for the first time, I felt really angry
at Spirit for putting me in this position and continuing to
raise the bar. There's no way back, no other way, all I can
do is keep breathing and keep going. I cannot silence this
relentless calling, yet I feel totally unworthy—unprepared,
small, daunted—in accepting it. It's so powerful, it makes
me feel like I am losing all connection with the real world. I
keep trying to find a place of balance between the two, but
I have a strong premonition that I need to heed Spirit. I'm
so glad to join you all in a few days, to be in a community
that gets me, and that can help me see more clearly.*

The responses from the women in the group were generous
and nurturing. One of them, *Unci* Grace, sent me this passage
from Marianne Williamson's, *A Return to Love:* "Our deepest fear
is not that we are inadequate. Our deepest fear is that we are powerful beyond measure."

Her words rang true and began to puncture through the
transparent illusion of my fears. I'd never considered the real reasons for my fears until she said it.

Another *Unci* alluded to Rumi's collection of poems, *A Moth
to the Flame.* I wasn't clear if she was implying that being consumed
by fire and burning misaligned parts of the self was a good thing,
a necessary thing or something to be cautious of, but I appreciated
the depth of our connection. They once again had mysteriously
shown up during the most tumultuous and demanding stretches
along my journey, and I couldn't wait to join them in ceremony.

While popping my birth control pill that night, it occurred to
me that we were scheduled to be together in retreat in the middle
of my menstrual flow. The timing of my period had been a private
affair and a non-issue my entire life. I never needed to calculate
in the past if it would interfere with my daily activities, but the
importance of honoring Lakota traditions—that women couldn't
participate in ceremony during their menstrual flow—wedged
itself into my consciousness.

I couldn't just push it back down. That would defeat the purpose of seeking out and immersing myself in these sacred rituals and indigenous teachings.

You've got to be freaking kidding me! Is this some kind of cosmic joke? Didn't you hear? No more tests! I'm sick of them, I shouted to the sky as the reality of my dilemma sank in.

Could I just not tell? No one would know that I'd be menstruating. It's not like there will be a period police patrolling the vicinity. What if I just take another week of pills that pushed my period out for a week? I wouldn't be lying about it and could still be a part of the group during sacred ceremony.

Just call the indigenous woman—what's her name again?—the one who Kay recommended, instead of doing something out of desperation that would go against these teachings. Mary Attu. Yes, that's her name. Call her and ask how important it is to be isolated in a separate lodge during your moon time, what meaning it holds in this modern day and age. That may give you some idea what to do.

"Hi, Mary. I'm a client of Kay. She recommended that I call you to ask for guidance regarding my involvement with a Lakota-guided spiritual group," I said.

"Kay's my star sister!" Mary said. "We've known each other from a time long before this one. How wonderful!"

Her dynamic energy and uninhibited expansiveness were contagious. It reminded me of my interactions with Paloma. I thought for a minute how to introduce myself to Mary, but all convention flew out of my mind.

"*I'm Rainbow Crystal Woman, and I've been getting a lot of fives and sevens lately,*" I said to my own bewilderment.

"Ah, you're crow!" Mary exclaimed.

"*Yes, yes, I'm crow,*" I said excitedly. It felt as if Rainbow Crystal Woman had hijacked my voice and body, was speaking in code, and knew exactly what to say to connect to Mary.

"That's beautiful! *The Rainbow within the Crystal is the Ancient Spirit of Life* which lives deep in the heart of Mother Earth. She resides in the seventh direction. Bless your path! Many people know of the medicine wheel's four directions, but there's also up and down, Father Sky and Mother Earth, and the seventh sacred direction is within, where rainbow colors disperse from white light. The number five is also in the middle, in the center of the four directions where Crow lives. Crow is the keeper of sacred law and a magical shapeshifter, similar to the different rays of the rainbow before they manifest in form," she said.

"That makes so much sense. I balanced an amethyst crystal egg in the center of a medicine wheel drawn on a kapemni, an 'As above, so below' Lakota symbol in my first sweat lodge ceremony. That's how I got the name, Rainbow Crystal Woman," I said. I realized in this instant that this point of balance is what Paloma called the Zero Point, the source of all unrealized potential. Bursts of elation spiked in my heart and throughout body.

"We worked for this. We've earned this ancient connection. All happens for a reason, a season, a lifetime, or a life change," Mary said, sounding silly and serious at the same time.

We? As in she and I? How did we earn this connection?

Her unflinching confidence shrunk my looming concerns into little raisins. I felt irreverent and foolish for asking if artificially pushing my period out by taking extra pills was a possibility, but did so anyway.

Mary listened patiently while I fumbled to get my question out. She seemed confused. Before she had a chance to reply, I'd gathered that being isolated in the moon lodge was an empowered time and an honor.

"The moon lodge protects others from the great power that's released and accessible to women when the veil lifts during this time of the month. They can be thrown off by it in her presence, that's how powerful it is," Mary said.

Much to my surprise, my painful longing to be in ceremony with the rest of the group had faded into a faint, dull ache. The depth of connection and union with the divine that Mary embodied and was transmitting to me was so captivating, it flipped my moping about sitting out in the moon lodge by myself on its head.

Curiosity about this ancient solitary experience seeped in, and I began to see it as an honor too. Suddenly, my old concerns about the masculine structures in the group popped to the foreground.

"Kay suggested that I talk to you about my confusion about the Red Road, my Rainbow Path, and my calling. I don't feel like they're in conflict when I'm talking to you, but there are times when I feel resistance to what I'm being taught by my teacher. He was taught the Lakota ways by Joe Eagle Elk medicine man. The lessons that came through were all very beautiful and have been so transformative. I can't imagine giving this depth of connection up, but, at the same time, I can't imagine giving up all the other colors of the rainbow either, even though I don't have the skills to deepen my connection to them," I said.

"I taught Lakota school children at the Rosebud reservation for many years and was taught the Lakota traditions by several elders, including an one-hundred-year-old Lakota *unci*," Mary said, as if verifying her credentials.

"Because of my close spiritual connection to Crazy Horse (the most noble, revered, and fierce nineteenth century Lakota freedom fighter amongst the Lakota), I was given two personal stones he wore and a rare picture of him (there are very few pictures of Crazy Horse, some experts even say that none of the pictures in books right now are authenticated). I'm going to smoke a pipe for you, okay? I will call you right back," Mary said.

"Okay," I said.

Click.

Smoke a pipe? As in pray and ask for guidance?

"White Clouds Running Bear. That's who you're dealing with," she said when she called back about fifteen minutes later.

White Clouds Running Bear? She must be referring to Tim.

"As soon as the sun is out of sight and hidden behind the clouds, Bear goes running," she said, confident that this insight would solve all my problems. "And you, my dear, are radiant. I'll teach you everything I know about being a pipe carrier. I'm one of the few Aleutian medicine women who still makes spirit dolls, and sews and tans medicine pouches the old-fashioned way. My grandmother taught me the traditional ways ever since I was a little girl," she said proudly.

Wait. What did she mean? That I don't go running when I don't have tangible proof? My cognitive mind wanted to move slower to integrate it, but my intuitive mind was moving on a different track and pace, and totally at ease with this way of relating.

"What's your favorite color? I'm going to make you a medicine pouch," she said.

"That's so kind of you. Lavender, my wedding color," I said.

"See there. Lavender is the color of the within direction, the seventh direction, your place. What's your address? I'll mail it when it's done," she said.

"Please, let me pay you for your generosity and guidance," I asked. My head was spinning, but my body felt calmer than it had in a long time.

"No need. It's my pleasure to make it for you. I'm going to fill it with love and medicine. Just enjoy it," she said.

I couldn't tell if I was the nutcase for letting myself be so taken in by Mary Attu's magic, medicine, and faith in me, if she was the nut and had bewitched me, or if we both had a few screws loose. Whatever I'd been concerned about had gone up in smoke and had been replaced by a confidence in subtle truths that normally felt feather-light, fleeting, frightening, and flimsy. Infused with her power, they felt as solid and majestic as a canyon of massive rock and stone.

Chapter 17

 SEVEN COSMIC SISTERS

Stop acting so small. You are the Universe in
ecstatic motion . . .
—Rumi

THE DAYS LEADING UP TO THE retreat gradually morphed into a spontaneous city vision quest that continued to disintegrate my usual sense of self and professional identity. As soon as the kids and Robert had gone to bed, I turned my computer on and tried to reconnect with Rainbow Crystal Woman, eager to write my way back to the magical portal and the secret underground tunnels that we'd tumbled into.

The bird still pecked on my window every afternoon for about an hour. Since the rest of the women were still having their own bizarre encounters with spirit guides too, I regarded and embraced the pecking as a mysterious induction into the spiritual realms. My Awarradam spirit guides had appeared right before our first gathering in a similar fashion, leading me down a path that I may not have embraced if they hadn't encouraged me to trust my feelings and lean into the process.

I went about my daily tasks as usual, but poignant lines from Paloma's paper popped up in my awareness like the pecking sounds of the bird. This one—*we have nothing to lose that won't be lost in death anyway*—became my mantra. I latched onto it whenever I wanted to unplug out of my normal way of thinking and acting. It baffled me that these private acts of defiance felt so dangerous, like diving off a cliff without my usual safety net of comfort, approval, inclusion, connection, and certainty.

No matter how often I'd been dropped or let down by this safety net of convention, giving into the urge to fly and relying on wings I'd never used before seemed much scarier. I proceeded in spite of my fears, no longer willing to betray myself. I recited my mantra, took a deep breath, leaped into the growing gaps between the rigid frames of reality, and dissolved into the vast unknown of the eternal here-and-now while everyone was fast asleep. Freely roaming into the vastness of my mind reminded me of my jungle adventures as a child.

I typed up the flow of my thoughts and drifted deeper and deeper into a state of extreme relaxation and plant-like stillness. I remembered Kay's suggestions to visualize the sun's rays coming through the top of my head and into the power chakra to hold some of that ancient light in me and to open another seven layers of receptive satellites above my crown chakra. When I envisioned what she recommended while sitting behind my desk, it seemed as if my body was photosynthesizing the sun's rays, and life-giving energy was directly entering my veins through an invisible IV tube, drop by drop.

No longer craving food or rest, I fasted during the days that followed and slept only a few hours per night, my body strangely able to run on light, love, and air as long as I remained receptive and regulated my autonomic system and metabolism with slow, steady, mindful breaths. I sometimes reached peaks of such exhilarating highs, I wondered if I was tapping into a part of my soul and potential described by people on month-long fasts and hunger strikes, or in extreme near-death situations.

Especially in the wee hours of the night when my mind toggled between sleeping, dreaming, and being wide awake, I was shown how light and dark interacted with each other in our world.

Through intuitive insight, I realized that I knew on some level that beaming my potent, bright light into the Universe was risky. It triggered envy, pain, aggression, and rage in prisoners of darkness, unseen entities lurking in the distant shadows. This darkness had led to the murders of warriors of light, such as John F. Kennedy and Martin Luther King, Jr., and the death threats that many others like them around the globe receive when they become too visible and prominent. This big picture perspective of my fears resonated and reassured me that I wasn't crazy. This was the reason why I hid my five-year-old self in the pitch-black ocean.

The next night, I made a connection with unfamiliar beings and was able to look at our level of consciousness through their eyes. I sensed that they were extraterrestrials from a dimension that felt foreign to me. Because they were nothing like the creepy, scary aliens I'd seen in movies, my first reaction was to doubt myself. I set out to type, "here's where the *skeptic* in me is stepping in." My fingers ended up typing, "here's where the *psychic* in me is stepping in." I looked at the screen and freaked out. It felt like a glitch in my brain and body, an extraction of my erroneous assessment and an insertion of the truth at a speed outside of time and space. The energy around these beings was so extremely loving and powerful, I welcomed the correction and surrendered to the experience.

For a few moments, I could see us, humans, through their eyes. We looked like ants to them in terms of our consciousness. They had no intention to hurt us and saw us as part of the mysterious grand scheme of life. Their souls were filled with light, profound compassion, love, goodwill, and a longing to connect. I begged them for help in bridging the chasm between our states of mind and their advanced consciousness and compassion.

When morning came around, I attended to my daily work and activities in cruise-control mode. I probably didn't seem all that different to Robert, just more thoughtful and reflective, sometimes a little out there, similar to how I seemed when I prepared myself and purged old patterns for the first retreat.

Like Paloma, I was good at doing loads of deep introspection without anyone noticing. I preferred to keep my soul secrets and magical experiences to myself until I was certain people were able to hear and honor them. During this spontaneous vision quest, I was once again detecting uncanny, synchronistic signs that were guiding me throughout the day: resonant lyrics from songs playing on the radio, passages on how to read hidden codes and symbols in the book, *The Da Vinci Code*, that my cousin for no particular reason lent to me, a phrase on a billboard, something a client or a group member said or did, a toy given to me by my kids. Each "aha" moment shot waves of profound, connective ecstasy throughout my body. By the end of the day, the serendipitous signs had greatly increased in frequency, entering my consciousness in an almost steady flow.

Isn't this what we call delusions of reference and depersonalization? And when we label clients as psychotic, hallucinating, manic, and grandiose because they attribute personal meaning to random events, visions, and conversations that are not perceived by others? What's the difference between me and someone who's really crazy or dangerous? the watchful clinician in me questioned.

A clear and simple answer emerged. Those struggling with psychotic disorders were dealing with the same debilitating threats of persecution, annihilation anxiety, and fears of death that had terrorized me before. The only difference: *Paloma's and Mary's rolemodeling and Rainbow Crystal Woman's immense reservoir of love and compassion had made it possible for you to maintain your clarity and ground in the present moment while moving through the chaotic and intense dissolution of your usual self.* Rather than running on paranoia, agitation, adrenaline, or other stress hormones associated with annihilation terror, I learned how to regulate the physiological spikes in my body and remain open to wise guidance.

I intuited that the synchronistic signs and metaphoric clues coming through were just the tip of an iceberg. They were neither good nor bad, just ripples of energy directing us to old, neglected wounds and unresolved pain in need of reintegration and healing. Viewed through the cloudy, polarizing lens of fear, however, the lingering imprints of these old wounds appeared as malicious visions and voices, replaying some old horror story in our dreams, thoughts or lives.

A shot of passion and bliss accompanied this insight while driving home. The power running through my system didn't fit into any conceptualization of what it meant to be "human." Being infused with the presence of Rainbow Crystal Woman in the past was similar to replacing a tentative, flickering inner lightbulb with a super bright, halogen one. What I was experiencing now was offering me a completely new understanding of myself. This current connection felt more like having ingested the sun and shining rays of light into every dark corner of my inner world and surroundings. The ancient spirit of Rainbow Crystal Women was fully merging with me, purifying my mind, heart, body, and soul and invoking sensations that were unfamiliar to me.

The energy pumping through me was majestic, serene, fearless, and riveting, both masculine in its structure, directness, and strength, and feminine in its creative receptivity, organic flow, and ability to surrender to an infinite source of love and light. My split consciousness confused me to no end. My old self was hiding between my legs like a young child, in awe of this new, fierce me, and the new me, as ancient as the sun, was in awe of the novelty of being in my familiar body.

That evening, I walked through my house like a stranger, examining and collecting objects with special meaning and resonance: Terrance's ninja turtle towel that would serve as an altar cloth (in a flash I understood that they represented a band of spirit warriors fighting for earth, aka turtle island), a lavender ring with a turtle and trinity of stars on its shell, given to me by Jade after I picked her up from preschool earlier that day, a bowl with carved love birds from Robert's parents, the two little crystal buffaloes that I had bought in Mt. Shasta, dolphin coasters, reminding me of my hypnobirthing session and rebirth, a candle set labeled with the elements, another pair of candle holders decorated with spirals, favorite greeting cards from Robert, art with rainbow images, and the books, *The Da Vince Code, Buffalo Calf Woman Comes Singing: The Spirit Song of a Rainbow Medicine Woman*, and one about indigenous Spider Woman tales, given to me by the doula who'd helped me to make and paint my body cast.

On the kitchen floor, in the stillness of the dark night, I arranged all the items in the shape of an elaborate medicine wheel on the towel, lit the candles, and held a ceremony while a spider strolled by and stayed put on my little stack of books. I experienced myself as a powerful healer and thanked Grandmother Spider for joining me in ceremony and blessing my altar. When done with my ritual, I packed my new altar pieces in a hard case, Samsonite suitcase along with the towel and a drum with a spiral drawing representing the galactic center and spirals of life. Its circular shape and the linear beater were the feminine and masculine forces that brought forth the heartbeat in all of life. In between these sacred objects, I stuffed a few clothes, necessities, and toiletries.

I was scheduled to leave for Connecticut the next morning. It also happened to be the day Paloma was graduating. I examined the clothes in my closet and put on a long black dress with a print of three, earth-toned diamond shapes stacked on top of one another. They looked like "As above, so below" *kapemnis*, covering the front side of my body from my heart to my womb. A woven jacket with deer silhouettes lining a rim of triangular patterns and a favorite jaguar print hat completed my eccentric outfit. I'd never given this kind of thought to my clothes before but liked the sense of empowerment it gave me. I felt prepared to face whatever was waiting for me on the other side of the country.

I found Robert in Jade's room. He was getting her dressed in a cute Hawaiian number, graciously accepting double-duty responsibilities during the next few days, even before I was gone.

"I love that dress on her. I just got a flash memory that we were together in a previous life in old Polynesia. That's why we went to Hawaii during each of my pregnancies and why we gave both of them Hawaiian middle names," I said with a big grin on my face. Robert seemed too preoccupied to fully take in what I said.

"I'll get breakfast ready," I said and slipped out.

A few minutes later, he sat the kids down behind the bar and handed Terrance his toast on a Spiderman plate.

"See that? You're my Spiderman. Grandma Spider walked over my altar yesterday and delivered the message that the best way to fight dark, sticky webs is to build a stronger web of light. That's precisely what I'll be doing with Tim and the rest of his group at this retreat. And you're my sweetest partner-in-crime, holding down the fort at home," I said, leaning toward him with puckered lips.

Robert looked a bit puzzled, but was able to switch gears to an intuitive level of interacting, attributing my figurative speech to the upcoming retreat. Even if he didn't quite understand, he generally trusted the guidance that came through, especially when I was doing deep work. I probably didn't sound all that different than when I claimed that Rainbow Crystal Woman suggested that I get off the pill and we go to Mt. Shasta to get pregnant.

After I said goodbye to the three of them and drove off, my heart plummeted into an abyss of agony. It felt as if my usual sense of self and energetic presence shot out of my body, and pangs of anguish, panic, despair, helplessness, shock, anger, and profound concern whirled through me like falling dominoes. My heart was beating at triple speed as I looked down on my devastated children and Robert with excruciating heartbreak imagining that they'd just received news of my death. In less than a few seconds, relief brought on by a sense of spaciousness, acceptance, trust, and reassurance that they'd be just fine descended on me. It gently smoothed out the tight constrictions and filled me up with a peaceful sense of mysterious order, fearlessness, and love. In the midst of my euphoric unfolding, I knew that this was a very bizarre experience, most similar to accounts that I'd read of people having a near-death experience, but it didn't really faze me.

While this was happening, my hands and feet kicked into automatic pilot and drove me to the airport with just enough alertness to avoid any mishaps or accidents. The rest of my expanded self operated according to the wishes of Rainbow Crystal Woman. She demoted my usual self through this near-death experience and inhabited my mind and body more fully than before. Meaningful events of spiritual significance flashed in front of me, all in a blink of eye. This process felt very unsatisfactory to my cognitive mind, like swallowing a delicious banquet whole without the chance to taste, chew, or sort through it. I had a sense that I'd get to regurgitate and digest it later.

On my drive, a bird crashed straight into my windshield. It rolled onto the freeway, dead, while my car crawled along in a traffic jam.

This is what Paloma meant when she said that she sometimes felt like a bird in flight, and that she was going to evaporate on her graduation day, I realized.

Another potent boost of high-frequency energy jolted through me and filled every hair-fine crack in my subtle body with invincibility and brilliance. I wondered if she felt this powerful when I'd called her on the phone.

Serendipitous signs continued to accompany me to the airport. It dawned on me that my spirit guides were trying to reach me through a game of charades. I needed to string the clues together and unearth their message.

As I pulled into the airport's parking lot, two rabbits on their hind legs, as if frozen in their tracks, just stared at me. *That must be White Clouds Running Bear and a second rabbit just as afraid as him.* They were warning me what to expect: that my email messages and attempts to update Tim and the women may not have gone over well. In rambling emails, I'd told them about the contact I'd made with the beings from other dimensions, asking if they could be spirit guides, and I also wrote them that Rainbow Crystal Woman or an ancient spirit had entered my body.

In regard to the ancient spirit visiting me: I'd heard that dancers were often possessed by some kind of deity during *Winti* rituals. I was confident that Tim and my *hunka,* of all people, would be most open to a bit of mystery moving through me, but I was getting a dreadful sense that I was wrong. My experience was more far out than what they were accustomed to and the clouds were covering the sun. My heart was so full of love and optimism, I couldn't imagine how this could pose a barrier for very long. They'd realize that I was filled with love and light as soon as we'd meet face to face again.

I parked and got on the shuttle bus. In my spaced-out elation, I forgot my suitcase on the bus. I decided to wait for it to come back around, but felt increasingly more nervous about missing my flight as time went by.

Did I gather my sacred altar objects and most meaningful experiences in one place only to discover that I'm overattached to them and that they don't define me? The moment this clicked and softly settled into my body as a *yes* and I was willing to leave them behind, the shuttle swung around the corner. I retrieved my suitcase, ran inside, and boarded my plane in the nick of time.

Upon my late-night arrival at the Super 8 Motel in Connecticut, I was informed that the women from the retreat had canceled their reservations the day before. Perhaps it had to do with me having my period and needing to be separated from the get-go, and not because they were worried about my mental state after reading my letter. They didn't say why and hadn't left a message or any contact information for me.

My usual self would've been indignant at this very unprofessional behavior. I instead heard, *This is necessary for your learning. You're not alone. You and your seven cosmic sisters are the Super 8.* I was intrigued, eager to know who these seven cosmic sisters were.

Mary Attu immediately came to mind because of the way she described her connection to her star sister, Kay. That's two right there. On that same star sister wavelength appeared Brooke Medicine Eagle, Paloma, and Nancy, a psychologist who once in a while covered for Alan whenever he was on vacation. She'd said that Paloma was "meant to cross my path" when she heard about our interactions in group meetings. Her bold claim meant a lot to me. Mimi Stern, a body worker and friend, was my sixth cosmic sister. She'd listened to and helped me to integrate the bizarre incidents along my journey for years. My last and newest cosmic sister, Linda Joy Myers, a spiritual memoir writing coach, had written an ad in the same resource guide with Kay's information. I'd not decided yet what kind of book would be best, but it looked like I was being guided to this kind of genre.

Each of these seven cosmic sisters provided affirmation for Kay's reading: that my book project and psychic channeled writing were a gift from the ancestors. I still wasn't totally clear on what their main message was except for showing that inhibiting my clients' and my intuition was undermining our fullest potential and mental health instead of protecting either one of us from harm.

On the lobby counter was a brochure with HBO movies currently showing in the rooms. One of these movies was *The Matrix*. Not really a sci-fi type, I never quite understood what all the hype regarding this blockbuster was all about. But when my new eyes locked onto Neo, Morpheus and Trinity, an epiphany burst in my mind like a drop of food coloring in a glass of water.

Paloma's description of institutional spider webs was analogous to the workings of the matrix, keeping us asleep in pods like zombies. The traumas of soulless, modern life made it easy to succumb to paralyzing systems of fear that sucked the life out of us and vilified our intuitive impulses as untrustworthy, uncivilized, primal instincts. We'd learned to turn against ourselves, attacking ourselves like an autoimmune disease by viewing our own longings, screams, and attempts to awaken as psychological disorders and irresponsible acts of rebellion. But as Mouse, the youngest crew member on the Zion, said, "To deny our own impulses is to deny the very thing that makes us human."

I took my suitcase to my room and ventured back out, in search of food. A rare, deep-purple, anemone flower, associated with anticipation and new beginnings, sat in a vase on the table. It was the same one Robert had uploaded as a screen saver on my computer years ago, knowing that I loved the color indigo, the color of our third eye chakra and intuition. I choked up, feeling his love and presence. I wondered what time it was in California, and, as I looked at the clock on the wall, about to strike midnight, I received the message, *humanity is transitioning into a new cycle of evolution. Just like the hands on the clock move from twelve to one, not thirteen, we move in circles and cycles, not in a line. This last supper and your inner experiences are characteristic of what happens during the last phase of an old era before entering the next level of consciousness. In this new era, you'll see the return of sacred feminine energy, both in yourself and in society.*

I went to bed and slept like a rock, not the least concerned how the next day would unfurl. Around nine in the morning, I received a call from the front desk. Two people—Amy, the indigo college student who I'd met three years ago, and her fiancé, Mike—were waiting for me up-front. I wore the same outfit I had on the day before and greeted them as if this had been our arrangement all along, my expanded heart too enormous to feel slighted for being left by myself at the hotel. I put my suitcase with my altar pieces in the trunk while they explained that we were heading out to a remote piece of land that belongs to a friend for our sweat lodge ceremony.

"This arrangement was necessary, because you can't have two altars in a ceremony," Mike said on the way there.

Two altars, what are they talking about? *Eh, did you forget what you filled your suitcase with?* emerged from deep within. I remembered, but didn't put two and two together. Did they see me as a ceremony leader with my own altar? My labeling mind had been turned off and my actions felt as natural and innately driven as searching for food might be for a hungry animal. I got the distinct sense that Tim and the group understood better than I did what was awakening and emerging inside of me.

Perhaps this was Tim's way of blessing my rainbow path and endorsing me as a leader for indigos and rainbow children, while at the same time holding firm that my rainbow ways couldn't mix with his and the ways of the Red Road. I still wasn't convinced that we couldn't find a way to harmoniously work together. I also couldn't wrap my mind around being in charge of my own altar and leading some tribe of my own. I had zero experience and had so much yet to learn.

"*Whatever happened to the seventh ceremony, the throwing of the cosmic ball, one of the ceremonies that White Buffalo Woman brought back? Only six of the rites-—the keeping of the soul, the sweat lodge, the vision quest, the sun dance, the making of relatives, and the coming of age ceremonies—are regularly practiced,"* I asked Amy and Mike. Tim had shared this tidbit of information three years ago. I had not given it any thought and I was surprised that I remembered all the details. I had no clue why I brought it up, but I had a hunch that it mattered a lot to the ancient spirit inside of me.

This ceremony involved a young girl, who represented innocence and clarity, standing in the center of a four-quadrant playing field and throwing up a red ball, Mother Earth, in each of the four directions. Two blue circles were painted around the ball, symbolizing the coming together of heaven and earth, "As above, so below."

Neither Amy nor Mike knew much about this game and probably also wondered why this was significant now. I got a flash of insight that humans needed to get in the game and keep a closer eye on the cosmic ball, which symbolized the sacred and the Great Mystery, insert: *Wakan Tanka.* I also wondered if we needed to empower more young women like Paloma, who was like the young girl in the center of the game, a keeper of innocence and wisdom.

As we approached the retreat site, the spirit inside of me kicked into full gear and all my doubts and concerns about leading my own ceremony faded into the background. This me was as daring, uninhibited, undaunted, and in charge of my voice and body as she was on the phone with Mary.

We pulled into a long driveway and parked by a modest home, surrounded by a pretty meadow, mature trees, and high grasses. A sweat lodge, covered with a dark-plastic tarp had been set up near a fire, colorful prayer flags were waving in each of the four directions, and about a dozen or more participants were scattered in bunches, preparing for ceremony.

I recognized a few of the *unci's* as I got out of the car, their expressions reserved and lukewarm. Amy and Mike walked up to Tim, who greeted me with a sideways glance and nod. I overheard one of them say, "Yes, we're dealing with coyote."

Who me? Coyote? As in the sly and cunning fox? No wonder they left me there all by myself! They don't trust me! my usual self thought. This sharp reaction faded as soon as Rainbow Crystal Woman stepped back in.

James, who looked like the owner of the land, was standing next to Tim. *Ah, that must be rabbit number two.* I offered him a slight smile. His two unleashed, agitated Rottweilers were snarling by his side and about to have me for lunch if I made just one wrong move.

The sight of these ferocious watch dogs would have typically scared me out of my wits. I probably would not even have gotten out of the car to begin with. The new me approached the dogs with alpha self-assurance and poise and picked up a tennis ball lying on the ground.

In a flash, I remembered what Tim had said at our first retreat three years ago. Shamans and medicine healers are tricksters, Coyote-like, because of their comfort with paradox and their tendency to reveal our shadow parts in surprising, tricky, and playful ways. They're feared by some people because they tend to disrupt order and reveal the things that we'd rather avoid, bursting our bubbles of illusion and forcing us to remove our masks of deception. I sensed that Tim and James, who I hadn't met before, weren't sure yet if I could be trusted with Coyote's power. James relied on his dogs to test my integrity and help discern if I had harmful intentions.

I tossed the ball up and down in my hand and cooed, "You just want your ball, huh? No one wants to play this game with you? Come here, I'll play with you," treating these watch dogs as if they were adorable puppies.

I threw the ball as far as I could to the other side of the yard, delighted to see the dogs chase after it. I noticed Tim's bewilderment, and heard a voice inside of me say, *Hello, dear old friend . . . so good to see you again . . . Let the games begin.* I had a distinct sense that we'd known each other long ago in another time and space and used to play this cosmic game together.

I scanned the land and noticed that one side bordered a lake. The water pulled me toward it like a magnet. I walked to the lake's edge with the grace and authority of a great leader. I stroked the wind, kneeled down and greeted the water, then cupped it and slowly poured it onto the land while blessing it.

I could feel the antennae and satellite dishes above my crown working. They were super lit. I captured the message, *Tim and James are scared of you, Coyote, because you provoke what's in their shadow. This is what Mary meant with White Clouds Running Bear. They fear the unknown and are relying on form and structure as a crutch. Coyote welcomes the shadow and creates fluid new structures and opportunities for growth in the moment.*

That made sense. I realized that this must be the same wariness and fear that people projected on Paloma when she didn't shrink her light and power in public and challenged many social rules.

I walked to a small group of *unci's* who were hard at work. *Unci* Grace, who'd sent me the poem about being more afraid of our light than our darkness, invited me to join them. They were stringing red prayer ties, each one filled with a teaspoon of tobacco, along a medicine hoop. I counted. There were seven in each quadrant, twenty-eight total.

I watched and copied what the women were doing, but, when I got to my number eight, my hands refused to make another red tie. I instead reached for a piece of black cloth. I cut out seven small squares and, after tying those up, I cut out seven yellow squares, and seven white squares, and proceeded until the four quadrants of my hoop of prayer ties were in the colors of the medicine wheel. The women around me gave me disapproving glances but didn't say anything.

Mike came around with a bag that looked like a magician's hat. He asked us each to pull out one of the larger prayer flags that were inside of it. The women around me pulled out red, black, and yellow, blue, and green flags. I pulled out a white flag.

Mike nodded knowingly. I could read his mind. *Your light is in your shadow*, were his thoughts. What does that mean? Was that a bad thing? Could I inflict harm because of that? How? No answer.

The big campfire called out to me. I walked toward it and unwittingly stepped on a trail of tobacco that had already been laid between the fire and the sweat lodge. According to ceremonial rules and sweat lodge etiquette, this was a serious sign of disrespect. James jumped up and charged me.

"You crossed the line!" he bellowed.

I held my hoop of prayer flags around both wrists, palms facing the open fire.

"Because it's not a line. It's a circle," I said and stood my ground.

Laser beams of wrath shot out of the eyes of a few of the men and burned into me for what seemed like an eternity. James approached me, took my jaguar hat off my head, and carefully examined it. I had a sense that the fierceness associated with Jaguar energy was scaring him. I calmly took it back and threw my beloved hat into the fire. This gesture meant to prove that I was willing to sacrifice my possessions and any arrogance or aggression that I may be harboring; I showed everyone the *kapemnis* and deer, representing compassion and gentleness, on my woven jacket. That seemed to instill trust in my positive intentions and relax them a bit. They returned to their activities while I thanked and honored the fire.[4]

I asked Amy if I could get my suitcase. She led me to a section of the land next to the lodge where I could do as I pleased. After braiding my hair by the edge of the water, I laid out my books and cards in a medicine wheel formation, then added the rest of my sacred objects onto my ninja turtle towel and around, creating a large, open-air altar. The dogs fetched and ran back and forth with the cosmic ball while we held our complimentary ceremonies on the two separate parts of the land. On one side, Tim led ceremonies in the dark womb of Mother Earth, the sweat lodge, and, on the other side, barefoot, birthed new ceremonies into life in the ancient bright light of the sun and Father Sky, allowing inspiration to move me just like I did during my dance audition when I portrayed a tree.

I danced and worshiped the sun, as Kay recommended that I do. A small garden snake with black and red rings, symbolic of the sacred feminine, sneaked up and remained completely still, again staring right at me, while drumming, chanting, and sounds, simulating the throwing up of anguish and agony, waxed and waned on the other side of the land.

---

4. *The Fire Ceremony was the most fundamental and important of all Mayan rituals. Mayan mythology is rich in jaguar lore. The Jaguar God of Terrestial Fire personifies the number seven, is assumed to be the night sun, and is usually called Jaguar God of the Underworld.*

We reconvened in the late afternoon. Some of the women came over to my side and examined my altar. James stood at a distance and looked on. I slowly walked to him and informed him that I'd never bled so much before during my moon cycle.

He stiffened up and sneered, "So what?"

"It means that your land is sacred, and I blessed it with my blood just like the indigenous women, who ran through the fields to fertilize the land during their moon, have done for generations."

James nodded. He seemed grateful but was still suspicious of me.

"Here, this is for you. I found it right here," I said, pointing to the ground. I gave him a white rock that nature had carved and sanded down into the crude shape of a little buffalo.

"Is that one of the buffaloes that you got at Mt. Shasta?" Amy asked. I felt as if I were some kind of quack.

"No, they're right there," I said, pointing to the buffaloes still on my altar. James accepted the buffalo rock reluctantly, examining it with his fingernail.

We gathered in James' living room. A DVD case of the movie, *The Matrix*, sat next to his television.

"This is how we get out of the matrix," I said to James, referring to our ceremonies, as if we'd been undercover secret agents on a similar assignment for lifetimes. He didn't need to respond. I sensed the shift and softening in his body.

The rest of the group still didn't know what to make of my peculiar behavior. When they passed the peace pipe around in a closing ceremony that included me, I had a coughing fit, not ever having smoked in my life. It was a clear sign to everyone that I didn't belong in this group and that the Red Road wasn't right for me.

I didn't understand. Why was I trying so hard to fit in and remain attached to this group when I kept getting messages that I needed to move on and find my own power? *You're learning the ancient lessons of the moon lodge ceremony. This is how women learn to cut emotional ties and be separate from the group. Your empathic capacities sometimes cause you to foster umbilical cord-like connections that are similar to the lianas that suffocated you in your childhood dream. It's particularly hard for women to cut these ties, even if the cutting would benefit them and everyone else in the long run.*

Amy and Mike drove me back without saying a word. I wasn't sure if they'd pick me up the next morning, but I assumed so and didn't ask, feeling completely at peace with the progression of each new moment and discovering this information tomorrow.

"Someone named Gerry is here to see you," the receptionist informed me close to nine in the morning the next day. Gerry, one of the male elders, was waiting for me in the lobby. He was a gentle and kind man and informed me that we were going to the campus.

I only took a small album with pictures from Awarradam with me. Mike and Amy were waiting in the car. Gerry was open to hearing about my Awarradam experience during the drive. He enjoyed my pictures and was particularly intrigued by my close-up shot of a rare rainforest mushroom covered by a web that looked like a bride's veil.

To my surprise, the energy of the rest of the group was more intense than the day before. I noticed their empowered garb. They were wearing medicine pouches around their necks and totems of their guides were on their clothing. I wondered what Rainbow Crystal Woman was up to. I'd done exactly the opposite. I'd deliberately put on a plain, casual outfit without any symbols on it.

They looked at me fiercely, as if trying to scare me off. Was my energy and the power running through me somehow harming them, as Mary had explained to me? They were trying to stand their ground with the help of their guides and seemed caught off guard by my neutral, guide-free appearance. That moment, I realized what the ancient spirit inside of me was trying to convey. The Rainbow energy that I was holding onto was not associated with any spiritual or cultural form or structure. It ran freely through my body and filled me with as much power, light, clarity, and ecstasy as it did the day before, regardless of my external appearance.

Unci Grace approached me and sat by me. My heart beamed with love.

"My fierce, protective mother bear is coming out and has

a special request. Please, don't disrupt our ceremonies. We have spent a long time practicing and preparing for them. We will be holding them right in there," she said, pointing to a closed door.

"Most certainly. I have no intention of doing so," I said. Why did she think I'd do such a thing? I still had difficulty identifying my agenda. It took great focus for my usual self to regain some control and speculate what the reasons for the tension in our dynamics were about.

"In the dark lodge yesterday, while looking through my mole eyes, Great Spirit was saying to me that our empowered objects didn't really matter all that much. What mattered was the genuine intention in our heart," she said. I nodded, realizing that Tim, James, and the ancient spirit inside of me were having some sort of chess match between the Red Road and the Rainbow Path. *Unci* Grace said what I wanted him and the group to understand about the role of physical form in the material world so that they would include me in their group and share their teachings with millennials and indigo types like Paloma and me, who were trustworthy even if less steeped in one tradition.

When the group was holding their ceremonies inside the classroom, I remained by myself in a small library and adjoining student lounge that was plastered from wall to wall with book cases, cork boards, posters with inspirational slogans, art, and community resources. There were enough interesting books and resources in there to keep me busy for hours.

Every so often, the group took a break from drumming and singing and interacted with me. A few of the women approached me and asked me questions, like "Would you rather visit Alaska during months of darkness or the Eiffel Tower in Paris?" "Would you rather work with dying cancer patients or with newborn babies?"

They seemed proud of themselves for coming up with tricky questions to test my intentions. Their energy fields were on high alert, treating me as if I were from outer space. The ancient spirit in me was confused by their transparency and lack of sophistication and wanted to show them some real magic, as if they were kids at an elementary school. My old self felt a twinge of hurt due to their lack of trust but was more intrigued by the lack of social skills that this ancient spirit inside of me was portraying.

Instead of responding directly to their questions, I somehow manifested my answers and pointed to one of the posters, slogans, resources, or books that we happened to be standing or walking by, thinking that I was channeling a unique, divine gift that would make a positive impression on them. My answer to the first question was, THE DARKER THE NIGHT, THE BRIGHTER THE STARS, printed on a poster. It was also the perfect answer for White Clouds Running Bear's deeper issue. I realized that Paloma had described experiences that were similar to this. She had discovered that her purpose in life was to deliver gifts of love and guidance to whoever she happened to be interacting with.

"These answers are emerging out of Zero Point gravity, the source of unmanifested potential. This is what Paloma, the student I wrote you about, said to me. She's an indigo, like you," I said to Amy. Because the gifts of guidance came directly from their own study area, I assumed that gifting them their own wisdom would win their trust back.

"You need to offer these rainbow and indigo children their own altar," Amy said, to my surprise. How come she didn't feel confined by the structures of this Red Road?

The next day, Gerry forgot to pick up a cake that was decorated with a red web. I reluctantly agreed with Tim's subtle hints that I was distracting this tribe with my own web: my presence, power, stories, and picture of the mushroom. I began to understand the problem of having my light in my shadow.

Someone asked Tim where the sage was, and he responded, "It's in the closet." He paused, then enunciated slowly for everyone to hear, "The *sage* is in the *closet*." They reconvened in ceremony and apparently cracked some kind of code.

While they were drumming and chanting in the other room, I felt my new self deflate like a balloon and my old self inflate back in my body, aching so much for my children and Robert that I searched for a phone and made a collect call. I hadn't missed them much the last few days and hadn't even called.

When Tim and the rest of the group came out—vigorously dancing, chanting, and drumming around me—it was obvious that they'd ousted whatever had been in me and had lured my old self back in my body. Tim announced, "These are the risks of trying to do this powerful work alone. This is why the Red Road is superior."

Unci Deb was crying and looked at me despairingly, her eyes and frown apologizing that it had come to this, sad that we never had a chance to connect and that this was a final goodbye. I gave her a reassuring look that I was fine, that it was meant to go this way, my heart and body as committed as theirs to a larger cause we shared. My heart felt at peace with this quick and clear telepathic exchange even though it operated outside of my thinking mind.

I found Gerry and shielded myself behind him. I asked him if he could take me back to the hotel, relieved that I was going home the next day. I left the building like a celebrity escaping from a dancing paparazzi mob that used rattles and drums rather than cameras.

Gerry was as kind and compassionate as he'd always been and comforted me by asking about and listening to stories about my family. He wished me well and encouraged me again to guide my students and clients by creating my own rituals and healing models. Aware that he was representing the entire group, I could tell that they had my best intentions in mind. I reluctantly accepted that this clean cut was the best course of action for all involved.

My presence and behavior must have come across as entitled, self-centered, disruptive, and imposing, but I still wished they'd give me a little bit more time and support to understand what was happening. I was more sure than ever that I was about to unearth a treasure, a profound understanding, buried deep inside of me that could potentially benefit many, and I had nowhere else to turn. I'd come so far, it was hard to give up on it, but I was also learning that closed doors were as helpful as open ones in revealing my path.

On the way back from the airport, I felt compelled to call Paloma. Our work had naturally ended as her graduation neared, and we had spent her last sessions reviewing the progress she'd made in all areas of her life, but especially in regard to her relationships and work. She didn't have any concerns or reservations about me writing a book about our journey: whenever I double-checked if she was still okay about this, she reassured me with a wise compassionate look that she was.

It felt important to tell her about the bird even though we'd already said our goodbyes, and she was about to move to Mexico to join her partner. I trusted that she'd get why I felt propelled to call.

"Your will has been done," rolled off my tongue when I heard her voice on the other line. The ancient spirit resurfaced and relayed these strange words to Paloma's wise inner guidance. Paloma graciously accepted them. I informed her that a bird had flown into my windshield and "evaporated" on my way to the retreat on the day of her graduation, just like she had predicted. I asked her what it meant to her.

"It signified the death of my small, fearful self," she said.

"That's precisely what happened to me too these last days," I said.

Paloma appreciated the call and the acknowledgement of her psychic and healing abilities, her impact on me, and most of all her precision in timing. After we hung up, my mind drifted to my most important childhood dreams, early premonitions that foretold my future path just like Paloma's prophecy. Reawakening after being killed in my dream had felt like a huge breakthrough, along with the intuitive understanding that I'd lived many times before and had accumulated wisdom, like honey in a beehive, that no one could harm or hamper in this lifetime.

My dreams and insights, once just flashlights, were now as powerful as floodlights, beaming a new clarity and lived experience into every level of my being. These mysterious, peak experiences of aliveness could not be reproduced, measured, or tested in a research study. They were sacred, spontaneous, unique, complex and paradoxical, both terrifying and uplifting, hard and inspiring aspects of my heroic, mythical story. They both triggered and supported my journey of transformation. Dismissing and missing the central thread of these very intimate and personal experiences felt like stealing my soul and all that gave my life purpose and meaning. No wonder Dr. Meehl's comment—that anyone who trusted their personal experiences more than hardcore research was self-deceived—bothered me so deeply.

I was thrilled to see Robert and the kids when I arrived home in the early evening. It felt as if I'd returned from the dead. I inhaled the smell of their hair and age, Jade not even a year old and Terrance four and a half. Smiling broadly at Robert, I cradled their sweet little bodies in mine, savored the ring of their adorable voices and their every move, then sneaked into bed with them, never ever wanting to let go of them again.

Chapter 18

 **HOMEBOUND**

> *Our ancestors worshipped the Sun and they*
> *were not that foolish. It makes sense to revere the*
> *Sun and the stars for we are their children . . .*
> *For small creatures such as we, the vastness is*
> *bearable only through love.*
> —Carl Sagan

THE WEEK FOLLOWING MY game-changing retreat, I met with Mimi, the massage therapist who'd been most effective in grounding and centering me back in my body whenever I felt overwhelmed and needed a reset.

"Guess what? You were one of my seven cosmic sisters keeping me company when I was left all by myself in a Super 8 in Connecticut!" I said while her magical hands dissolved knots and generated cascades of tingly sensations up and down my back.

"What did you say?" she asked, abruptly halting my heavenly indulgence. "Hold on. I have to show you something. You won't believe this."

She retrieved a small painting of seven cloaked heads of indigenous women in a starry sky and placed it in my hands.

"I got this from Standing Deer, a medicine man and artist from the Tiwa tribe, when I visited their pueblo in Taos, New Mexico. The members of this tribe believe that they're from the Pleiades stars, the Seven Sisters!"

Yes! That's where I am from! I heard a familiar voice—after a week of silence—inside of me say.

"No way . . . I had no idea that my seven cosmic sisters were a constellation of stars. I thought they were actual people. Perhaps they are actual people with links to these stars. You won't believe what all happened in Connecticut. This is making it even more mindboggling."

I told Mimi in bits and pieces what happened. It was very difficult to sequence and recount all the events into a coherent story, even though there wasn't a single moment when I'd blacked out. My mind was functioning like a child's brain, able to read the big words in a story, but still lacking depth, breadth, and complexity to fully integrate what happened into a larger spiritual theme. I often derailed or sounded like a broken record, painfully aware of the gaps that Paloma tended to close.

My intuition was still as sharp as a hound dog's. I caught a whiff of promising clues that led me down an enticing trail. First stop: back to Paloma. I was certain that she wouldn't mind if I emailed her and asked her if she'd ever heard of the Pleiades. Sure enough, she emailed me back that she had an inexplicable, mysterious connection to the Pleiades and had considered getting a tattoo of the seven stars. Her new partner had speckle birthmarks on her arm that were in the shape of the Pleiadian constellation. I shared that the Pleiades had been a big guiding force for me as well in the past few days and had come through in codes and symbols.

The gaps in my mind prevented me from asking what they represented to her and her girlfriend. I wished I'd asked her if they were the "home" that she felt drawn to in Kay's workshop, but perhaps I didn't on purpose. I was aware enough to only get information that could close important gaps and to refrain from exploiting her psychic gifts for information to put myself at ease.

My uncertainties about the future and the unknown were

my rocks to remove out of the river. Mimi's and Paloma's feedback had offered me enough direction to look to the skies and stars for further guidance. Over the course of the next three weeks, I followed clue after clue until a good number of puzzle pieces fell into place on the day before a rare cosmic event. It evoked strong pangs to reach out to Tim and the *hunka* group and apologize for my disruptive and disrespectful behavior during our last gathering, but most of all to share what I'd discovered. I suspected that this new information would greatly interest them and mend our relationships.

In an email, I explained that it felt as if my body had been taken over by an *iyeska*, a medicine person, who was trying to convey an important, coded message to us, using sacred numbers and ancient Mayan astrology.

The message that came through is consistent with your previous message about divine feminine energy returning to Mother Earth. It's just much more detailed. When I read The Da Vinci Code, I discovered that Venus was referred to as the five-pointed star, because of its pentagram trajectory. I Googled "Venus," which happens to be my birth planet. Tomorrow, June 8, 2004, is the day of the first Internet broadcasted Venus transit. This transit occurs only twice every 112 or so years.

Venus is known for her divine feminine energy and was a central component of Mayan cosmology. So were the Pleiades, the Seven Sisters, who kept me company during my late-night supper at Super 8 on May 13th (5/13), the symbolic death of an old, unbalanced, masculine era. The number thirteen was a root number for the Mayan. It represents the number of actual moon cycles in a year and the number of weeks per season.

It is both a prime number and the eighth number in the crucial Fibonacci series, which has a mysterious, parallel relationship with the Golden Ratio, 1.618, the formula that is at the root of the divine feminine spiral patterns found throughout nature. Earth and Venus, sister planets, have a phase locked orbital cycle that is based on a 13:8 ratio and has been associated with the Golden Ratio. This is derived from the fact that Venus revolves around the sun 1.6 times faster than Earth so that 13 Venus revolutions is equal to 8 years.

From there on, I was guided to the astrological and spiritual meaning of this rare event, which is a precursor to a much bigger planetary and galactic transit and cycle that I had prior to this day never been interested in nor aware of. The Mayans and other ancients, like the Tibetans, consider the upcoming transit on December 21, 2012 to be a historical transition into a new era, the Golden Age, the most spiritually pregnant time for transformative growth for the planet and all of her children. It marks the return of the Great Mother, a new wave of creative energy from the galactic center, and the return of the feathered serpent, Quetzalcoatl, the Mayan symbol of heaven-earth, "As above, so below," similar to the meaning of the kapemni. This amazingly only happens once every 13 baktun, every 5125 years.

At the bottom of my email, I wrote that I hoped to stay in touch but would understand if they preferred that I no longer contacted them. Tim wrote a very short email back, stating that I was a beautiful person and beyond gifted. Not knowing what to make of my energy was distracting. The ceremonies were hard and required all his attention, but he promised that he'd be a wiser man in handling this kind of situation in the future.

After this email, I never heard from him or any of the women ever again. As disappointing as this was, the emptiness that I thought I'd feel was filled with knowing and the affirmation from Tim that he meant well and had done the best that he could under the circumstances. He was doing me a favor by honoring our distinct callings and was releasing me to Mary and the Universe to further assist me along my journey. I felt the same way toward Paloma, trusting that the Universe had new teachers and experiences lined up for her that were better equipped to guide her along her path.

After this brief exchange with Tim, I mustered the courage to cut my ties and divorce the psychotherapy group while we were at it. It was an amicable one, one of mutual respect and appreciation for our different worldviews. I was trying too hard to make it work instead of going with the flow and the guidance that suited me.

I gratefully fell into Mary's loving arms. I'd told her what had happened with White Clouds Running Bear in Connecticut and shared my discoveries about the Seven Sisters, Venus, and 2012. She didn't even wince and sent me letters in her best cursive handwriting in envelopes decorated with heart stickers and heart drawings, proud of the leaps and bounds of progress that I'd made and reminding me of a favorite elementary school teacher. In one of her lovely letters, she wrote:

> *Dear One, Rainbow Crystal Woman,*
> *Bless you and thank you for the cards, notes, photos, and writing. You touch my life, heart, and spirit. I smiled inside and out when you said I am the Wind beneath your Wings. My friend wrote a book about me based on eleven years of letters. The title: Daughter of the Wind. In short time, there will be other items and teachings sent to you. Enclosed is a medicine bag for you filled with cedar, sage, sweetgrass, and juniper for cleansing, clearing, peace protection, and spirit. Also, a stone from New Mexico, a sacred land, that helps with truth, trust, and thanksgiving.*
>
> *In the pictures, I see the radiance of life and spirit in you—what a gift to the people! This medicine bag made for you is the only one ever to be made. I have not used these colors in flower design ever before. This just shows how special you are and the radiance and power within you. The flower is the symbol of the beauty of earth. Gold (center of flower) is to represent Sun. Sun is the radiance and life of the Creator. Purple (petals) is*

where you stand. Green (leaves)—earth color, symbol for
golden eagle and healing.
        You are so growing and I am so proud of you. Love
you, and you live in my heart and in my prayers always
and in all ways, forever.

Over the phone, she shared with me that the prayer ties had
been done in all red for only the last fifty years or so for protection
and fierceness. She also informed me of the close connection the
Lakota people have with the Seven Sisters. The elders believed that
their ancestors and White Buffalo Calf Woman descended from
the Pleiades.

"You were visited by an ancient spirit who wanted to teach
you about the spirit of Mother Earth' crystal heart—the rainbow—
because it's also the spirit of our pure, crystalline selves, our life
essence before it enters human form. That's why, in ancient times,
the prayer ties were traditionally done in the colors of the medicine wheel, and the last three of the twenty-eight ties were done in
green, blue, and lavender to reflect the seven rainbow colors of all
the sacred directions," she said, pleased with this proof that I was
indeed Rainbow Crystal Woman.

She didn't seem concerned that I was spontaneously sum-
moned and overtaken by this ancient spirit nor find it necessary to
understand what exactly happened. I could have connected with
energy from a past-life self, a self with a parallel life in some other
dimension, an ancient Pleiadian visitor braiding in its essence with
mine to cover more distance, like in a relay race, or an overarch-
ing oversoul, with bits and pieces that fit all of the above. I got the
sense that these bleed-throughs and visitations were quite typical
in her expanded reality and that I'd get better in discerning what
was what in my negotiations how and when to share my mind and
body over time.

"The old ways are making a comeback in sensitive rainbow
people like you. You don't need to know anything. You can be as
dumb as dirt like me. You just need to be a willing pioneer to bring
forth catalytic change, renewed choice, and consciousness. This

was prophesized by the Mayans, Hopi, Lakota, and many other indigenous groups," she said.

"Can I ask you a question? I'm writing a memoir and feel torn about sharing information about indigenous people and cultures, not sure if it's sensitive and needs to be protected. I don't want to contribute to the exploitation of sacred cultural traditions and information that belong to native people. At the same time, all of this is a key to my story and development, and when I check in, I hear, 'Yes. This must be included.' What do you think?"

"It's your soul's purpose to teach and write about the wisdom of the ancients to help reclaim the indigenous soul of all of humanity. It doesn't belong to anyone. Many different groups who have never met safe-keep it in similar ways because of direct guidance by the spirits. They've chosen you because you're holding it with respect and offering it as a gift to help the people. That's what matters. They're blessing your path," she said.

"Okay. In that case, I will," I said. I felt relieved and told myself to stop looking for external validation and approval. It was derailing me. Mary's love, calls, gifts, poems, and letters made up for a hundred support groups. I couldn't believe my good fortune, wondering if I was dreaming whenever she enveloped me in her other-worldly love. Sadly, my dream lasted only a few weeks. She told me out of the blue in a phone conversation that she couldn't stay in contact anymore. She'd gotten too sick.

This news came as a complete shock. I didn't even know that she was sick or what was ailing her. The timing and nature of our relationship was so strange, I wondered for a brief moment if she'd changed her mind and just wanted to get rid of me or if this was really the truth. I went with my gut and decided to believe what she'd told me at face value. I expressed my deepest appreciation for all of her gifts and guidance—which I would cherish forever— and wished her well in her recovery. I refrained from prying about whether her illness was life-threatening, if I could check in with her sometime in the future, or if I could expect to hear from her when she felt better. I took my cues from her and respected her need for privacy, but got the sense that she lavished me with so much wisdom and love because the end was near. Letting go of the person who understood my ancient self better than anyone else felt like another lesson in loss, in learning to live with the mysteries of life and the unknown, and in remaining open to guidance and answers.

I stared at a picture that she'd sent me. An attractive, light-skinned, mixed indigenous woman, appearing to be in her mid-sixties, stared back at me. She was standing proudly in front of two faded pictures that were hanging on the wall behind her. I guessed that one of them was the picture of Crazy Horse that she'd told me about. I placed her picture on my altar, read her letters, and felt her intense, oceanic, undefended, crystal-clear love for me. Sadness was too faint to form into tears. For almost a year, her image and letters filled me up with love, wisdom, strength, and hope whenever I felt alone and lost.

At work, I discovered that I was no longer debilitated by fears of harming clients thanks to the powerful and effective work that I'd done with Paloma and Mary. Alas, I was far from done. Underneath the old, tarry layers of self-doubt and fears of hurting my clients was an even older layer of fear that was just as bizarre and paralyzing, if not more, than my preoccupation with the standards of care in my field.

Fears that I'd hurt my small children—if I advanced my spiritual growth—loomed in my peripheral awareness. I'd projected these fears onto my clients because I didn't have children yet when they first emerged. The deeper roots in regard to these old fears were slowly unraveling. I became concerned about my aloof feelings toward my children when I had my near-death experience and felt taken over by Rainbow Crystal Woman's spirit. I was so completely insulated in bliss during that intense time that I could have died and been at peace with crossing over. I wondered if my old self would have found my way back if Tim and the group hadn't drummed me back into my body.

My fears that I'd bliss out again, neglect, and somehow harm my children if I pursued further training were reinforced by synchronistic "threats" and "warnings"—i.e. a strong gush of wind out of nowhere violently slamming a door into Terrance, Jade tripping and hitting her head on the corner of a table—the minute I decided to make a move, do research, or look for a new teacher. These occurrences stopped me in my tracks and submerged me back into my idle mode.

Thanks to Mary's confidence in me, I'd gained greater trust in my intuition and in the process. It was heartbreaking to discover in a Google search that she had indeed died within a year of our last conversation and was gone for good, but it at least affirmed my gut impressions that she'd told me the truth about her condition. I dared to believe all the other information that she shared with me as well. And I could sense her presence, grounding and showing me how to patiently wait for something to shift and ripen, and guiding me toward deeper understanding when the time was right.

It was *Apoh*'s—my grandmother in Hong Kong—sudden stroke that booted me out of my stifling fear. Life was too short and precious, and the thought of dying with unfinished business scared me more than the risk of making a mistake and hurting my kids.

I actively looked for and found a reputable shamanic teacher who could help me make sense of it all: Michael Harner. After word that *Apoh* was getting worse instead of better, Ma, Pa, and I hopped on a plane to bid her farewell. Our trip overlapped with Harner's shamanism workshop that I'd planned to attend and had already paid for. I received a raincheck from the same teaching institution, allowing me to attend the next shamanic healing seminar, offered by Isa Gucciardi of the Foundation of the Sacred Stream, a few months later.

On my way to Isa's workshop, I had a vision of a deer. Minutes later, I drove by a deer grazing next to the freeway. I smiled, grateful for this encouraging sign. Deer and turtle had been the first two animal spirit guides that I'd spontaneously connected to while on retreat with Tim in 2001, and Standing Deer had introduced me to the Seven Sisters in his painting.

Isa taught us the ins and outs of shamanic journeying: how to safely enter and leave non-ordinary realms and meet a helping guide. I probably would not have picked her as a teacher on my own accord and thanked *Apoh* for leading me to her. Her teaching style was exactly what I'd yearned for all these years, combining traditional teachings and external structure with enough spacious flexibility and freedom to anchor in my truest self.

Drum-guided shamanic journeying felt like riding a bike. Once I let go of my inhibitions, my soul began to merge and shapeshift with power animals and spirit guides before I received formal instructions how to do so. They approached me like a group of enthusiastic and rowdy dogs, finally freed from their cages and eager to play with me.

During my first official journey, for instance, I immediately transformed into Anansi, the trickster spider and West African deity of knowledge and stories. I crawled on my tree guide, the giant, sacred *kankantri* tree that had made a big impression on me in Awarradam, and spun a thread that guided me down in the lower world. I had an epiphany. I trusted the invisible, thin thread that I was dangling from with my life. I crawled onto a web, my home, and stumbled upon another revelation: this delicate, almost invisible web held all the meaningful events in my life together. I saw with fresh eyes that it was my life-giving source, connecting me to my external world and offering me food and nourishment to survive. The spider's essence and web's meaning shifted from being a metaphor to an embodied sensation, intimately related to my physical survival.

On the journey about my birth, I saw a flash of a jaguar's tail enter in the "vulva," a vertical, lip-lined slit, of my tree. The next moment, I was the jaguar, my body agile, sleek, and strong. Jaguar took me deep into the cracks of the earth where I was born and shapeshifted into a green seed. I was purposefully sown in very rich and fertile Suriname soil to feed off its spiritual energy and was supported and held in place by my parents' heritages and ancestral roots representing humanity's red, black, yellow, and white racial groups. This jaguar energy was very present in the spirit of the ancient healer who'd taken over my body during Tim's second retreat. I felt protected, guided, and loved beyond comprehension, getting a sense that the remarkable circumstances around my birth had been chosen with great intention to optimize the success of my mission.

Each subsequent journey widened and expanded my understanding of myself in a whole new light, incorporating core missing pieces that strengthened my rainbow convictions and path. I understood the importance of ancestral traditions and lineages in passing along wisdom, but also began to see these as cultural and physical forms that some of us, like Paloma, did not necessarily need to access to embody wisdom that they'd carried over from lifetimes. At last, I'd found a teacher and a holistic modality—depth hypnosis, a combination of shamanic healing, transpersonal psychology, Buddhist psychology, and energy medicine—whose teachings deeply resonated and allowed me to be everything I was born to be. My gifts and skills blossomed, but my fears of hurting my children still returned every now and then during my year-long certification training.

When Jade, about two years old, began to have night terrors, kicking and screeching inconsolably in the middle of the night as if under a wicked spell, I was certain that she was tuning into the same trauma that I'd skirted for so long. Even when I held her in my arms, it sometimes took up to ten minutes to break the trance and reassure her that she was safe.

I felt increasingly more helpless, desperate, and ready to try anything to help her. In a healing session guided by Sacred Stream teacher and practitioner, Laura Chandler, I gave into my fears, agony, and guilt while imagining Jade's pain and was spontaneously transported to a different time and space.

"Look at your hands, what's around you, and tell me what you are experiencing," Laura said.

I looked at my dress, apron, and my surroundings, and concluded that I'd landed in a past-life in the Dark Ages in France.

"I'm an herbalist, a peasant in a small village in France. I was accused of witchcraft. Someone in the community felt threatened by my healing powers," I said, in shock, and at the same time intrigued by how real this felt. It was very different than empathizing with a character in a movie. I was the character in this scene, going through it with the same embodied self-awareness I experienced being Loraine. It was also different than when the ancient spirit visited me. There was just one of me in this body, and we were in a totally different scene that felt incredibly realistic.

"A man's dragging me out of my home, catching me completely off guard . . . the children are screaming . . . I'm much more worried about them than myself . . ." I said, feeling completely frantic and about to lose my mind. Laura fast-forwarded me to my death to minimize my suffering.

"I was killed like many of the other women accused of being witches at that time. . . . Right before I died, I dug deep in my knowing that I was light, not a body, and held onto that with all of my might. . . . It buffered the trauma and pain to my body, because I knew that harming my physical body couldn't really harm the real me or extinguish my light. . . . But my kids, a school-aged boy and a girl, were horrified and greatly suffered as a result of my death," I said, sobbing with guilt and heartbreak as I looked down at them.

"Do you recognize them?" Laura asked.

"Oh my. . . . They are Terrance and Jade. Disheveled and dirty, but the same feisty Terrance who came into the world, kicking and resisting. His Chinese name means warrior of the Tao. In this past life, he became politically active in adulthood and organized community meetings to put a stop to these witch hunts, but Jade, as sensitive as now, was utterly devastated and lost for a long time. Wow. My husband back then, a gentle white man with a reddish beard, is Robert, my husband now. He took care of our kids but felt empty and missed me terribly," I said, not able to stop the tears from streaming. There was so much grief, heartbreak, love, and strength swirling in his heart while tackling day after empty day. Everything made so much sense. No wonder he was so set on being with me when we first met. We'd come back to finish unfinished business together. Terrance's birth marked the frustration of pushing against resistance that was as thick and rigid as a wall, and Jade's birth showed what our female bodies and our divine creative wombs were capable of when healed and honored in the right way.

After this session, I no longer felt afraid of hurting my children. Realizing that I wasn't the one who'd hurt them in the past felt like huge weight falling off my shoulders. I'd blamed myself then and my whole life now for what happened because the sequence of events and overwhelming pain made everything foggy. I was able to resolve my fears of my own death in my childhood dreams, just like I had right before I was killed, but I wasn't able to access and clear the deep anguish, guilt, buried rage, and fear of doing harm to others that I'd associated with expanding out again.

Yes, that's correct. You were profoundly triggered by insinuations that you could hurt someone else if you acted and spoke in accordance to your truth and power and silenced yourself for your parents', your clients', and eventually your kids' sake.

My intentions now were fueled by nothing but love. I relaxed more fully in myself and my convictions. Whenever Jade woke up in a night terror, I hugged and cradled her in my arms with great consciousness and hope that something would click to ground her more fully in this life. More than anything, I wanted her to trust that I would not be persecuted and taken from her for speaking and living my truth.

Jade's night terrors subsided but never completely went away. As she got older, she was able to describe what she was experiencing: feeling lost, orphaned, and wandering alone in harsh, unforgiving landscapes in the middle of the night, sometimes finding shelter in a cave, other times daring to knock on a stranger's door, hoping to be taken in, all the while searching for me and missing me terribly. I held and comforted her, swaying her in my arms and singing lullabies until her body melted in mine and her panic and wailing stopped.

It bothered me that I was able to help clients with psychic bleed-throughs from early childhood or past-life traumas. I was able to use holistic and intuitive interventions to help them to discern what was going on and extract meaning, guidance, and gifts out of their most challenging experiences. Yet, I still didn't know how to help my own daughter and alleviate her suffering.

I began to feel terribly homesick for Suriname, my motherland, and had a flash of insight that reconnecting to my rainforest home may offer me some guidance. Terrance didn't have nightmares like Jade, but, every once in a while, he also expressed concern about my physical safety. They weren't concerned about Robert, even though he was into road biking which was much riskier than what I did on any given day.

I longed to show both of them what had rooted me as a child. They were now old enough to explore and absorb the mystical energy of this special place known for making life-changing impressions on first-time visitors. Robert was just as excited about this idea when I proposed it.

We bought tickets and a few months later traveled from San Francisco to Suriname, enduring long lay-overs and delays. Jade, almost eight, and Terrance, eleven, embraced all the mayhem and third-world inconveniences with curiosity and enthusiasm. They enjoyed meeting their relatives, touring around the city, driving past our childhood homes, and making a day-trip to Saramacca to my beloved *boitie*. Not much had changed in the decade and a half since Robert and I last visited.

After we'd been in Suriname for about a week, I felt intense tugging to visit Galibi, an indigenous village on the far north-eastern tip of Suriname. Thousands of female *aitkantis*, the leatherback sea-turtle, returned to this protected and uninhabited beach area, their birth place, every year to lay their eggs. They managed to find their way home after making twelve thousand mile, epic journeys around many of the world's continents, foraging mostly on jellyfish for two years straight.

This part of the country seemed completely shrouded in mystery when I was a child, and too remote and off-limits to develop disappointing longings for. Fortunately, there was no reason to ignore these stunted longings now. The kids wouldn't let me, espe-

Jade, Tapoka, and Terrance

cially after I told them about the possibility of meeting a mythical *aitkanti*, technically earth's last dinosaur, who lived alongside the rest of the dinosaurs some 110,000–245,000 year ago.

We were able to join an eco-tour that left early the next morning from Paramaribo, the capital. Our trip took four hours by bus over bumpy road and an hour and a half by boat. Our modest lodging was smack in middle of Christiaankondre, a World Wildlife Fund-sponsored nature reserve in the indigenous village at Galibi. The kids enjoyed our cabana on the beach and the petting zoo, where a tarantula, snake, wild raccoon, spider monkey, baby sloth, and toucan freely wandered in and out of their cages and around one another. The zookeeper, Tapoka, and his pet spider monkey looked on, each in their endearing, made-to-size hammock. Tapoka gave Jade the nickname WWF, after watching her handle and dote on each of the animals. *"Meti lobi meti, bodies love bodies,"* he commented.

I smiled. I recognized so much of my child self in her. In just a few days, Suriname's wildlife and natural world had enchanted them both beyond my wildest dreams. They were mesmerized and entrenched in wonder, just like I was as a child, and as spirited and lit up as the sun.

Our best chance of seeing an *aitkanti*—which meant "eight sides" in Surinamese Creole, the number of sections on its shell—was to leave in the wee hours of the morning. They nested on the deserted shores of our neighboring country, French Guiana.

While crossing the mouth of the Marowijne River at four in the early morning, at least five shooting stars swiped across the densely speckled night sky all around us like lit-up magic markers.

"I hope that means that our wish will be granted," I said to Terrance, who was so excited, he hardly slept. August was the last month of the nesting season, and the chance of running into a pregnant *aitkanti* this late in the year was slim.

We disembarked the boat in pitch black and walked along a long, rugged beach, encountering some dried seaweed and broken turtle egg shells scattered in bunches. Not a single *aitkanti* around. We had about an hour window to run into one, and I was dragging my feet, counting the minutes with each heavy step toward the halfway turning point.

Most kids from Suriname had, like me, never been to Galibi or seen an *aitkanti* in real life, but some of us knew that *aitkantis* had special powers. They were living, breathing proof that magic was real: they were like auntie Gerda's dog, Kazan, who amazingly found his way back home after being sold to someone on the other side of town. Except that *aitkantis* were even more incredible. My soul knew that these hard-to-track phantoms of the sea shared my primal attachment to my homeland, incomprehensibly adamant and accurate in their instinctual ability to nest and root their off-spring in the same dirt that they first crawled out of.

My restless heart couldn't bear the thought of returning to California without a single *aitkanti* sighting, well-aware that it may take years before we'd be able to go on an elaborate excursion like this again as a family.

"There!" our local guide shouted, while pointing to an immense, crouched shadow several feet from the glimmering squiggles of the Atlantic Ocean.

Like thieves in the night, our small group of adults and children slowly approached the seven-foot-long, one thousand pound, prehistoric walking fossil until we were just a few steps away. For a few eternal minutes, Robert and I squeezed hands, drunk on awe. The kids squatted to get a closer look. Like out-of-place humans in a Jurassic Park scene, we watched this massive *aitkanti* lay her last eggs, rhythmically cover them with sand, huff with exhaustion, then scoot her aqua-dynamic, slick body back into the sloshing sea with the majestic sovereignty and ancient wisdom you'd expect from the last living dinosaur.

Perhaps it was the muggy heat of Galibi, perhaps it was my mind tuning into the vast mysteries of the rainforest, sky, and sea while at arm's length with this navigational marvel. While walking back to the boat, a resolute knowing that *aitkanti* had been my inner compass and primary animal spirit guide throughout the years surged through my being. She had guided me along my journey, somehow sharpening my intuitive acuity to perceive guidance from the stars, the sun, the sea, and the land and cosmically timed my mission.

As the ancient and learned one, her inner compass had provided clarity to all the other ancestral, spirit, and animal guides, relying on her staunch sense of True North—home—as their common denominator. The more I learned from our very knowledgeable guide about *aitkantis'* special abilities, the more convinced I became that she was Crow, Anansi, and Coyote in marine form. They were *iyeskas*, tricksters, and shapeshifters of the skies, trees, and the land: she was the magician of the sea. Even her physical sex wasn't fixed. It was determined by egg incubation temperature and her environment.

Shaman means "seer in the dark." Diving into the ocean's unknown abyss up to 50 times a day to depths of 1,200 meters or 4,000 feet—deeper than all other sea turtles and the majority of marine mammals—definitely qualified her as seer in the dark and elusive keeper of mysteries of the deep black.

My heart sent out a huge hug of gratitude to my *aitkanti* guide for solidifying what needed to be solidified within my soul. Right before reaching our boat, our guide noticed two late-bloomers dig their way out of their sandy womb. Exhausted, they wobbled clumsily toward their new liquid home, accompanied by Terrance and Jade who were scooting their "flippers" along their bellies to show them the way. I asked and prayed that this encounter would activate their *aitkanti*-selves, just like returning home to Suriname did for me.

Our silent, contemplative boat ride was topped by a delicious meal and a late morning nap. We reconvened for the afternoon celebrations attended by everyone from the village. We sat in the front row, Robert to my left and Terrance and Jade to my right.

"Welcome everyone!" a village leader said. "I hope you'll enjoy our traditional dances and the beautiful yellow dresses of the dancers, symbolizing life-giving warmth and light from the sun." A small group of female dancers and male drummers began to sing, drum, and move in staccato patterns, all the while paying homage to the sun and the moon, the sea and the animals, the smallest flower and the biggest tree.

Through a play-dance ritual, a circle of grandmothers, mothers, and daughters reenacted an important legend passed down from generation to generation. Centuries ago, the female ancestors of these women abandoned the tribal men—their husbands, fathers, brothers, cousins, and uncles—who were feasting in secret on some game that they had caught after days of hunting. The incensed women fled with their daughters and sons and as many possessions as they could fit in boats, shooting arrows at the men who were chasing them. They resettled in a different area along the northern coast of Suriname.

"Spanish explorers from long ago who encountered these women-run tribes named them, and later this entire region, the *Amazon* after the fierce female warriors from Greek mythology," the announcer said.

The dancers approached the women in the audience and took us by the hand. Robert smiled and gave me a nod of encouragement. While joining the women in dance, I sensed *aitkanti's* presence, a gentle steadfastness and unrelenting fierceness that was palpable and radiated out from the women's no nonsense demeanor and convictions. A profound sense of knowing, *You have arrived, you are home,* welled up from the ground and flowed into my body while dancing and spiraling into trance, sinking into a deeper, richer experience of home beyond space and time: a sacred feminine web of life that extended from the milky way above all the way to oceanic whirlpools below. I danced until my feet and every cell in my body pulsed with knowing that home could never again be ripped out of my bosom.

On an ordinary school night, not long after we returned to California, I was getting Jade and Terrance ready for bed.

"Mom, are you afraid of dying?" Jade asked me. Terrance's ears perked up, equally curious about this topic.

"Why do you want to know? Do you think I'm sick or going to die?" I asked.

"I don't know. I'm just afraid of you dying," she said.

"Me too sometimes," Terrance said.

"Well, I'm very healthy and plan to be around until you're tired of having me around," I said, trying to reassure them. How could I liberate them from this past-life wound, fear, and pain that was still hurting them and help them realize deep in their souls that this was a new life? That we won? I wanted to tell them not to ever let anyone scare them in staying small, because not even death could break us or keep us apart.

How could I explain to them that I loved them so much, I longed to soothe their little hearts with great motherly pangs ever since I was a child and that I'd willingly travel to the ends of the earth and to the stars and back, again and again, just to have them safe and sound in my arms again? I wanted them to know that they didn't need to compromise. It was possible to break out of the double bind and enjoy the best of both worlds: they could bravely expand to challenge as much as they're called to transform within our world and vast multiverse, and remain as heart connected and small as they wished to be within their intimate circles of love.

How could I say all that without cheating them from discovering their path and the mysteries of life for themselves? I sat on the bed as I did every night for story time, and signaled for them to come snuggle under my wings—as they liked to call my arms—in our cozy nest.

"I think I have an answer to your question. If I thought of myself as just a leaf, I would be terrified of dying," I said. "But because I think of myself as a tree, I know that I'm actually gathering my strengths during the winter even when I appear to be dying to everyone else," I said. They had pensive looks on their faces.

"I know that I'll burst with new leaves and new life again in the spring. I think it's the same way with humans. It may look like we're dying, but we really aren't. We're just taking a break, and return fresh and a little bigger and stronger the next season," I said.

Jade looked up at me, squeezed her little arms around me, and said, "And after we die, I'll find you again, just like your remote control key finds your car, right?"

"Yes, you will. You already have," I said and pulled her toward me, unable to hold back my tears. I felt her sink into a deep state of calmness and peace.

Second chances couldn't get any sweeter than this.

Appendix and References

 BEHIND THE SCENES

> *All shore areas and beaches are doorways between
> the human world and the spirit world.*
> *The sea turtle is especially the keeper of the doors
> between dimensions, and its appearance heralds
> a time of new wonders and rewards if
> we maintain courage.*
> *New dimensions are opening for us.*
> —Ted Andrews

FOLLOWING THE CUES FROM THE Seven Sisters, I joined Linda Joy Myers' memoir-writing course after I returned from my second spiritual retreat in Connecticut in 2004. Only after some of the writers shared their heartfelt, riveting, and beautifully crafted pieces with the group did I realize what I'd gotten myself into. I was learning for the first time what memoir writing really entailed. In rigorous academic settings, my writing ranged from good to strong. Among these talented writers, it was bland, dense, intellectual, analytical, and impersonal. It took a while for me to get why: as an academic, I'd learned to dart around the most important word in memoir writing—"I"—as if it had cooties.

My strengths were my clarity, intuition, and professional insider perspectives. I realized that if I wanted to do my voice, story, and the gift of wisdom that were coming through justice, I needed to shift gears and fully embrace this genre of writing, even if it felt like embarking upon a whole new area of study.

I conceded and tentatively began to tell my story from a personal perspective, a huge and awkward first step for me. But, in all honesty, even if someone had told me about the steep learning curve ahead and the many, long-winded twists and turns it would take for me to arrive where I am today, it probably would not have mattered.

I never expected that the writing of my memoir would be guided in the same way my heroine's journey and story were. Theoretical articles, books, and research often crossed my path and deepened my understanding of concepts that I was addressing in my memoir, chapter by chapter. These occurrences provided information that I was on the right track. Taking notes and organizing this guidance filled up the painful gap between my two worlds and bridged it with my sheer existence.

I saved these writings and suspect that especially hardcore academics and deep thinkers will appreciate this distilled, behind-the-scenes string of highlights that kept me going and offered me clarity, strength, and energy, like fresh runners in a relay race.

Early on, I was obsessed by the Golden Rule, "What cannot be communicated to the (m)other cannot be communicated to the self," coined by the father of attachment theory, John Bowlby. Even though I agreed that we were social beings and significantly shaped by our most important and earliest relationships, I felt greatly cheated by this Golden Rule, which informed the basic premise of almost every therapeutic setting I'd been in.

The Golden Rule dismissed my Golden Truth. During most of my upbringing, my mother called me *eigenwijs,* confusing my tendency to have the last word with a stubborn self-righteousness. She strongly discouraged what felt like an obligation to me: to give voice to subtle and important truths that society sliced off and abandoned in the shadows. My imaginary friends, nature spirits, and my soul knew that these were the jewels in life that glistened the most.

I noticed that cause and effect laws, foundational to the Golden Rule, sometimes mysteriously bended to support me. Artists, writers, mystics, animals, nature guides, and teachers, in person or in books, provided me words and cognitive understanding at the right times so that I could articulate what I was feeling and experiencing. Not only did these friends and guides become the mirrors I most trusted, their mirroring seemed to guide me along a path of new openings, versions of myself, and potential that creative self-exploration and memoir writing invoked in me.

Even though these intangible guides didn't have the prominent presence of my parents, they bumped up the ladder of mirroring impact because each and every one of our interactions felt extraordinary and special. I didn't need to have a conceptual understanding of synchrodestiny—which is what Deepak Chopra calls the synchronistic signs that line our path of purpose and destiny—nor was it necessary for an adult to tell me that these peak experiences were the shiny breadcrumbs to follow in life. This understanding seemed as natural to me as eating when hungry.

Needless to say, I was dumbfounded when this aspect of myself and reality felt the most threatened in my clinical psychology graduate program. Each time I tried to flesh out in my head why I felt unsafe—speaking these "last words" to myself out of fear that they'd just get picked apart in a class or supervision setting in my field—some kind of mind-blowing, miraculous guidance would appear and validate my concerns.

One quiet afternoon, still in the throes of Bowlby's Golden Rule, I found a brochure about the book, *Attachment in Psychotherapy*, by Dr. David Wallin in my office mailbox. These words on the brochure, "The Stance Toward Experience," jumped out at me. Dr. Wallin proclaimed that "mindfulness" or "non-judgmental, mindful awareness" toward experience was the answer to breaking habitual and subconscious attachment patterns. I got his book the same day. This line on the first page shot a spike of energy through my body, "the stance of the self toward experience predicts attachment security better than the facts of personal history themselves." This was what I'd been looking for. A few pages later, he elaborated:

Mindfulness and secure attachment alike are capable of generating—though by very different routes—the same invaluable resource, namely an internalized secure base. Secure attachment relationships in childhood and psychotherapy help develop this reassuring internal presence by providing us with experiences of being recognized, understood, and cared for that can subsequently be internalized. Mindfulness can potentially develop a comparable reassuring internal presence by offering us (glimpsed or sustained) experiences of the selfless, or universal, Self that is simply awareness.[5]

Maybe a year later, I attended a "Mindfulness and the Brain" seminar presented by Drs. Jack Kornfield, author of *A Path with Heart*, and Daniel Siegel, author of *Mindsight*. I learned that some of the participants in Dr. Siegel's pioneering interpersonal neuro-biology research study developed coherent and integrated stories about themselves and formed healthy relationships with others as adults, despite their diminished attachment experiences as chil-dren. Their secret: they treated themselves with care and respect, like a best friend.

Even though neither one of these experts had an explanation why some children were better at this than others, I felt heartened in knowing that my loyal relationship with my core self and imag-inary guides was not an idiosynchratic exception to the Golden Rule that I only practiced and benefited from. It was a sign that I was onto something important.

Around this time frame, I started to feel impatient with my slow progress as a writer, wondering if I should just "whip out" what I had rather than give my message unlimited space to per-colate and unfold on its own accord. I felt reinvigorated when Dr. Kornfield informed us that famous psychiatrist, Carl Gustav Jung, took fifteen years to integrate his profound ideas. His solitary soul-searching came to a dramatic halt when a friend gave him a

---

5. *Reprinted from* Attachment in Psychotherapy *(p. 6), by David J. Wallin, 2007, New York, NY: The Guilford Press. Copyright © 2007 by David J. Wallin. Reprinted with permission.*

small book about Taoist philosophy that encouraged him to reveal his watershed ideas to Western psychiatry. I never caught the title of the book, but I reminded myself that bridging Western psychology and holistic, indigenous, and non-dualistic worldviews was no easy task, not even for Carl Jung, and to be kind to myself.

The following weekend, I attended a workshop on Tai Chi and Qigong, "Ancient Pathways to Modern Health," by Dr. Michael Mayer, and learned that many of the principles behind Tai Chi were extracted from a little Taoist book called *The Secret of the Golden Flower*. The alchemical symbolism of gold—the transmutation of base metals and matter into a precious metal—and the symbol of the flower or lotus—the uncontaminated truth-body rising out of mud —were beautiful and profound. It took a few moments for it to dawn on me that these perspectives aligned with my Golden Truth, and, more importantly, that my Hakka Chinese name, Gam Lan, meant Golden Flower!

I rushed home and had only one thing on my mind. After a few Internet searches, I discovered that *The Secret of the Golden Flower* was indeed the book that inspired Dr. Carl Jung many decades ago to end his long sabbatical and span the wide chasm between Eastern and Western schools of thought. It took at least a week for me to absorb this immense gift of support and integrate it with my sense of self. Doing so fortified my level of commitment another nudge.

A comprehensive meta-analysis of key mindfulness studies, "Meeting of Meditative Disciplines and Western Psychology," by renowned psychiatrist Roger Walsh and psychologist Shauna Shapiro (American Psychologist, 2006) crossed my path next. They claimed that Western psychology tends to peg uncategorized data into existing categories, contributing to an "assimilative integration that feeds the global 'colonization of the mind'" and "undermines the growth and credibility of other psychologies." I liked their audacity. They acknowledged that the potential harm of being too conservative and protective of the status quo could pose as big of a problem as being too progressive and risk-taking with new ideas.

The revolutionary authors also celebrated the added value of outliers, who weren't appreciated in fields that predominantly relied on robust group norms to make their strongest arguments. These mavericks detected that tucked in the margins of Western psychology were "the transpersonal states described by meditative psychologies, yoga, and shamanism—peak and plateau experiences, the numinous experience, the holotropic experience, and cosmic consciousness, occurring spontaneously especially in exceptionally healthy individuals, who may confer significant psychological benefits."

They asked psychologists to consider a renaissance of phenomenological case-studies by "gifted meditators," whose "introspective sensitivity may make them exceptional observers of subjective states and mental processes." These meditators could offer us "precise phenomenological accounts of the subjective effects of pharmacological and other therapies."

"It takes only one black swan to prove that not all swans are white," was the phrase that rang in my ears during that period. It was a phrase that was often used by professors in my research methods and statistics classes to remind students that there was no such thing as "scientific proof," no matter how statistically significant our analyses or how large our body of research. All we are doing is showing how likely two different events are to occur at the same time through the use of statistical probability measurements. We need just one exception to the rule, however, to disprove a long-held assumption about reality and completely overhaul the order of business in a field.

Psychiatrist Judith Orloff is a black swan who did just that. She revealed in her book, *Second Sight* (2010), that she treated her intuition like a "shameful secret" and stopped dreaming altogether when she was a graduate student in medical school. Even within the safe perimeters of her own thriving private practice years later, she still dismissed her intuitive hunches until it was almost too late. Only after she incorrectly disregarded an inexplicable, strong visceral sense that one of her clients was about to commit suicide did she muster up the courage to reclaim and integrate her intuitive and psychic talents back into her work. Her story and her clear example of the potential harm that can result when not listening to our intuition as healers made an indelible mark on me and reassured me that the mental health field was ready for an up-close and personal review.

Another pioneering meta-analysis, "The Weirdest People in the World" (Behavioral and Brain Sciences, 2010), by researchers Henrich, Heine, and Norenzayan illuminated why I had such a strong reaction as a graduate student when I was first introduced to Dr. Paul Meehl's conviction that any clinician who considered "personal experience to be more valid than research studies was self-deceived." These researchers found that 96 percent of psychological participants in studies published in top journals were from Western, Educated, Industrialized, Rich, Democratic (WEIRD) societies, made up only 12 percent of the world's population, and were "particularly unusual" and frequently "outliers" compared to non-Western research participants. Most affirming to me was this line, "The sharp self-enhancing biases of Westerners are less pronounced in much of the rest of the world, although self-enhancement has long been discussed as if it were a fundamental aspect of human psychology."

Interestingly, the studies done on university professors produced the same results, which could explain the ardent fears about self-serving bias among academics and social scientists, like Dr. Meehl. His famous seventy-two-page rant, entitled, "Why I Don't Attend Case Conferences," outlined dozens of "mental fallacies" committed by "feeble-minded psychologists" at case-conferences, and has become a classic must-read for everyone on the road to becoming a practicing psychologist. While his attempts to remedy inherent bias and fundamental human flaw through hardcore quantitative research were noteworthy, I wasn't convinced that they'd remedied the self-enhancing, culture-bound biases that are still operating in many researchers' blind spots and experimental designs.

Dr. Meehl's papers still sounded arrogant to me, and I didn't understand how someone like him could become one of the youngest presidents of the American Psychological Association. It sent the message that being prolific and intelligent was more important than being compassionate and wise. I felt quite disillusioned by this, expecting this sort of thing to occur in business or politics, not in a healing profession like ours.

There was something else about Dr. Meehl that inexplicably upended my sense of universal order and contributed to my self-doubt that ignited the storyline of my memoir. Even after I was done with my first draft, I sporadically read writings about or by him in search of some mysterious missing link. This link seemed to pertain to matters beyond the scope of the book and my personal story, and I did not understand why it still had a grip on my soul.

In the early days of the Internet, only Wikipedia-like descriptions and long lists of impressive accomplishments, positions, and publications popped up when I typed keywords like "Meehl" and "biography" in my Google search box. Adding "criticism" to my search produced lots of critique given by him, none of him. Perhaps because of the political zeitgeist, it finally occurred to me in the summer of 2016 during a two-week deep writing retreat to add "narcissism" as a keyword to my Google search. This is how I discovered the real Dr. Paul Meehl and the answers I'd been seeking for almost two decades after he first crawled under my skin.

In an obscure, hard-cover, encyclopedia-sized journal called, *A History of Psychology in Autobiography* (Stanford University Press, 1989, out of print and going for $577, used), Dr. Meehl had made a fifty-three-page autobiographical contribution, reflecting on his personal and professional life with much greater insight and integrated hindsight than anything I'd read about him.

He wrote that he'd inherited his father's "brain genes" and identified strongly with his claim that, "if a man was dumb, he might just as well be dead." When he was eleven, his father, described as an excessively industrious bank clerk, committed suicide after embezzling money to play the stock market. As if that wasn't tragic enough, Dr. Meehl stated that "at age sixteen I suffered a second object loss when my mother died of ether pneumonia. . . . This episode of gross medical bungling permanently immunized me from the childlike faith in physicians' omniscience that one finds among most persons, included educated ones. . . . It has also helped me to avoid dogmatism about my own diagnostic inferences, to which I am tempted by my self-concept as a naturally gifted and well-trained clinician."

It finally made sense to me why he was so mistrustful of the "diagnostic inferences" of all clinicians, including his own. He wanted to prevent others from experiencing the childhood horror he endured and relied on his intellect and actuarian research to prevent human error in predicting risks. "Voltaire said that in contemplating human affairs, those endowed with an excess of feeling are moved to weep, those with an excess of intellect, to laugh. I am clearly of the second sort. . . . A frenzied egalitarian could say that I have substituted an elitism of intellect for the more common snobberies of race, family, or money, a point I cheerfully concede."

Much to my surprise, he was fascinated by parapsychology and extrasensory perception, i.e. the "extrascientific ways of knowing," the "metaphysical mind-body program," religion, and mental health. These contradictory interests and reflections on mysticism had been published in "papers that [he] was proud of for their high level conceptualization, but which few psychologists have read or even heard of."

Even though he wasn't easily swayed by the views of others and usually did the swaying, he wasn't very influential in creating a following in this area. He became more cautious and reserved when his "peculiar" and "bizarre" interests became the brunt of jokes and criticism, but openly asserted that, "I'm inclined to think that there's something to telepathy, and if forced to bet a large sum one way of another, I would wager affirmatively." I was beyond delighted by this validation.

Learning about the "ambivalent regrets" that he had about his professional life and the endearing humility that he developed later in life helped me to lay whatever unfinished business existed between us to rest. I developed gratitude for the triggering words that so sharply provoked me the first time I read them and irked me in ways that defied logic, "Any clinician who considered personal experience to be more valid than research studies was self-deceived . . . We are bound as human beings to make 'fundamental attribution errors'—giving ourselves too much credit for positive outcomes, and only a 'hard-nosed' skeptic and critical thinker with statistically significant data can remedy this unfavorable, unreliable human condition that's prone to self-serving bias."

These words fueled the archeological excavation of my soul and ultimately helped me to discover and reclaim what mattered the most to me—my intuitive healing wisdom. Never in a million years did I anticipate that Dr. Meehl would be the ascended master I'd meet at the end of this road, providing me the affirmative mirroring about the state of the mental health field that I longed for all these years. Because of the power of his own healing intuition, his unwavering search for truth, and his commitment to service, he had the foresight to record his hero's journey, self-reflections, and epiphanies as a gift for us and the next generation, even if parts of his self-discoveries were self-incriminating.

He wrote that he was at sixty-eight a "somewhat disappointed man," aware of the "note of petulance creeping into [his] scholarly publications, for which [he] has been faulted" and expressed concern about the "narcissistic rewards" that he'd been entrusted. I was touched by the devotion to his soul's redemption and that he—despite the emotional buffer that his ego and intellect had provided him all of his life—listened to his heart and his pain to reset the course of his life. I connected to his big heart and soul, cherished our otherworldly telepathic bond, and felt honored to revive these last words of his that are buried in an archaic book that's hardly ever read. I believe they're offering the kind of guidance he'd emphasize if he were still alive today, guidance that would reset and redeem the soul of our field:

> The profession has delivered such ego-pellets to me somewhat more than I deserve. . . . I sometimes think that professional recognition came to me too early for my own good. . . . In the relatively short time I was treating patients, I had the nagging background thought that what I found interesting and scientifically defensible

didn't necessarily relate closely with how much I helped the person. . . . I'm more likely today to rely on leverage from the 'relationship' and a mixture of common sense, intuition, and bits and pieces of psychodynamics (their early relationships with caretakers) than I am to proceed with some grand strategy.

⊠ ACKNOWLEDGMENTS

WRITING THIS BOOK WAS a collective effort, not only in honoring and translating ancestral guidance and wisdom, but also in regarding and incorporating teachings from many mentors, holy medicine men and women, nature spirits, and consciousness pioneers—young and old, dead and alive, human and non-human, supportive and challenging—who assisted with its creation.

I'm particularly grateful for the support of visionaries, healers, and teachers, like Brooke Medicine Eagle (www.medicineeagle.com), Mary Attu, Standing Deer, Maria Root, Kay Taylor, Mimi Stern, Donna Morrish, Isa Gucciardi, and my mentors and supervisors at the Pacific Graduate School of Psychology (now Palo Alto University), the UC Davis Counseling Center, and the many psychotherapy, spiritual, consultation and writing groups I've been a part of. The catalytic interplay of their unique contributions inspired this work of art that I had the privilege of incubating and birthing into the world.

I'd like to thank Brooke Warner, my publisher at She Writes Press, for blazing a new trail for women writers like me. Her empowering and revolutionary hybrid publishing model offered me the creative freedom and support I needed to do my best work. So has her She Writes Press team of editors, designers, and fellow writers, and my project manager, Cait Levin, who have each exceeded my expectations.

I'm especially indebted to my editor, Liz Kracht. From the start, she envisioned the bigger and juicier potential of my story and the importance of building momentum and credibility from the ground up. Her coaching and editing style helped me to sharpen my writing skills and craft, particularly in bringing scenes to life using lay language. I'm also thrilled with the alluring cover design by Tabitha Lahr. It captures the mysterious unpeeling of layers to reveal my most sacred, vulnerable self and deepest wisdom and truths.

I'm grateful to be alive during this time of great transition and change and for the expertise, feedback, integrity, and comradery of the many pioneering healers, psychotherapists, academics, researchers, writers, artists, and change-makers that I've had the good fortune to dream with, to laugh and cry with, to grow with, to write and create with, and to help serve the world with both in online and face-to-face groups. They often provided the creative spark, clarity, words of encouragement, validation, or insight that kept me going.

I thank my clients, in particular, from the bottom of my heart for entrusting me with their healing journeys, bright light, and courageous struggles. They make it possible for me to do daily work that fills my heart with deep meaning, awe, humility, and joy. I'm grateful to have witnessed the unfolding of their sacred relationships with divine guidance and spirit guides over the years and for the many lessons and insights I gathered as a result.

This book would not be as poignant, groundbreaking, and powerful without the tremendous contributions made by Paloma (pseudonym). I can't thank her enough for being a brave maverick, often a few steps ahead of me in exploring the unconventional path of our shared spiritual calling. She understood before I did that writing about our experiences would liberate both of us and shape the story that needed to be told. After she ended therapy with me in 2004, she received a prestigious scholarship and graduated with a master's degree in gender studies. She's currently living in Mexico where she continues to find joy in her spiritual community, train in mindfulness, and practice for the benefit of all beings. She had the opportunity to read the book right before it went into print, thanked me for believing her, and felt honored to be part of the story.

Over the years, my loving family, my in-laws, and my friends, both near and far, kept me sane and kept me going. They never stopped believing in me and my book but also made it easy to stop talking and thinking about it. I thank them for being my anchors, early readers, cheerleaders, and ground. I'm so grateful for visual artist and life-long friend, Nicole Van Straatum, who created my magical book trailer and couldn't have captured the essence of my story and the mystical traditions at Galibi and Brokopondo in Suriname any better. A big thank-you and shout out to Myrysji Tours and the people of Galibi as well as the people from Awarradam for sharing their ancestral stories, traditions, and dances and for their stewardship of the land, the animals, and the sacred feminine.

I'm especially thankful to my parents, Jules and Josta Tjenalooi for their love, encouragement, and countless sacrifices. Their courage and actions formed the backbone of my story. I hold a special place in my heart for my aunties, uncles, and cousins from the Dieterstraat and for my surrogate father and our matchmaker, Uncle Henk *Treurniet,* Don't Mourn, who has always been a dreamer, a romantic, and a stubborn idealist who still insists that what matters most in life is love.

Last but not least, I dedicate this book to my soul team, my dear husband of twenty-five years, Robert, and my precious children, Terrance and Jade. Their crucial roles in the story and their unwavering, day-to-day, practical support made it possible for me to write this book, which I hope will one day be read and enjoyed by their children and their children's children. Thanks to their love, humor, and willingness to roll with the punches, I had the much-needed creative space, energy, and time to deeply focus, listen, stretch beyond the usual limits of my daily routines, and offer you this "gift from the ancestors."

ABOUT THE AUTHOR

Author photo © Robert Van Tuyl

LORAINE VAN TUYL, PhD, CHT, holistic psychologist, shamanic healer, Depth Hypnosis practitioner, and author, is happiest when exploring how the natural world relates to our true nature in healing sessions, on the page, and in her journeys and dreams. She has guided visionaries, educators, healers, artists, change-makers, and therapists from the Native American Health Center, the UC Berkeley Counseling Center, and at her private practice, the Sacred Healing Well, where she seamlessly weaves modern psychotherapeutic and ancient practices into her holistic approach. She has been an ordained minister at the Foundation of the Sacred Stream, the largest credentialing wisdom school in the larger San Francisco Bay Area, for more than a decade. Her creative outlets these days involve providing holistic mental health resources to the Healing the Waters Within online community, serving Gaia and Standing Rock Water Protectors, working on her next book, Awaken your Amazon Spiritual Warrior by Renaturing your Denatured Soul, and designing Learn to Be (a) Well retreats for nature wisdom keepers. More information about her Awaken your Amazon Spiritual Warrior courses and mystical Costa Rica retreats can be found here: www.retreatsfornaturewisdomkeepers.com.

SELECTED TTILES FROM SHE WRITES PRESS

She Writes Press is an independent publishing company founded to serve women writers everywhere. Visit us at www.shewritespress.com.

This Trip Will Change Your Life: A Shaman's Story of Spirit Evolution by Jennifer B. Monahan. $16.95, 978-1-63152-111-9. One woman's inspirational story of finding her life purpose and the messages and training she received from the spirit world as she became a shamanic healer.

Change Maker: How My Brother's Death Woke Up My Life by Rebecca Austill-Clausen. $16.95, 978-1-63152-130-0. Rebecca Austill-Clausen was workaholic businesswoman with no prior psychic experience when she discovered that she could talk with her dead brother, not to mention multiple other spirits—and a whole new world opened up to her.

Renewable: One Woman's Search for Simplicity, Faithfulness, and Hope by Eileen Flanagan. $16.95, 978-1-63152-968-9. At age forty-nine, Eileen Flanagan had an aching feeling that she wasn't living up to her youthful ideals or potential, so she started trying to change the world—and in doing so, she found the courage to change her life.

Motherlines: Letters of Love, Longing, and Liberation by Patricia Reis. $16.95, 978-1-63152-121-8. In her midlife search for meaning, and longing for maternal connection, Patricia Reis encounters uncommon women who inspire her journey and discovers an unlikely confidante in her aunt, a free-spirited Franciscan nun.

Think Better. Live Better. 5 Steps to Create the Life You Deserve by Francine Huss. $16.95, 978-1-938314-66-7. With the help of this guide, readers will learn to cultivate more creative thoughts, realign their mindset, and gain a new perspective on life.

Learning to Eat Along the Way by Margaret Bendet. $16.95, 978-1-63152-997-9. After interviewing an Indian holy man, newspaper reporter Margaret Bendet follows him in pursuit of enlightenment and ends up facing demons that were inside her all along.